Innovating in a global crisis

For Cens
and
Shelley

Innovating in a global crisis

Riding the whirlwind of recession

Fons Trompenaars and Charles Hampden-Turner

First published in 2009 by
Infinite Ideas Limited
36 St Giles
Oxford, OX1 3LD
United Kingdom
www.infideas.com

A CIP catalogue record for this book is available from the British Library

ISBN 978–1–906821–23–4

Brand and product names are trademarks or registered trademarks of their respective owners.

Cover designed by Baseline Arts Ltd, Oxford
Typeset by Sparks, Oxford – www.sparkspublishing.com
Printed and bound by TJ International Limited, Padstow, Cornwall

The paper used in this book is FSC certified. FSC (the Forest Stewardship Council) is an international network to promote the responsible management of the world's forests.

Mixed Sources
Product group from well-managed forests and other controlled sources
www.fsc.org Cert no. SGS-COC-2482
© 1996 Forest Stewardship Council
FSC

CONTENTS

PREFACE

This book is intended to fill a gap in the market between books that show how to develop more creative people, and those that show how organisations can create a culture of innovation that can harness this creativity. In the increasingly oligopolistic world of business, in which old ideas can be copied and replicated at lower and lower costs, it is the constant renewal of creative solutions that is the ultimate differentiator of survivors.

Much has been written (separately) about creativity and innovation. Much has also been written about corporate culture and mechanistic and structural approaches to innovation in organisations. What is severely lacking is a single body of knowledge in the form of an easily digestible book that integrates these subjects.

The core philosophy of this book is thus the connection between the development of people first as individuals, then as teams and then across the organisation (which contributes to the long-term sustainability of the organisation) and the constant renewal of talent and motivation of its workforce.

As you will discover, to apply the concepts presented in this book you will need a change in mindset in the way you approach problems – away from more simplistic linear and bi-modal ideas, characteristic of Western cultures. Weighing the relative merits of 'this *or* that' action along a linear scale where you can only have more of one at the expense of the other, or assuming that action is limited in choosing between 'this *or* that', too often results from the consumer idea of choice and from suffering from (Cartesian-based) Western education. Do you want tea *or* coffee?

To become more creative and to harness the talent of being creative requires us to think in terms of asking 'Can we have our cake *and* eat it?' or, more succinctly, as explained throughout this book, 'How can we combine and not simply choose between options to open up new avenues to deal with today's fast-changing world?' So it is not about choosing a beer *or* a whisky, but asking if we can combine the two (as in a 'chaser') to create something more.

Organisations often focus on systems and process changes. But the key message from this book is the importance of behaviours and actions by leaders and managers that can lead to a supportive climate that respects and reinforces creativity and innovation essential to the longer-term sustainability of the organisation. When creativity is put in the context of realising business objectives and solving business issues, its results are greatly enhanced.

The authors have an exceptional talent for blending rigorous research with professional practice so that one informs the other within an entertaining and easy-to-read format. This book will therefore be of value to managers to help them understand how their behaviours have consequences for the working context of their employees and thereby how they can synergise the needs of the organisation with the needs of the individual employee and secure the best for all. It will also be of value to individual employees and students of business and management who need to learn and understand the increasing importance of these 'soft issues' of work and organisations, over and above functional disciplines and business economics.

This book includes a comprehensive exploration of creativity and innovation from this new perspective with a business focus. You can test yourself on some of the profiling instruments described in this book and access interactive case studies and further content at www.ridingthewhirlwind.com.

Professor Peter Woolliams, PhD
Emeritus Professor, Anglia Ruskin University, UK

ACKNOWLEDGEMENTS

Fons writes:

It all started on the evening of 13 October 2005 when I was invited to join a Gala dinner of Abbott Diagnostics in Wiesbaden. Because there was no 'Dutch table', I was asked if I would join the Scandinavian table, where Norwegians, Swedes and Danes were hospitable enough to invite both me and the Finns. At the end of the evening, one of the Swedish clients wished me good luck and told me that I would most probably see him next year in Stockholm. Indeed, I had been invited to a bestseller conference, but how did he know this? 'Haven't you seen the programme?' No, I said. 'But you are on stage with John Cleese.' WHAT? With John Cleese? *The* John Cleese ...? YES!

And indeed, on 1 June 2006 I was on stage with John Cleese, who talked about creativity, while I talked about the importance of diversity for innovation. It inspires me, particularly because his presentation complemented (in the broad sense of the word) my own so well. We travelled together on the train to Gothenburg, and the idea was born to do some joint workshops and seminars in the fall of 2007. What better way to prepare than to write a book?

The first part of the book integrates more traditional thoughts on creativity into our culture and dilemma framework. The following chapters draw heavily on the work of Charles Hampden-Turner, whose creative mind continues to be a main source of inspiration. And it was very much inspired by the dialogues I had with Peter Woolliams, who contributed and did the final editing. Here the question becomes 'where does

---

co-authorship start and editing stop?' It's a grey area. Thank you, Peter, for all the support you gave me.

Thank you David Lewis for the great graphic support. Your talents go beyond being a good graphic artist; you have an unusual talent to capture in drawings that which we couldn't say in words.

And last but not least, a big thank you to John Cleese, who keeps on reminding me that the ultimate creative act is to make people laugh – then they realise that humour is the ultimate way to appreciate opposite ends of a spectrum.

As I write this on a terrace looking out over Darling Harbour in Sydney, I realise how important it has been to test my concepts in front of large audiences. Thank you to all the organisations that have allowed me to speak on the creation of a innovative culture – in particular AHRI, the professional organisation of HR managers of Australia, for allowing me to withdraw for a moment and test the latest idea on 1,400 of their members.

Fons Trompenaars

INTRODUCTION

1

'Life is a bursting unity of opposition barely held.'
'A nation should be just as full of conflict as it can contain ... but of
course, it must contain.'

Robert Frost

Introduction: Innovation in tough times

Since the first edition of this book was published the global economy has
lurched from boom to bust. This raises an interesting question. Is innovation a phenomenon of boom times? Is this book being reissued in a totally
unsuitable environment? It is tempting to think so. Consider what boom
times do to enhance innovation.

Unencumbered with fears about survival and in a confident and
expansive mood innovators are free to seek *self-fulfilment*, to produce
goods of outstanding *quality* despite the cost, to attain ever-higher levels
of *complexity* to *supply* customers at every *opportunity* that those good
times provide. In this mood we proclaim the triumph of *free enterprise*;
we take on *responsibility* for *ourselves* and *learn best practices* along the
way. Certain words above have been italicised because we are going to
look into these more carefully.

Quite a different atmosphere takes hold when boom turns to bust,
an atmosphere that we might think was wholly unsuited to innovation

so that we must, for the duration of this recession, dismiss it from our minds.

Encumbered with fears about survival and in a pessimistic mood of contraction and retrenchment, innovators must consider dire *necessity* and the *cost* not quality of what they produce. The need is to *simplify* products and pare these down to what customers *demand* and nothing more. These are *crisis* times where opportunities are scarce and the *risk of loss* high. Decades of free enterprise are being replaced by *socialism* and public ownership as bank after bank is *rescued*, and *negative feedback* testifies to egregious *errors*.

Surely innovation could not survive such terrible times? Has the time come to lay books like this aside? Not if you grasp that the boom led to the bust, that these two highly contrasting phenomena are in fact joined together, so that the second follows inexorably on the first. While the boom appeared to favour us all and shower us with blessings, the grim aftermath was being generated even as we basked in the sunshine. It was William Blake who called for 'the marriage of Heaven and Hell'. It was Kipling who wrote 'If you can meet with Triumph and Disaster and treat those two impostors just the same'. The problem is not this recession or the busting of our affluence; the problem is boom–bust as a total phenomenon. The triumphal surge in confidence achieved in boom times is very much part of the problem.

The definition of innovation as self-fulfilling, ebullient, confident, free and full of learning is a cliché and as such the antithesis of genuine innovation, a false god we worship until we are struck down. The misery of the recession or bust is also a cliché and we would be wise to search within it for the seeds of wisdom we can find. For the reconciliation of boom–bust, bubble-recession is a *sustainable form of capitalism* that eschews the headlong rushes to disaster we seem unable to halt.

Genuine innovation takes the characteristics we find in a boom and marries or reconciles them with the characteristics we find in a bust. If these pairs of contrasting attributes can be joined so as to qualify each other, then perhaps our economic system will cease to lurch from one extreme to another. Let us look at some of the contrasting characteristics that we earlier italicised.

Self-fulfilment and necessity

Babson College in Massachusetts and the London Business School have jointly sponsored the GEM studies, which examine the level of entrepreneurship and innovation across the world, nation by nation, culture by culture. They have discovered two contrasting drivers of innovation: self-fulfilment, more common in affluent countries, and necessity, more typical of poorer developing economies. In the latter case you invent a means of survival in the face of hunger and dire poverty. You need your family to survive and 'necessity is the mother of invention'.

While we do not doubt that the relative salience of self-fulfilment and dire necessity differ across the globe, we question whether these two drivers were ever separate in the first place. Israel is one of the most entrepreneurial nations on earth and so is Taiwan but, given that both are surrounded by potential enemies, is not their self-fulfilment shadowed by necessity? There are reasons to envy an entrepreneur who can go into any business he or she chooses and so fulfil deep desires. But once this choice has been made and commitment entered into, necessity is everywhere!

A dozen decisions must be made before you go to sleep, the bank calls in your loan, the receivers are ringing your bell. While there is more self-fulfilment in a boom and more necessity in a bust, the interaction between the two and the need to reconcile them never goes away.

High quality and low cost

The notion that one must make a stark choice between high quality and low cost is a fallacy. No less an authority than Michael Porter at Harvard Business School argues that there are two 'generic' strategies for all businesses. They must either create a premium product and/or service, valuable because no one else, or very few, can supply it, or they must produce the lowest-cost service and drive those that cannot match their low price out of business. Porter warns us not to confuse such strategies but keep them distinctive.

Yet genuine innovations find a way of combining low cost with high quality. W. Edwards Deming always insisted that low cost was an aspect of high quality, something parsimonious designed into a product. Toyota has long insisted that its chassis and wheelbase are highly standardised across as many types of vehicle as possible, so as to lower costs, while the super-structure mounted on this platform should be customised and of high quality. The Lexus is an example. Dell Computers also buys cheap components by the millions, but designs these into a system custom-designed for each corporate client. The modules are low cost, while their combinations are unique and of premium value.

Complexity and simplicity

Much is made of the Knowledge Revolution and how products grow in complexity by leaps and bounds. In boom times, it may not matter too much that customers are over-served, that technologies they use have three times as many functions as they can possibly understand or learn to use. But in tough times it matters a lot and it is in recessions that mini-mills replace integrated steel mills even faster, that cheaper, simpler computers with smaller disc drives replace their fatter predecessors.

According to Clayton Christiansen, of 129 electronic companies using disc drives 109 went bankrupt because a smaller, simpler, cheaper alternative replaced them. In many cases the customers over-served by the complex machines collapsed too. One secret behind the inexorable advance of Asia is that they provide simpler alternatives for their less affluent domestic customers, which are then preferred globally. Cannon Copier produced a simpler, cheaper alternative to Xerox.

Supply and demand

The cliché about innovation is that it is something new supplied to customers, the better mouse trap so that 'men beat a path to your door'. But when recessions bite and customers are hurting it pays to look into their mind-sets and locate their 'pain-points'. This is the argument of Adrian

Slywotski in *How to Grow When Markets Don't*. Of course, much innovation is concerned with new forms of supply but by no means all.

Cardinal Drugs found itself in a rather wretched, low-margin industry, supplying packaged drugs to hospital pharmacies. It is difficult to add value to bulk pills ordered from pharmaceutical companies. Then the company decided to 'follow the pill' and see what happened in the hospitals receiving these. It discovered a rare mess. Hospitals were chronically under-staffed because there was a nationwide shortage of registered pharmacists. Hundreds of pills were going missing and if patients became addicted the hospital was legally responsible. Nor were pills being accurately invoiced to the patients' accounts.

Armed with this information Cardinal offered to staff and run hospital pharmacies itself. It supplied pill-dispensing machines which only disgorged a measured quantity when it recognised the signature and fingerprint of an authorised person and a registered patient to whom the cost was billed. The mark-up on these activities was 22% or higher, all discoverable when investigating customer distress and the demand that pain cease, all of which abound in recessions.

Opportunity and crisis

There is a famous Japanese *kanji,* a composite pictorial letter, which combines the idea of crisis with the opportunities to be found within this crisis. Any crisis is an opportunity to meet that crisis. Although temperatures in Helsinki plunge as much as 20 to 30 degrees below freezing in winter, it loses fewer days to bad weather than almost any other capital. Because of the danger of being frozen in a broken down vehicle at night, Finns not only drive cars of the highest reliability, but they also carry two Nokia mobile phones lest one fails. Deaths from such crises are rare. The opportunities to remedy the crises are many.

Similarly, the status, the competence and the salaries of Holland's civil engineers stand very high. For centuries they saved their country from the sea. They now sell the skills born of crisis across the world.

Free enterprise and socialism

When the Berlin wall collapsed it seemed to everyone that free enterprise had triumphed. There was but one superpower, the USA, but one viable economic system. Reagan and Thatcher had sounded the trumpet and the walls of Jericho had tumbled down. All this seems to be a long time ago. Today the rubble of the wall has given way to the rubble of our triumphalism.

And Socialism is back with a vengeance! Bush, the arch-conservative has done more to advance public ownership than the most ambitious communist. He puts Castro in the shade. Capital markets are plunged into unforgettable disgrace.

Yet the chance for creating some innovative solutions show distinct signs of hope. Obama will probably bail out the American auto industry but only if they innovate in the next three years to an extent greater than the last thirty years. He wants alternative fuels: ethanol, hydrogen, steam, electricity. He wants an attack on global warming, with wind, tidal, thermal, solar and other renewable sources of energy. The challenges of clean drinking water, proper nutrition, affordable medicine and world pandemics all need to be urgently addressed. Perhaps it is time to give an opportunity to the acceptable face of government-sponsored innovation, so as to replace the unacceptable arse of capitalism with its million-dollar bonuses for failure.

Self-responsibility and being rescued

The wonderful thing about boom times and asset bubbles is how these celebrate our values of independence and self-responsibility. 'I am the master of my fate. I am the captain of my soul,' we shout in joy as the bubble expands. But what a terrible fate, what disgrace to be rescued by the very institution of government that we have been telling to leave us alone for decades! Being rescued by taxpayers is an abject experience.

But if we can overcome our shame, there are some important lessons. Business owes its very existence to the public amidst which it resides. After this experience perhaps business will be more public spirited than before, keener to serve the public that has assured its continuing existence at great expense to itself and the rising generation. Perhaps business will be more ready to contribute to issues of public survival, the environment, the health system and other issues of social responsibility. After all, it is using our money. It has had 'the free lunch' it always told us did not exist and now owes us! The innovation that becomes possible when you broaden your objectives and consider society as a whole may prove a powerful stimulus.

Learning from best practice and negative feedback from serious errors

Clearly, leading or imitating the best practices in your industry is the more comfortable way to learn and in boom times managers give much attention to this form of learning. When the economy busts there comes a flood of negative feedback and we are confronted by our errors, rendered more serious and more punitive by hard times.

While it is very hard when our own chickens come home to roost, it is also very salutary. The statement 'you only learn from negative feedback' is somewhat exaggerated. We learn something from having our hypotheses vindicated. It is nevertheless true that from negative feedback we learn most and the lessons, however painful, are very, very important. We learn that we have been wrong perhaps for decades and must now pay the penalty, that the capitalism we cheered for was unsustainable, that the wealth we thought we had was ephemeral, that unless we change our ways, history will repeat itself.

As any student of innovation will tell you, dissatisfaction with the status quo is the beginning of all innovation, so the fact that the current edifice has crashed allows us to build anew.

In the pages of the book you will encounter again and again the fact that polarisations are recipes for sterility. High quality–Low cost, Simplicity–Complexity, Supply–Demand and so on need to be reconfirmed and artfully reconnected. Where we fail to do this, the pendulum will swing, suddenly and violently, from boom to bust, from bubbling to bursting, from bravado to bathos. The most urgent innovative task is to design a free-enterprise system that sustains us long-term. We have just been reminded of the costs of failure.

The structure of this book

The aim of this book is to offer a new set of approaches to the leaders to make their organisations more innovative and thereby more sustainable in the increasingly turbulent future.

We will deal with three crucial levels of the innovative culture: the individual, the team and the organisation. An organisation cannot be innovative if there are no creative individuals working to fulfil their personal dreams. Yet you can put creative individuals together and end up with a team that is actually very *un*creative. Creative people need to have people with complementary competences around them to make the team inventive. And haven't we all seen organisations where the Research and Development (R&D) and marketing teams are (separately) excellent, but the organisation is dysfunctional because they can't work together? Indeed, an innovative organisation needs to develop a pattern of interactions where individuals and teams work effectively together for the larger objective of the organisation.

The second and third chapters focus on individual creativity and how to enhance it, but from a new perspective. They cover the tensions with which the creative person needs to deal, such as the quandary between our rushed 'hare brain' and the more reflective, investigating 'tortoise mind', as originally discussed by Guy Claxton. We revisit the well-established psychological frameworks that are closely linked to creativity, such as the Myers Briggs Type Indicator typology (MBTI), Kolb's Learning Style Inventory and even Kirton's Adaptation-Innovation Inventory (KAI). The concern is to draw attention to the fact that all of these (and other) frameworks are essentially based on linear models that cannot fully capture a person's creativity. We offer both practical and conceptual arguments supporting the premise that the creative individual essentially reconciles what seem to be mutually exclusive poles that underlie these models. Exercises and alternative measurement tools show how effective the concept and practice of 'dilemma reconciliation' can be for your organisation.

The work of comedy writers such as John Cleese (including *Monty Python* and *Fawlty Towers*), John Sullivan (*Only Fools and Horses*) and Matt Groening (*The Simpsons*) and that of ourselves as academic con-

sultants (consulting daily in the largest and most successful international organisations in the world), are quite different, but complementary.
We seem to have one thing in common: the functional use of humour.
Like Arthur Koestler, they all believe that humour is very much linked
with creativity. Why? Because humour is the process of discovering that
two apparently opposite logics turn out both to be logical. That is what
makes you laugh. So this book will try to take utmost advantage of this
both theoretically and practically.

The fourth, fifth and sixth chapters deal primarily with how to encourage and facilitate inventions from teams that consist of individuals
with complementary talents. We begin from a description of the eight
roles of the innovative team as described by Meredith Belbin, but we will
extend the basic model by also describing the reconciliation of the main
characteristics across those roles. You might have a team that is not inventive even though all roles are covered. Again, it is important that, for
example, roles like the idea-generating Plant are challenged by the role
of the Monitor-Evaluator. We focus on how to find the particular roles
and facilitate the tensions between the roles. The role of the Chair – as
the reconciler in chief – gets particular mention.

The seventh chapter is devoted to the patterns of interactions one
needs to create to get the whole organisation innovating. Yes, the creation of an innovative culture assumes creative individuals and inventive
teams. But these are just necessary pre-conditions, and are not sufficient
alone. The dynamics that exist between teams (as well as between individuals in teams) are crucial. This chapter is underpinned by the research
we have undertaken at THT (Trompenaars Hampden-Turner), into several thousand dilemmas of the participants at our workshops over the
past ten years. We use this evidence to discuss not only the many dilemmas that need to be reconciled but also how to create what we will define
as an integral culture of innovation. This culture consists of a focus on
adaptation/flexibility, tasks/goals, structure/reliability *and* loyalty/com-
mitment. We show the results of hundreds of organisations – ones that
are innovative compared to those who struggle – and how their respective cultures differ.

Chapter 7 shows that innovation can actually be taught at a major
Asian university. However, the classroom must let out upon a larger eco-

system that includes a Learning Journey to foreign lands. In addition, we have designed a methodology to define, capture and assess the values of an innovative pedagogy. We show that conventional education, even in a good school, falls far short of the creative ideal, but that teaching students to resolve dilemmas leads to dozens of entrepreneurial start-ups as well as an enthusiastic learning experience.

The eighth and ninth chapters propose some ideas and actions for leaders and managers to help their organisations innovate.

We trust you will enjoy the book and have fun reading it.

Fons and Charles

INDIVIDUAL CREATIVITY: HARES, TORTOISES AND WHAT JUNG MEANT

'There is a phrase I learned in college called "Having a healthy disregard for the impossible". That is a really cool phrase. You should try to do things that most people would not'

Larry Page, co-founder of Google Inc.

The creation of a culture of innovation often starts with the individual. There are few innovative organisations that don't have some unusually creative individuals. They are constantly challenging the organisation's routines, irritating their more conservative colleagues and making many mistakes on their way, from which they constantly learn.

People like actors and sculptors sometimes think that they all have creativity. Many people are in favour of creativity but many who extol it cannot do it. It takes no creativity to invoke the process. Many can be creative internally. You simply take the ideas you remember and recombine them, like jiggling a kaleidoscope and choosing the best images. But to be creative as the world sees this and produce a useful product without precedent is much harder and requires *innovation,* the transformation of creativity into valued use. We need to overcome the prevailing wisdom that creativity is possessed by only a gifted few.

What kind of special competence(s) does the creative person possess? And is it innate or can you teach it? A great deal of effort has been made to try and define creativity. Early Greek philosophers thought it was a mystical inspiration from the seven muses and later Freud viewed creativity as resulting from the tension between conscious reality and unconscious.

One of the problems is the enormous range of implicit notions, that is, what people think creativity is implicitly, rather what has been explored systematically and rigorously through scientific research. Many of us have various ideas about creativity often based on 'great man' theories (such as Leonardo da Vinci or Einstein) but cannot explicitly state what this is. Most of the explicit theories generated in the field of creativity have focused on identifying how much creativity a person possesses rather than what it is. This approach is interested in measuring the capacity or ability to create, evaluating the 'correctness' of responses. Ability or level of creativity might be measured by fluency, flexibility, originality and elaboration; it is specific to the situation being examined. This is called the *level approach*. Thus we might contrive an instrument that 'measures' how much creativity a person has based on the following dimensions:[1]

- Remote associations: the capacity to make connections between things that don't initially appear to have connections
- Perspective: the capacity to shift one's perspective on a situation in terms of space and time and other people
- Curiosity: the desire to discover something beyond the status quo and see if this can be improved
- Boldness: the confidence to push boundaries beyond accepted conventions and the ability to eliminate fear of what others think of you
- Complexity: the capacity to carry large quantities of data and to be able to manage and manipulate the relationships between information
- Persistence: the capacity to force oneself to keep trying and derive more and stronger solutions even when good ones have already been generated
- Abstraction: the capacity to abstract concepts from experience and then discover new concrete applications.

Since the 1950s, researchers have focused on understanding how people manifest their creativity. This is called the *style approach*. It recognises

---

1   As used by CREAX NV, Belgium, in their 'Creativity' Profiling tool

that people express their creativity in different ways or cognitive styles. The style approach aims to answer the question 'How are you creative?'

The need for identifying highly creative individuals generated an impressive amount of research that focused on the level approach. This situation reinforced a commonly held belief that creativity is limited to a minority capable of generating creative thinking. A corollary of this argument is that geniuses use cognitive processes that are radically different from those employed by most individuals. Most researchers conclude that we are all, or can be, creative to a lesser or greater degree if we are given the opportunity.

In summary, the spectrum of components that various authors come to include when defining creativity comprises four characteristics:

1   They always involve thinking or behaving imaginatively.
2   Overall this imaginative activity is purposeful: that is, it is directed to achieving an objective.
3   These processes must generate something original.
4   The outcome must be of value in relation to the objective.

Imagination is definitely a key part of creativity. But are all imaginative ideas creative? Suppose someone imagined a green and white spotted lion. Would this be creative? It may be that no one has conjured up a lion like this before. But what is the point of the idea? If someone thinks of an imaginative idea like this and then does not take it any further, are they creative? Creative people are purposeful as well as imaginative. Their imaginative activity is directed at achieving an objective (although this objective may change over time). Imaginative activity can only be creative if it is of value in relation to its purpose. This means asking questions such as, 'Does it do the job?', 'Is it aesthetically pleasing?', 'Is it a valid solution?', 'Is it useful?'

Sometimes our views about what is worthwhile and valuable may differ. Sharing judgments together can provide useful insight into what other people value. An act can be highly imaginative and original, but harm someone or destroy something. Are we happy with this kind of creativity?

An additional aspect has to do with dissecting creative thought into a process of dual exchanges through the interaction of two types of thinking – convergence and divergence. Definitions of divergent thinking usually include the ability to elaborate and to think of diverse and original ideas with fluency and speed. Ideating and brainstorming are premiere examples of this type of thinking. Convergent thinking is defined as the ability to use logical and evaluative thinking to critique and narrow ideas to ones best suited for given situations, or set criteria. We use this type of thinking when we make crucial and well-formed decisions after appraising an array of ideas, information, or alternatives. One needs to be able to weave in and out of divergent and convergent thought patterns in arriving at an appropriate conclusion specific for a given situation.

Once the level of creativity could be identified[2], consistently and reliably, the next wave of research examined whether or not those levels of creativity could be enhanced. Torrance[3] and Torrance and Presbury[4] identified a total of 384 studies that examined the effectiveness of creativity training. The majority of these studies concluded that creativity can be enhanced through formal training. Perhaps one of the most extensive studies on the effects of creativity training was conducted by Parnes and Noller[5].

Creative people are more…	Creative people are less…
Intuitive	Sensing
Perceiving	Judging
Thinking	Feeling
Extrovert	Introvert
Tortoise brain	Hare brain
Lateral	Vertical
Risk taking	Securing
Hunting	Gathering
Individualistic	Consensus seeking
Right brain	Left brain
Etc.	Etc.

2 Guilford, J.P., *Way beyond the IQ*, Buffalo, NY: Beady Limited, 1977; Torrance, E. P., *Torrance tests of creative thinking: Norms and technical manual*, Bensenville, IL: Scholastic Testing Service, 1974

3 Torrance, E.P., 'Can we teach children to think creatively?', *Journal of Creative Behavior 6*, pp.236–262, 1972

4 Torrance, E.P. and Presbury, J., 'Criteria of success of 242 recent experimental studies of creativity', *Creative Child Quarterly 30*, pp.15–19, 1984

5 Parnes, S. J. and Noller, R.B., 'Applied creativity: The creative studies project Part 11', *Journal of Creative Behavior 6*, pp. 164–186, 1972

Unfortunately, the various measures are most often represented on linear-scale models, where one orientation excludes the other. Let's try it.

We argue that there might indeed be relationships between certain dominant orientations and the creative competence of an individual, but an important point has been missed. 'Stop!' some would say. Many have done solid research that shows a correlation between certain of the above preferences and creativity. Take the work of Kirton, the renowned British psychologist, who developed the well-regarded instrument, the KAI Inventory[6]. This measures individual styles of problem definition and solving. Kirton conducted a study showing the relationship between the KAI and the MBTI. The primary correlations of the KAI were with the MBTI's Sensing-Intuiting (S-N) and Judging-Perceiving (J-P) scales (Thinking-Feeling and Introvert-Extrovert were not highly correlated)[7]. Other studies went further, and one claimed that all four MBTI preferences correlate with creativity. Creative individuals tend to be more intuitive (N) than sensory (S), more perceiving (P) than judging (J), more extroverted (E) than introverted (I) and more thinking (T) than feeling (F)[8].

We don't dispute the relationship (statistical reliability) between these characteristics and preferences. However, we have found that the essence of the creative process is not in one or other position of a continuum, but in how the opposites of the scale interact. How are the faculties of imagination, holism, emotions and connectedness of our right brain interacting through our *corpus callosum* with the preferences of our left brain to be realistic, analytic and rational? Creative people integrate *all* those faculties and, in the process, discover new ideas and solutions.

Let's see what that means for the major models of distinctive orientations in the human brain. In this chapter we will look at the hare brain and the tortoise mind, the intriguing formulation of Guy Claxton, before

---

6 Kirton, M.J., *Journal of Applied Psychology* 61, pp.622–629, 1980

7 Kirton, M.J., 'Adaptors and innovators: A description of a measure', *Journal of Applied Psychology* 61, pp.622–629, 1976. Kirton, M.J., *Manual of the Kirton Adaption-Innovation Inventory*, London, England: National Foundation for Educational Research, 1977

8 Thorne, Avril and Gough, Harrison, *Portraits of Type: An MBTI Research Compendium*, Palo Alto, California: Consulting Psychologists Press Inc, 1991

turning to our new slant on the work of Carl G. Jung, and our modifica-
tions to the MBTI. In Chapter 3 we will re-examine some well-known
learning processes, including the role of humour in the culture of creativity. We'll examine how powerful these ways of looking at reality are and,
in addition, extend them by going beyond their inherently linear scales.

Hare brain and tortoise mind

Guy Claxton[9] makes a fundamental distinction between 'hare brain' and
'tortoise mind'. Hare brain, with its faster thought-processing speed,
is analytical, calculating, self-conscious, and language-dependent (and
given to 'monkey chatter' in its worse moments). As Claxton emphasises,
'hare brain' is the right tool for many situations, but not all.

But when creative solutions are needed, when a problem is fuzzy and
imprecise, then the much slower, pondering and meditative strengths of
the 'tortoise mind' give answers. Others have named this 'tortoise mind'
as intuition, or the unconscious, and the id. Claxton goes on to name it
the 'undermind'.

Based on research of electrical activity of the brain, Claxton describes that the brain unconsciously initiates action one-third of a second
before conscious intention, which in turn precedes action by one-fifth of
a second. The obvious question is, does the 'undermind' will things to
happen that the conscious mind can only veto, not initiate? And who in-
structs the undermind, if it might not be our conscious mind? This would
seem to violate the notion of human 'free will'.

Freud suggested the hidden, unconscious mind, the id, was the pressure cooker for much neurotic pain. Claxton wants us to see the undermind 'tortoise mind' as a wondrous endowment of the brain and ever the
equal of the conscious mind, the 'hare brain'.

Beyond the reach of conscious language, the undermind, to do its
best, needs time to ponder and meditate. Claxton suggests that among
religions, Buddhism best cultivates the undermind.

---

9 Claxton, Guy, *Hare Brain, Tortoise Mind: How Intelligence Increases When You
   Think Less,* Harper Perennial, 2000

Confusion has to become our friend

Thus Claxton explores why intelligence increases when you think less. He builds a thesis on the dichotomy between the privileged mode of intelligence-conscious, result-oriented problem solving and the less respectable unconscious intelligence. This unconscious, or 'undermind', approaches problems playfully, examines the questions themselves and keeps us in touch with our poetic nature. His multidisciplinary approach is beautifully executed, with a constant dialogue on the virtues of intuition and a peaceful mind drawing on the works of poets, novelists and Buddhist teachings. In the West, 'intelligence' is measured by how well we can verbalise and enumerate what we do, and therefore much of human capability suffers when put under the spotlight of conscious attention. He contrasts this Western approach with the actions of the 'unconscious intelligence', claiming that much of our best thinking takes place below consciousness.

That is why in management we go from one fad to another, because in the long term none of them seem to work. Management writers often say there are just five points, or seven habits, written in a very concise, rational way. You get excited, but the next day you have forgotten 50%, and by the next Tuesday 98%. The problem in business is that these commandments leave no room for the tortoise mind – a terribly dangerous development that stifles creativity and innovation and inevitably leads to bad decision making. These commandments are the widely held, but misguided, beliefs that being decisive means making decisions quickly, that fast is always better, and that we should think of our minds as being like computers. Sadly, most of us today believe that a computer is of more use to us than a wise person.

If you want to change your behaviour or incorporate a new habit, you have to continually practise and 'live' it for 30 to 40 days after you first learn it – otherwise it is gone forever. It is in the ongoing practice that you finally understand what was meant on that PowerPoint slide that was flashed up in front of you. And it seems very much like learning to speak a language. You start with some words and some basic grammar, then you get the holistic feel for the structure and flow of the language.

And when you go to a shop and speak to the shopkeeper in her local language, do you still calculate the total cost of what you are buying in your mother tongue? It takes time to 'think' and 'calculate' in the new language.

Guy Claxton noted that to clarify by hare brain, you need to refer to the sort of deliberate, conscious thinking that we do when we apply reason and logic to known data. By tortoise mind he refers to a less purposeful, clear-cut, making less assumptions, more playful, more dreamy way of experiencing; we mull things over, we ponder a problem, we bear the problem in mind when we see the world go by. These leisurely ways of knowing are part of our intelligence. Hare brain works best when the problem is known and so is the answer. All the info is there to solve the problem. But real-world problems are not like that. When the problem is complex the tortoise mind works best. You may need measurements but you don't have them. In our Western culture, things that can't be measured are often ignored. Problems which are a bit dubious and loaded with assumptions are often either avoided or disregarded as not serious. In tortoise mind we like 'big buzzing confusions', where the measurements and data don't match. Answers are not clear-cut.

However, hare brain can solve small creative problems. The Japanese educational system stops people thinking for themselves. Yet, the Japanese are very good in solving tiny incremental problems. But when you want a new picture, you need tortoise mind. The hare brain tends to look within the imaginary frame, while our tortoise mind invites us to think outside of the box, to leave our self-imposed assumptions. Creativity is inviting the tortoise mind to overcome your hare brain assumptions. These assumptions are what Scheerer calls 'fixations'. In our normal mode of operation we are so used to thinking mechanistically, linearly, conservatively and with no full inspiration, we take the problem and 'kill it'. And when it doesn't work we attack even more aggressively, with the same approach. Insight is often delayed or thwarted by 'fixation' on an inappropriate solution. Hare brain seems to dominate our automatic pilot. There are more sources of fixation. Here are some exercises that show it.

The match problem
Six matches must be assembled to form four congruent equilateral triangles each side of which is equal to the length of the matches.

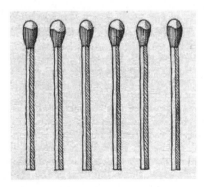

Solution: The match problem is solved by building a three-dimensional pyramid. Most people assume that matches must lie flat.

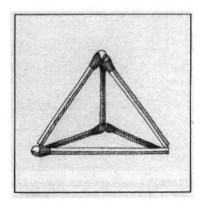

We see that the matches problem cannot be solved, as one assumes that the matches must lie in one plane, and virtually everyone who tries it assumes just that. The assumption is implicit. And the solution is obvious when one 'reformulates' or 're-centres' one thoughts. This is exactly what happens with the next riddle as well.

Perceptual fixation exercise:
Place element B on element A in such a way that two closed figures are formed.

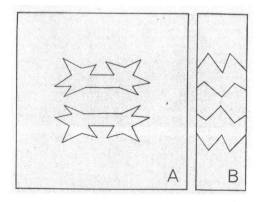

Solution: Recentering also solves this problem. The abstract shapes of A are broken up and rotated 90 degrees, B then fits properly.

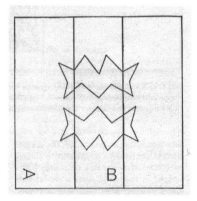

Sheerer quotes some experiments where fixation has been reported to be a function of involvement in a situation. When observers were given a conscious 'psychological distance', while watching 'subjects' running through the motions of solving problems, a significantly higher percentage of observers were able to solve the problem than those involved in the problem. And don't we all find this when watching games on television? Another reason for fixation is goal-directedness. A large majority of people are unwilling to accept a detour that delays the achievement of their goal and can be strengthened by too much motivation. A final quoted factor of fixation is habituation. In all cases fixation is overcome and insight attained by a sudden shift in the way the problem or the objects involved in it are viewed. It is our tortoise mind that can get hare habits and orientations broken.

Working together between hare brain and tortoise mind

Your hare brain you might easily conclude that it is in the tortoise mind that creativity is born. Yes, no doubt, using your tortoise mind made the difference. If you overcame your assumption that the matches should be lying flat, then it becomes easy. And if you overcome your assumption that the pictures need to be horizontal, the answer becomes obvious. But let's explore the following exercise. Here's a picture. What do you see?

Figure 2.1 What do you see?

Some people interpret the integrated picture as a skull and some as an older man drinking wine with a younger lady. Even looking at the integrated picture we can see the 'other image'. This might require you to let your mind drift (as in 'tortoise' mode). Both the hare brain of detail and analysis and the tortoise 'undermind' of the larger picture are in and of themselves deceptive. It is in the interplay between these orientations that we create our reality. Which you see first may be based on your expectation.

Figure 2.2 The whole picture in detail

Let's go back to the question we asked at the beginning of this chapter. What were the circumstances in which your best creative idea was born? Where did it happen?

Let us take a guess. You weren't working hard and pushing for the breakthrough. Neither were you just relaxing and meditating waiting for ideas to drop into your mind. You got to some great ideas when you used the tension between hard work and relaxation. It was on vacation, when you suddenly got the new ideas that could make that difficult project so much easier.

In a nutshell, Claxton describes the hare brain as logical, fast, machine-like thinking. The tortoise mind, on the other hand, is slower, less focused, less articulate, much more playful, almost dreamy. In his book, Claxton says that the two sides *need each other* to come up with not just ideas, but good ideas. It is important to note that you need the hare brain. You need to get the information first and work hard on it through the hare brain. Only with that work will you make the tortoise mind effective and creative. You only get the solutions because you work hard. You need to do the hare brain thinking first! Then you must think through the situation and finally, when you have the ideas, you need to evaluate them logically and systematically (hare brain again). It becomes a spiral, reconciling the tension between hare brain and tortoise mind.

You may think that you consciously make moment-to-moment decisions about your life. But Claxton convincingly demonstrates that the mysterious 'undermind' has more to do with who we are and what we do than our conscious, logical, linear mind. The 'd-mode', our *deliberative* thinking style – the one we perfect in our years of schooling – is the most commonly accepted model of how our minds work. However, the experimental evidence suggests that d-mode thinking has relatively little to do with how we make most of the decisions in our lives. The d-mode actually comes up with plausible reasons that justify our actions, but it isn't the *source* of those actions. The conscious mind's job is to focus attention on a particular problem and maintain a coherent sense of ourselves; but these processes all come after the fact of our inner decision making. People often seem happier with their decisions in the long run if they think less about them from the outset. It is in this sense that 'think less' makes one more intelligent.

How to create the conditions for tortoise mind

Often the only difference between creative and uncreative people is self-perception. Creative people see themselves as creative, and give themselves the freedom to create. Uncreative people do not think about creativity, and do not give themselves the opportunity to create anything new. Being creative may just be a matter of setting aside the time needed to take a step back. Ask yourself if there is a better way of doing something. Edward de Bono calls this a 'Creative Pause'. He suggests that this should be a short break of maybe only 30 seconds, but that this should be a habitual part of thinking. This needs self-discipline, as it is easy to forget. On a corporate level 3M and Google have successfully experimented with the notions of '15 or 20 percent time'. It is borrowed from the academic world, where professors are given an average one day a week to pursue private interests. At Google, individual employees are expected to allot 20 percent of their time to whatever ideas interest them most. It is the refocusing between projects that makes tortoise mind and hare brain interact creatively:

'The 20 percent rule was a way of encouraging innovation, and both Brin and Page (the two co-founders of Google FT) saw this as essential to establishing and maintaining the right culture and creating a place where bright technologists would want to work and be motivated to come up with breakthrough ideas ... People talk over lunch about the things they are playing with.'[10]

Much earlier 3M developed a 15 percent rule to spin innovation. The extra time to dream yielded, amongst other things, the idea for Post-it notes.

MBTI revisited

While few people would argue against the desirability of employing creative people, how to accurately identify creative people is less clear. There are instruments that claim to measure almost anything, so wouldn't it be wonderful if we could simply test a person's creativity? The goal of making personality traits measurable is the fundamental quest of professional tools that seek to offer an objective assessment. Of these, the champion is the MBTI instrument, the most widely used personality inventory in history, which is administered to over three million people a year[11]. Human Resources professionals depend on it when their clients need to make important business, career, or personal decisions.

One of Jung's most important discoveries was the realisation that, by understanding the way we typically process information, we can gain insights into why we act and feel the way we do. In particular, he noted that, in order to understand ourselves better, we need to understand the way we typically perceive, and then act upon, information. Jung identified two core psychological processes: *perceiving*, which involves receiving, or taking in, information; and *judging*, which involves processing that information (e.g. organising the information and coming to conclusions from it).

Jung identified two further ways of perceiving information, which he termed *sensing* and *intuiting*, and two alternative ways of judging

---

10 Vise, David A., *The Google Story*, fully updated edition, Pan Books 2005, p.7

11 Myers, Isabel *Gifts Differing*, Palo Alto, California: CPP Inc, 1995. And look at http://www.winovations.com/NFmbti.htm Myers, Isabel Briggs, and McCaulley, Mary H., *Manual: A Guide to the Development and Use of the Myers-Briggs Type Indicator*, Palo Alto, California: Consulting Psychologists Press Inc, 1992

information, which he termed *thinking* and *feeling*. Moreover, he noted that these four mental processes can be directed either at the external world of people and things, or at the internal world of subjective experience. He termed this attitude towards the outer world *extraversion*, and this attitude towards the inner world *introversion*. The attempt to find creativity in the traditional MBTI points to the fact that those who use 'the road less travelled' by their culture are more creative.

MBTI limitations

So, can this widely used instrument also give some clues to the creativity of the individual being evaluated?

One such variation of the basic tool that we have found to be particularly useful is the MBTI Creativity Index, or MBTI-CI. The MBTI-CI is calculated by taking MBTI scores and applying an algorithm, developed out of 30 years of creativity research at the Institute for Personality Assessment and Research (IPAR)[12].

Creative individuals tend to be more intuitive (N) than sensory (S), more perceiving than judging (J), more extroverted (E) than introverted (I) and more thinking (T) than feeling (F)[13]. In another study, the MBTI profiles of innovators varied greatly. The great majority had an ENT combination, while the split between judging and perceiving was approximately 50:50. Other studies have shown that up to 95% of senior corporate managers are STJs[14], with Americans tending to be an E type and British managers a dominant I type.

And the frequently occurring difference between innovators and managers is a source of potential conflict. Intuitives and sensers view the world very differently. A change will always seem greater to an ST than to an NT, because STs are typically more comfortable with continuous

---

12 Gough, Harrison, 'Studies of the Myers-Briggs Type Indicator in a personality assessment research institute', paper presented at the *Fourth National Conference on the Myers-Briggs Type Indicator*, Stanford University, California, July 1981

13 Thorne, Avril and Gough, Harrison, *Portraits of Type: An MBTI Research Compendium*, Palo Alto, California: Consulting Psychologists Press Inc, 1991

14 Kroeger, O. and Thuessen, J. *Type Talk at Work,* Dell Publishing: New York, pp. 394–399, 1992

change than with discontinuous change. An NT, however, may actually enjoy discontinuous change.

But what happens when users try to apply methodologies and instruments to measure things that go beyond the environment and delimitations in which they were developed?

Personality and creativity

What we really need to ask is why the underlying models were designed around mutually exclusive values in the first place. It is because our Western, hare brain way of thinking is based on Cartesian logic and forces us to say it is *either/or*, not to say *and … and*. This contradicts what Jung had in mind when he originally construed the underlying conceptual framework behind MBTI[15].

We want to consider how we can extend MBTI by slightly adjusting the context and thereby make it a more reliable instrument, measuring creativity far beyond any cultural preference.

Although there is some evidence that the typologies are statistically related to creativity, we believe that the assumptions on which the instrument is based prohibit its potential to measure creativity. We need a different approach, and a different context.

First of all, it needs to be redesigned into an Integrated Type Indicator that overcomes the limitation of the linear model; and secondly, we need to adjust the process in which it is embedded.

The big advantage of the MBTI is how readily recognisable it is. We have all encountered extroverts or overwhelming introverts at social gatherings. We have all tried to reason in vain with someone whose feelings are so strong that our efforts were useless, or have witnessed someone calculating while others visibly suffer in the process. The MBTI is a 'ready reckoner' of personality types, but there are serious problems of superficiality and of proper application.

The superficiality problem stems from *either/or* classifications. Is it really the case that we judge *or* perceive, think *or* feel, etc.? Jung himself arranged his 'opposite' archetypes in the shape of Tao and wrote of *effec-*

---

15 Jung, Carl G, *Psychological Types*, Routledge & Kegan Paul, 1971

tance through synthesis. He warned us that ESTJ was the dominant profile of relatively young, brash people in the practical world. He regarded these as the dominant Western industrial values. But is this related to the process of creation? Our research suggests not!

What Jung advocated was that we move *out* of this pattern and mature over time, especially in our later years. He believed that introversion should qualify extraversion, that intuitive faculties should guide sensing, that our feelings could tell us which thoughts were more profound and that good judgment was based on the fullness of perception. In short, Jung sought to *reconcile* his four functions, not polarise them. He regarded the less preferred end of any function as lying beneath the *persona* (the superficial character armour). Where personalities overemphasised their dominant preferences, they could be haunted by their 'shadow sides' – that is, the values that are repressed and pushed down into unconsciousness. But these values were always there, and all the more pervasive for being denied!

The problem of applicability is even more troublesome (in staff selection, for example). Suppose a company *is* predominantly ESTJ: does that mean that a candidate with this profile should be preferred or *not* preferred? Clearly he or she would 'fit in', but is this necessarily desirable, particularly if we are looking for innovation? Haven't we missed an opportunity to make the company more diverse? After all, customers come in every shape, size and type. Might it not be wise to match the preferences of our customer base with our employee base and listen to someone *different* for a change?

The problem of applicability doesn't end here either. Suppose we decided to achieve a balance. Should this be an aggregate balance (i.e. all employees), a departmental balance or a peer group balance? And where should this balance take place: *within* the personality or *between* personalities? Jung wanted a better balance and a synthesis within the personality, but the MBTI is of little use in this respect, because it fails to register our less preferred types. We are left with the possibility of creating balance within the group, but what do we do when the first INFPs we hire feel rejected by the ESTJs?

And might it be actually harmful to just accept your type as fixed? Might you not, like the tragic heroes of world drama, *overplay your winning combination*, go on doing what you have habitually done and not change? In our experience, those who administer the MBTI work hard to bring to the surface the less preferred type, and so make their subjects more whole – but are these efforts enough to compensate for the selective reinforcement of one's customary façade? Perhaps not.

It's also instructive to consider what the MBTI does *not* measure. It does not measure the capacity to reach out to another person with the opposite profile, and it does not measure how severely the 'shadow sides' are repressed within the candidate. Severe repression would, according to Jung, make it very difficult to communicate with someone with the characteristics you so dislike in yourself.

Can the MBTI be improved by extending the underlying model?

We have seen that the MBTI brilliantly measures four very important decisions but is unable to assess to what extent these contrasting types have been integrated *with* each other, as opposed to subordinated *to* each other. Might it be possible to *conserve* the best aspects of MBTI while inquiring about the extent to which introverted ideas have been extroverted, sense impressions have been intuited, feelings have been thought about and judgments formed on the basis of strong perceptions? And in this process of integration of opposites might we just find the key to creativity?

Given the millions of people who are interested in one way or another in MBTI profiles, it is important *not* to let all this measurement, coaching, mentoring and insight go to waste. We must, if possible, build on this famous instrument, not try to demolish it or replace it. This is what we have tried to do in our Integrated Type Indicator.

Our Integrated Type Indicator

If you are recruiting someone who has a slight preference for intuiting, what do you do if sensing is the organisation's preference for making a successful career? And in an international company, can MBTI be of help in finding creative people to stimulate innovation?

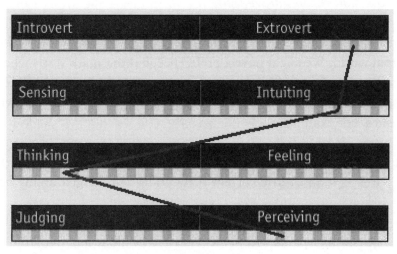

Figure 2.3 Classic MBTI – profile of a creative individual

Research has sought to correlate the MBTI scales with different job categories, functions and (national) cultures. There is evidence to suggest which dominant type best fits a marketing role, which type is found most often amongst successful managers and what is dominant in Asia versus the USA. And we have seen that considerable research has been focused on relating creativity to certain preferences on those MBTI categories.

However, since most of this research has been done in the USA, we are suddenly confronted with some interesting dilemmas that challenge this principle.

We have to remember that much of this type of research owes its origin to western thinking and research methodologies, even though it has been 'exported' across the world. When we begin to reflect on the philosophy of the underlying paradigms of inquiry and incorporate other types of logic, such as Yin Yang or Taoism, we soon realise that we have been restrictive in basing the profiling on bi-modal dimensions. We believe that the creative individual in the western world tends to start with thinking followed by feeling, intuiting followed by sensing, perceiving by judging and extroversion by introversion. In the Latin world, creativity tends to start with feeling, later checked by thinking, and in Asia there is a tendency to prefer intuition, introversion and perceiving followed by sensing, extroversion and judging. However, creativity exists in all environments; there is just a difference in preference about where to start.

Let's apply this thinking and new logic to the scales of Myers-Briggs.

Extroversion versus introversion

Creativity is where the inner world of energy is connected with the external world. We might have a preference, but the spark starts when the two 'energies' meet. So what we measure with the original MBTI type of question is preference only. We ask people to choose between two opposites. For example:

a) Most of my personal energy comes from the people I meet and greet. It is as if an electric current between us has charged up my batteries.
b) Most of my personal energy comes from ideas, feelings, and data generating sparks within me. I need to be alone and free from interruption to organise my ideas.

Obviously a) represents an extrovert and b) an introvert. But see what happens if we add the following two alternatives:

c) Most of my personal energy comes from the people I meet and greet, but in quieter moments, what I experienced through them starts generating within me.
d) Most of my personal energy comes from ideas, feelings and data generating sparks within me. But then comes the acid test, when I tell everyone what I have conceived.

These four options tell us much more than the two initial ones. They allow subjects to:

1) prefer introversion to the exclusion of extroversion;
2) prefer extroversion to the exclusion of introversion;
3) be extrovert and gather information before introvertly reflecting upon this;
4) be introvert and so excite themselves to tell others extrovertly.

Our contention is that answers c) and d) select more integrated personalities and are more creative in the process. Answer c) puts extroversion first and then takes the results inside. Answer d) puts introversion first but in a way that communicates it to the outside world to share with others. We believe that people who select c) and d) are not only more creative, but *more able to deal with people of the opposite persuasion.*

The choices can be tabulated as follows.

Figure 2.4 Extroversion/Introversion

Choices a) and b) each exclude their opposites, but choice c) feels in a way inclusive of thinking, while choice d) thinks in a way inclusive of feeling. Both paths culminate in reflecting on vivid experience at top right. We believe that inclusive or integrated choices reveal leadership potential and predict more effective performances.

Note how the integrated answers move across the continuum, while the polarised ones stay put.

Who are the creative heroes who symbolise the integration of an extrovert mode with subsequent introversion? Donald Schön called these Reflective Practitioners[16]. They first practise in the real world and later reflect on that practice. Perhaps the world's first Reflective Practitioner

16 Schön, D.A., *The Reflective Practitioner*, New York: Basic Books, 1983

was Hippocrates, a working physician in Athens whose experience culminated in the Hippocratic Oath, taken by doctors to this day and now over two thousand years old.

Note that the curve (c) starts with extroverted conduct, visiting patients in their homes, trying sometimes desperately to save lives. It then learns from and codifies this experience ex post facto.

Who are the creative leaders who symbolise the introverted style, which then acts boldly and decisively in an extroverted fashion? Western history's most illustrious example is probably Martin Luther. That he was initially introverted is in no doubt. He was a monk, much given to prayer, reflection and anguished confessions. He entered a monastery in 1505 and it was not until 1517 that he famously nailed his 95 theses to the church door in Wittenburg. We would have heard neither of Hippocrates nor of Luther had they not moved between types. In the case of Hippocrates, this was from extrovert practice to introvert codification; in the case of Martin Luther, it was from cloistered introversion to a famous act of extrovert defiance.

Thinking versus feeling

The MBTI tests for the relative dominance of thinking versus feeling by the following type of questions.

When I make a decision I think it is most important:

a) to make sure that I test the opinions of others
b) to reach a decisive conclusion.

The thinking personality marks b) and the feeling one a).

In all creative processes we combine logic and reason with what we believe to be right. We all use both modes for our innovations. Some start with what they believe to be fair and correct by pre-defined rules. Others prefer to start in a subjective manner based on what they believe to be right within their own value systems.

To capture the essence of the creative process we added two more possibilities:

c) to test the opinions of others before deciding.
d) to be decisive and thereby elicit others' opinions.

These four questions tell us much more than the two initial ones. They allow subjects to:

1) prefer feeling to thinking
2) prefer thinking to feeling
3) feel out opinions before thinking
4) think and so invite feelings to be expressed.

Our contention is that answers c) and d) select more integrated personalities and are more creative in the process. Answer c) puts feelings first and then thinks about these. Answer d) puts thinking first but in a way that elicits feelings. We believe that individuals selecting c) and d) are not only more creative, but *more able to deal with persons of the opposite persuasion.*

The choices can be tabulated as follows (see over). Choices a) and b) each exclude their opposites, but choice c) feels in a way inclusive of thinking, while choice d) thinks in a way inclusive of feeling. Both paths culminate in *thoughtful sensibility* at top right. We believe that inclusive or integrated choices reveal leadership potential and predict more effective performances.

Sensing versus intuiting

These two types are contrasting ways of processing information. Sensing looks at discrete, empirical facts and records observations. Intuiting looks into a whole phenomenon, interpreting its meaning and significance. Here we ask: *Which* option best describes how you manage?

a) In solving problems I like to analyse the situation and look hard at the facts. I believe these speak for themselves, needing no window dressing.
b) In solving problems, I like to gain deep insights into the meaning of the issue. Once I have grasped this I test my supposition against all available facts.

Figure 2.5 Feeling/Thinking

c) In solving problems, I like to gain deep insights into the meaning of the issue. Facts are dependent on context. Once I grasp the context the facts fall into place.

d) In solving problems I like to analyse the situation and look hard at the facts, but then I start to draw inferences, until the meaning of this issue is clear.

The integrated answers are b) and d). The polarised answers are a) and c). In d), the person starts with sensed facts and develops intuitions. In b), the person starts with deep intuitions and tests these against the available facts.

The greatest scientific example of the sensing type was Sir Isaac Newton. He convinced three centuries of science to look first at the facts and only then to draw cautious inferences. The real world was neither what we wanted it to be, nor influenced in any way by our wishes. We must humbly reflect God-given realities on the pupils of our eyes and not let our beliefs or conceits stand in the way. Only after we have made sure of all the facts should we start to draw inferences. This approach to the physical world is illustrated in in the anticlockwise spiral.

Yet science moves on, and theoretical physics is quite another challenge, needing intuition to disentangle its puzzling anomalies. Albert Ein-

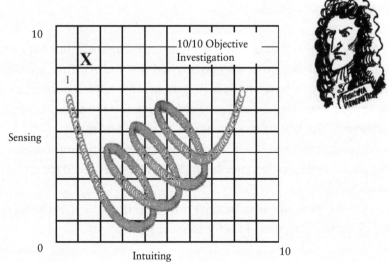

Figure 2.6 Isaac Newton

stein was famed for his intuitive powers and would cut himself shaving if an exciting intuition struck him. But none of this means that he ignored the available facts. Having gained his intuitions, he proceeded to test them – an example of how one type helps to verify the conjecture of another. The helix winding clockwise from intuition to sensing is illustrated in Figure 2.7.

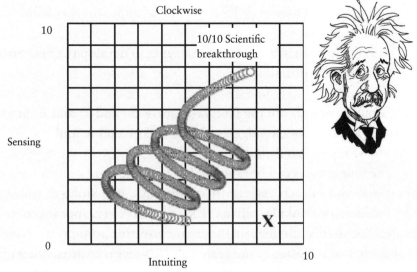

Figure 2.7 Einstein

Judging versus perceiving

A final example focuses on the preference between judging or perceiving. This is about how we perceive events and form judgments about them. Once you have made a judgment, this tends to foreclose further perceiving because you will probably act on that judgment. Some people judge very quickly; others always want more and more information. The perceiving preference leads to openness to experimentation and making mistakes, while a preference for judging leads to a need for structure and predictability.

Conventionally, instruments pose questions such as the following: *While* tackling an issue I prefer to work:

a)   in a structured and organised way
b)   flexibly and with the necessary improvisation.

In some cultural environments, such as Germanic cultures, there is a tendency to score higher on a), while b) would appeal more to the Latins. Thus in a team/group of both Germans **and** Latins, wouldn't the following be more effective to diagnose effective orientations?
While tackling an issue I prefer to work:

c)   in a structured way in order to stimulate improvisation within certain boundaries
d)   with the necessary improvisation, trying to develop the best procedures and organisation.

Here again c) and d) are the integrated answers and a) and b) are the polarised ones, in which judgment squashes perception and perception postpones judgment indefinitely.

The four choices can be tabulated as follows.
Choices a) and b) each exclude their opposites, but choice c) feels in a way inclusive of thinking, while choice d) thinks in a way inclusive of feeling. Both paths culminate in the error-correcting attitude at top right. We believe that inclusive or integrated choices reveal creativity potential and predict more innovative performances.

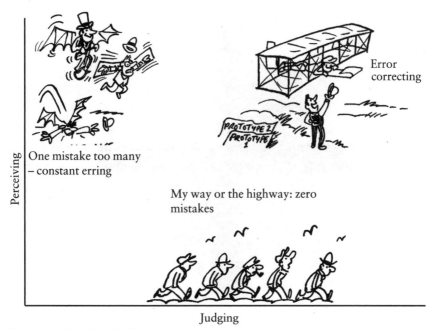

Figure 2.8 Perceiving/Judging

The Integrated Type Indicator model (ITI)

Let's summarise our conclusions. Like most social science instruments, MBTI-like scales attempt to measure object-like 'things'. The presence of extroversion, sensing, thinking and judging is thought to exclude introversion, intuiting, feeling and perceiving. In fact, all human minds contain both types – and they are not 'things' at all, but differences on a continuum along which we move continuously.

In our extended model of MBTI – the ITI – we use our own questions, which represent the two extreme opposing values for each conjugate pair. However, we also add two further choices that represent the clockwise and anticlockwise reconciliation of these extremes.

By combining the answers from a series of questions in this extended format, we can compute a profile that reveals the degree to which an individual seeks to integrate the extreme dimensions, and so shows that individual's potential for creativity.

From the relative shapes and sizes of the four blocks, you can tell the extent to which the ends of the four functions have been reconciled. Are candidates able to move from perceiving to making judgments, from

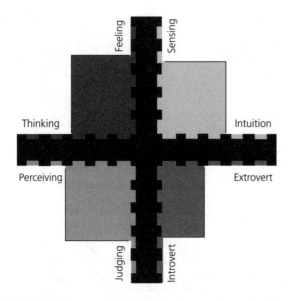

Figure 2.9 sample ITI profile

generating introverted thoughts and ideas to expressing these openly to others in extrovert ways? This capacity to move to and fro on the four continua is much more valuable to the organisation than getting stuck at one end or the other: you can't usefully process information from a fixed position.

If each variable is scaled from 1 to 10, then we can attain an integration score for a whole group, department or company, like this:

(Introvert + Extrovert) + (Sensing + Intuiting) + (Thinking + Feeling) + (Judging + Perceiving) ÷ 4 = Developing Creativity Potential

We have analysed responses to the web-based version of this ITI model. Taken by itself – that is, responses to this instrument alone – this model has already generated insights over and above the basic MBTI profile based on the traditional four linear scales. We have found that the instrument already has high validity and reliability – for example, design engineers in organisations such as the highly creative SatNav, TomTom and Siemens score above the mean on our index. However, the insights from our ITI are more usefully considered when combined (i.e. triangulated) with other measures we describe later.

Reconciliation: a new paradigm for creativity beyond cultural bias

Simply rejecting opposite orientations will get you nowhere. Abandoning your own extreme and adopting the other extreme is like trying to impress on your first date by acting out an unfamiliar role – and you'll soon be found out.

The integrated approach enables us to determine an individual's propensity for reconciling dilemmas, as a direct measure of creativity. We call this ability *innovative competence*. It transcends the single culture in which it may be measured and so provides a robust, generalisable model for all environments. Reconciliation is the real essence of the creative individual.

This ITI is different because it is underpinned by the recognition that, while managers work to accomplish this or that separate objective, creative leaders deal with *the dilemmas of seemingly 'opposed' objectives, which they continually seek to reconcile*. Given the importance of reconciling opposites, it is surprising that no instrument that measures this has been published before.

Published models of creativity tend to lack a coherent, underlying rationale or proposition that predicts effective innovative behaviours. These models tend to seek the same end, but through different approaches. Because of the methodology adopted, these are only prescriptive lists, like a series of ingredients for a recipe – you can only guess at what the dish is going to be. There is no underlying rationale or unifying theme that defines the holistic experience of the meal.

This creates considerable confusion for today's innovative leader. Which paradigm should s/he fit into? Which meanings should s/he espouse: his or her own or those of the foreign culture? Since most of our creativity theory comes from the USA and other English-speaking countries, there is a real danger of ethnocentrism. We do not know, for example, how the lists cited fare outside the USA, or how diverse conceptions of creativity may be. Do different cultures require different styles? Can we reasonably expect other cultures to follow a lead from outside those cultures?

We can see how creative leaders are able to reconcile opposites. Richard Branson can switch from being David in one business situation to Goliath in another. He reconciles the big player with the small player, so that the smaller player becomes big.

Our concern about applying any linear model across international boundaries might be explained by our own overdeveloped reconciliation profiles. But we insist that, with the combination of opposed orientations, today's leader can flourish in diversity. And no one has ever measured anything like that in us.

Please test yourself: www.ridingthewhirlwind.com

INDIVIDUAL CREATIVITY AS PROCESS

Up to now we have reviewed literature that treats creativity largely as a trait or function within personality. Creative persons have been found to think laterally rather than vertically, to think out of the box or frame, to think in third dimensions, to rely more on the right brain, to intuit rather than sense, to risk rather than secure. None of these findings is wrong but nor is it sufficient for a fuller understanding. *Creativity cannot be stereotyped as 'this not that'*. We cannot treat it like a dead butterfly stuck on a pin in a single posture. Yes, indeed, creative people are unusually high in their capacities to reframe and intuit but that is not *all* they are. They transcend stereotypes by integrating opposite endowments, thinking laterally in a way that joins and thereby uses vertical technologies, disordering the better to order, breaking frames to reframe, and risking resources to secure more of these.

The way to understand this is through *processes*. The person first perceives something, judges it to be interesting, dangerous or harmless and is then guided by that judgement to discover more. We suspend the original frame or box, think outside it and then institute a new frame. In this chapter we will be examining circular loops of learning, which feature highly contrasting values, and then encompass these in processes of creation and discovery.

Learning styles revisited

Inspired by the work of Kurt Lewin[1], Kolb[2] provides one of the most useful descriptive models of the adult learning process available.

Kolb believes that our different styles of learning derive from that segment of the loop with which each of us is more comfortable. Let us suppose that *active experimentation* (middle-left) is most engaging for a student. This leads her to *concrete experience* arising from her experiment, to *reflective observation* upon that experience, followed by attempts to abstract it conceptually. Another student might love *abstract conceptualisation* in which case he goes into an experimental mode in order to verify or falsify this and on around the circle. But there is nothing inevitable about this sequence. If the experiment does not adequately verify the abstraction then a wheel-within-a-wheel may circle until the two match. It is important to grasp that this system is open. New information may enter while experimenting, new experiences may require new reflections, while new models and abstractions may be needed to make sense of these. Novelty can enter at any point.

Concrete experience corresponds to 'knowledge by acquaintance', direct practical experience (or *apprehension*, in Kolb's terms), as opposed to 'knowledge about' something, which is theoretical, but perhaps more comprehensive (hence *comprehension*), represented by *abstract conceptualisation*. *Reflective observation* concentrates on what the experience means to the experiencer, (it is transformed by *intention*), while *active experimentation* transforms the theory of *abstract conceptualisation* by testing it in practice (by *extension*).

Kolb's model assumes that active experimentation and reflective observation are *opposite* modes, and that abstract conceptualisation and concrete experience are opposite modes, as described in Figures 3.1 and 3.2. By crossing or combining the four learning modes, four learning style types can be defined as follows:

1   Lewin, K., (1942) 'Field Theory and Learning' in Cartwright, D. (ed.), *Field Theory in Social Science: selected theoretical papers*, London: Social Science Paperbacks, 1951

2   Kolb, D., *Learning style inventory*, Boston, MA: McBer and Company, 1985

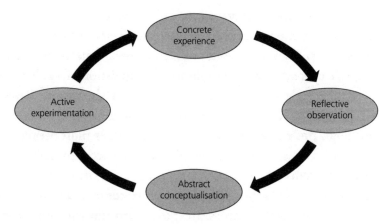

Figure 3.1 Kolb's learning styles

- *Divergers – reflective observation combined with concrete experience.* Divergers have opposite characteristics to convergers. Their greatest strengths are creativity and imagination. A person with this learning style is brilliant at viewing situations from many perspectives and at generating ideas. Research shows that divergers are interested in people and tend to be imaginative and emotional. They tend to be interested in the arts and often have humanities or liberal arts backgrounds. Counsellors, organisational development specialists and personnel managers tend to be divergers.

- *Assimilators – reflective observation combined with abstract conceptualisation.* Assimilators understand and create theories. They excel at inductive reasoning and in synthesising ideas into an integrated whole. This person, like the converger, is less interested in people and more concerned with abstract concepts, but is less concerned with the practical use of theories. For this person, it is more important that the theory should be logically sound and precise; in a situation where a theory or plan does not fit the 'facts', the assimilator would be likely to disregard or re-examine the facts. As a result, this learning style is more characteristic of the basic sciences and mathematics than the applied sciences. Assimilators often choose careers that involve research and planning.

- *Convergers – active experimentation combined with abstract conceptualisation.* Convergers' greatest strength is the practical application of ideas. They seem to do best in those situations where there is a single correct answer or solution to a question or problem, and where they can focus on specific problems or situations. Research on this style of learning shows that convergers are relatively unemotional, preferring to deal with things rather than people. They often choose to specialise in the physical sciences, engineering and computer sciences.

- *Accommodators – active experimentation combined with concrete experience.* Accommodators are polar opposites to assimilators. Their greatest strengths are executing plans and experiments and involving themselves in new experiences. They are risk-takers and excel in situations that require quick decisions and adaptations. In situations where a theory or plan does not fit the 'facts', they tend to discard it and try something else. They often solve problems in an intuitive trial-and-error manner, relying heavily on other people for information. Accommodators are at ease with people but may be seen as impatient and 'pushy'. Their educational background is often in practical fields such as business or education. They prefer 'action-oriented' jobs such as nursing, teaching, marketing or sales.

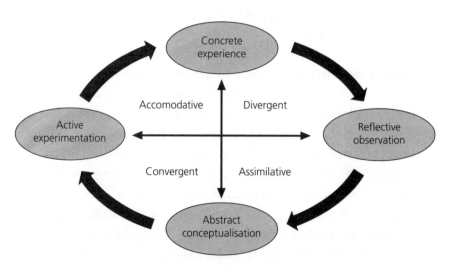

Figure 3.2 Four kinds of knowledge

Convergent and divergent styles

This distinction was first made by Getzels and Jackson[3] and was subsequently replicated by Hudson[4] in the UK. Hudson found that divergers were more creative but also largely liberal arts graduates with broad general knowledge, while convergers were typically science graduates with more specialised expertise in bodies of knowledge already codified. They had to endure the long convergent slog to the frontiers of knowledge. What this shows is that at the leading edge, or at the frontiers of science, a divergent art form is once more required, e.g. modelling an aesthetic and elegant double helix, but that the creative scientist will pass through a divergent phase and eventually converge upon the scientific solution to the problem. Hudson believed that convergent learners tended to be more highly valued in school, because most assessment approaches focus on convergent skills. Examples include applied mathematics, engineering and some aspects of language. Convergent knowledge is located in the quadrant between abstract conceptualisation and active experimentation.

Divergent knowledge, on the other hand, is (very broadly) claimed to be more about creativity: it is about the generation of a number of accounts of experience, such as in literature, history or art. Judgment about the quality of divergent knowledge and skills is much more difficult, because these are private areas. It is generated in the quadrant between *concrete experience* and *reflective observation*.

Assimilation and accommodation

It was Piaget who described assimilation and accommodation. These are, in his view, two dialectically related processes (i.e. opposing principles

---

3 Getzels, J.W. and Jackson, P.W., *Creativity and Imagination: Explorations with Gifted Children*, New York: Wiley, 1962

4 Hudson, L., *Contrary Imaginations; a psychological study of the English Schoolboy*, Harmondsworth: Penguin, 1966

– *thesis* and *antithesis* – between which a *synthesis* has to be negotiated) that describe the (roughly) different relationships between knowledge of the outside world and knowledge already held in our heads.

Kolb's approach to integrating these Piagetian ideas within the cycle is generally less successful than his application of Getzels, Jackson and Hudson. The search for new rules (abstract conceptualisation) to formalise observations (reflective observation) may well be an accommodative exercise, and very often trial-and-error learning (active experimentation) consists of moving from one known rule to another in the hope that one of them fits, so it is has an important element of assimilation. Nevertheless, the approach does help to focus attention on the relationship between the general and the particular. Assimilation includes fitting particular instances into general categories; accommodation is about working from the general principle to the particular application.

Broadly speaking, Kolb suggests that: practitioners of creative disciplines, such as the arts, are found in the *divergent* quadrant; pure scientists and mathematicians are in the *assimilative* quadrant; applied scientists and lawyers are in the *convergent* quadrant; and professionals who have to operate more intuitively, such as teachers, are in the *accommodative* quadrant. There are also differences in the location of specialists within the more general disciplines.

Learning styles and creativity

Kolb and Hudson took a useful step by integrating the extreme poles of their adjoining scales into new categorisations of personalities: respectively, the diverger, assimilator, converger and accommodator. However, our research indicates that the full creative process lies in the integration of the opposites and the encompassing within a loop of the entire learning process, i.e. the reconciliation of active experimentation and reflective observation, and of concrete experience and abstract conceptualisation. Again, where opposites connect, the creative juices flow.

As mentioned earlier, Donald Schön referred to the reconciliation of theory and practice as The Reflective Practitioner[5]. Educators have

---

5   Schön, D.A., *The Reflective Practitioner*, New York: Basic Books, 1983

become familiar with the concept of reflective practice through Schön's work[6]. This work has an historical foundation in a tradition of learning supported by Dewey, Lewin and Piaget, each of whom advocated that learning is dependent on the integration of experience with reflection and of theory with practice. Although each argued that experience underpins learning, they also maintained that learning can't take place without reflection.

Reflective practice is a mode that integrates action with reflection. It involves thinking about and critically analysing one's actions with the goal of improving one's professional practice.

But is this essential for creativity?

According to Schön, the stage is set for reflection when 'knowing-in-action' – the sort of knowledge that professionals come to depend on to perform their work spontaneously – produces an unexpected outcome or surprise.

This surprise can lead to one of two kinds of reflection:

- *reflection on action*, which occurs either following or by interrupting the activity, or
- *reflection in action*, which occurs during the activity (without interrupting it), by thinking about how to reshape the activity while it is underway.

Schön[7] says that, when reflecting in action, a professional becomes a researcher in the context of practice, freed from established theory and techniques and able to construct a new theory to fit the unique situation.

Before we can change professionals' theories or ideas about practice, we have to identify them. Acting before all the knowledge is in, because you cannot wait, involves knowing what is tacit, semi-conscious or encoded in your visceral reaction and hence latent. Not all professionals can describe or explain their own skills. This is why reflection is so important so that we learn from what was done intuitively and spontaneously. We must probe the mysteries of 'good judgement'.

---

6   Schön, D.A., *Educating The Reflective Practitioner*, San Francisco: Jossey-Bass, 1988
7   Schön, D.A., *The Reflective Practitioner*, p.51, New York: Basic Books, 1983

Reflective practice has both advantages and disadvantages. It can positively affect professional growth and development by leading to greater self-awareness, to the development of new knowledge about professional practice, and to a broader understanding of the problems that confront practitioners. However, it is a time-consuming process and may involve personal risk, because the questioning of practice requires that practitioners be open to an examination of beliefs, values and feelings about which there may be great sensitivity.

Schön[8] suggests that professionals learn to reflect in action by first learning to recognise and apply standard practice rules and techniques, then to reason from general rules to problematic cases characteristic of the profession, and only then to develop and test new forms of understanding and action when familiar patterns of doing things fail.

So in short, the reflective practitioner, in reconciling active experimentation with reflective observation, needs also to integrate abstractions with concrete experiences in order to be creative and avoid making the same mistakes forever.

This complementary process leads to what Lakoff calls the conceptualising experience or experiential conceptualisation.

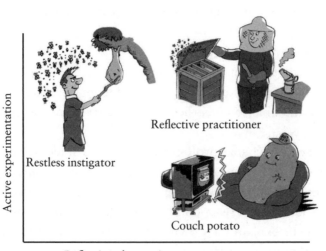

Figure 3.3 Reflective practitioner

8   Schön, D., *The Reflective Practitioner: How Professionals Think in Action*, Ashgate; New Ed edition (1991)

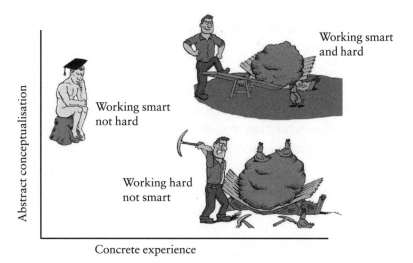

Figure 3.4 Abstract conceptualisation/Concrete experience

So, let's apply this logic of reconciliation to the full creative cycle, starting with a concrete experience, leading to all kinds of diverse possibilities (do they make sense in theory?), which are reflected upon through inductive assimilation.

Note that this also means that we have to ask different types of questions, to probe degrees of reconciliation, and abandon linear models.

Adaptors versus innovators

Kirton's KAI[9] measures individual styles of problem definition and solving. Style, in this case, refers to an adaptive, building or analogic problem-solving style versus an innovative or pioneering style. Kirton argues that:

> 'Adaptation-Innovation theory is located in the domain of cognitive function, specifically part of the strategic stable characteristic preferred style that people seek to bring about intended change ... there is a sharp distinction between style and the capacity or level of cognition of which a person is capable, whether this is inherent or learned. The latter describes

---

9 Kirton, M.J. (ed.), *Adaptors and Innovators: styles of creativity and problem solving*, revised edition, New York: Routledge, 1994

the "power of the engine"; the former the "manner in which it is driven".'[10]

One way to look at the KAI is as a measure of an individual's relation to their problem-solving style, whereas the MBTI is more of a measure of an individual's relation to their problem-solving style and social environment. According to Kirton, it follows that style is unrelated to technique.

In the list below, Jack Hipple (et al.) summarises the two groups and how each group is viewed by its opposites[11].

Table 3.1: Characteristics of adaptors and innovators

Adaptor	Innovator
Efficient, thorough, adaptable, methodical, organised, precise, reliable, dependable	Ingenious, original, independent, unconventional
Accepts problem definition	Challenges problem definition
Does things better	Does things differently
Concerned with resolving problems rather than finding them	Discovers problems and avenues for their solutions
Seeks solutions to problems in tried and understood ways	Manipulates problems by questioning existing assumptions
Reduces problems by improvement and greater efficiency, while aiming at continuity and stability	Is catalyst to unsettled groups, irreverent of their consensual views
Seems impervious to boredom; able to maintain high accuracy in long spells of detailed work	Capable of routine work (system maintenance) for only short bursts; quick to delegate routine tasks
Is an authority within established structures	Tends to take control in unstructured situations

How the 'other side' often sees extreme adaptors and innovators

Dogmatic, compliant, stuck in a rut, timid, conforming, and inflexible	Unsound, impractical, abrasive, undisciplined, insensitive, and one who loves to create confusion

10 Lakoff, George and Johnson, Mark, *Metaphors We Live By*, Chicago: University of Chicago Press, 1980

11 Kirton, M.J. (ed.), *Adaptors and Innovators: styles of creativity and problem solving*, revised edition, New York: Routledge, 1994

When collaborating with the 'other side'[12]:

Collaborating with innovators	Collaborating with adaptors
Supplies stability, order and continuity to the partnership	
Is sensitive to people, maintains group cohesion and co-operation	
Provides a safe base for the innovator's riskier operations	Supplies the task orientations, the break with the past and accepted theory
Appears insensitive to people, often threatens group cohesion and co-operation	
Provides dynamics to bring about radical change, without which institutions tend to ossify	

Kirton noted that some managers were able to initiate change that improved the current system, but were unable to identify opportunities outside the framework of the system[13]. Kirton calls this style 'adaptive'. Other managers were fluent at generating ideas that led to more radical change, but failed in getting their radical ideas accepted. Kirton termed this style 'innovative'. These observations gave rise to Kirton's hypothesis that there is a personality continuum called adaptor-innovator, which presumes two very different approaches to change[14]. The adaptor prefers to improve things while working within the given paradigm or structure. Adaptors are characterised by precision, reliability, efficiency, discipline, and conformity, and are safe and dependable in their work. The adaptor reduces problems by improvement and greater efficiency (see Table 2.1).

In Kirton's original KAI tool, a 32-item questionnaire was used to measure an individual's problem-solving style, on a scale from 32 to 160. A person with an adaptive style will usually score between 60 and 90, whereas a person with an innovative style will score between 110 and 140. In reality, whether an individual shows the characteristics of an adaptor or an innovator depends on context – where they are on the con-

---

12 Hipple, Jack (et al.), 'Can corporate innovation champions survive?', *Chemical Innovation Magazine*, Vol. 31, No. 11, pp.14–22, November 2001

13 Kirton, M.J. (ed.), *Adaptors and Innovators: styles of creativity and problem solving*, revised edition, p.11, New York: Routledge, 1994

14 Kirton, M. J., *Management initiative*, London: Acton Society Trust, 1961

tinuum relative to those with whom they interact. People with scores in the middle of a group, Kirton assumes, have some of both characteristics, and in some circumstances, they can function as 'bridgers'[15], people who are able to connect the strengths of innovators and adaptors.

For us the main weakness of Kirton's work is that it creates dichotomies and then falls in love with these, like the professor who diced cheese with a kitchen gadget and then wrote a learned dissertation on the cubic nature of cheese! These styles are much clarified by dichotomising and stereotyping them and the rude names the managers call each other are both recognisable and comic in their way. But the unexamined assumption that those who innovate cannot also adapt, and designing a questionnaire that stipulates that these strengths must subtract from one another is untenable in our view. It obscures the truth that the innovator is the instigator of a new sense of order to which she and others can now adapt[16].

Empirical evidence from our research

In order to provide empirical evidence for these bold conclusions, we asked some 250 managers from a variety of cultural backgrounds to complete our ITI and an adapted version of the KAI.

We found that creative people move more effectively *between* intuition and thinking, that innovators extrovertly publish their introverted calculation and constantly learn by oscillating *between* judging and perceiving, and finally check their feelings *through* thinking.

Moreover, certain individuals (mainly from north-west Europe and the USA) have a slight but significant preference for ISTJ, regardless of whether they were integrating or not, while most Asians started from INFP and most Latins from ENTP. The correlations between these pref-

---

15 Kirton, M. J., 'Adaptors and innovators: a description of a measure', *Journal of Applied Psychology 61*, pp.622–629, APA, Washington 1976

16 Kirton, M. J., *Applied Psychology, 61*, pp.622–629, 1980. Kirton, M. J., *Long Range Planning (UK)*, 17 (2), pp.137–143, 1984

erences and the KAI scores were much less strong than between KAI and the reconciliation between the extreme orientations described by Jung.

At any one moment, you are being *either* introvert *or* extrovert, intuiting *or* thinking, but wasn't Einstein's brilliance that he thought (later) *about* his intuitions? Suppose we took a whole minute of time. Might not some of us choose to place our individuality at the service of the community? In doing so, might we become *more* individual, yet also *more* communal? Isn't the question at least worth asking?

The important finding is that culture often determines the side that respondents start from. So we are not saying that one culture is more creative than another; only that their starting point for looking at a problem is different.

Not combining contrasting logics shows an absence of creativity. Values are appreciated through contrasts, sound and silence, failure and success, loving a person yet hating some of the things she does, dissenting passionately out of loyalty to the country you love.

Revisiting definitions of innovation and creativity

But do innovation and creativity really work like Kirton says? Our evidence suggests not. Let us distinguish Innovation I, as Kurton defines this, from Innovation II. The first concept is contrasted with adaptation and so includes none of it. The second is fused with adaptation and so includes the entire continuum of innovating-so-as-better-to-adapt. While Kurton believes adaptors can and should work with innovators, his mind is closed to the capacity to encompass both styles in one learning loop, within one person. The existence of entrepreneurs would belie this. They need to make their new ventures work in the real world.

So, instead of questions from Kirton's original KAI that are based on linear (Likert) scales, our 'integrated innovation indicator' asks questions like the following:

Q1 Which of the following four options best describes how you most frequently behave?

(a) I am efficient, thorough, adaptable, methodical, organised and precise and prefer to remain so without concession. (Scores 5 for adaptation and 0 for innovation)

(b) I am ingenious, original, independent, unconventional and unpredictable with no intention of being straitjacketed. (Scores 5 for innovation and 0 for adaptation)

(c) I am thoroughly efficient, precise and organised in testing out my own original and ingenious ideas. (Scores more than 5 by invoking Innovation II)

(d) I am ingenious, original and independent but still submit my new ventures to the most rigorous, methodical testing. (Scores more than 5 by invoking Innovation II)

Q2 Which of the following four options best describes you?

(a) I am more interested in solving our many current problems rather than going out and finding yet more! (Scores 5 for adaptation and 0 for innovation)

(b) I actively look for new problems to solve and contrast my own more ambitious ideals with current realities. (Scores 5 for innovation and 0 for adaptation)

(c) I like to solve existing problems and then ask whether these solutions might not have wider applicability. (Scores more than 5 by invoking Innovation II)

(d) I actively look for new problems because I suspect that in solving these, many current problems might resolve. (Scores more than 5 by invoking Innovation II)

Our research features the traditional choice between Innovation I and adaptation. This consists of the preference for one against the other in responses (a) and (b), while those scoring (c) and (d) understand that innovation requires many people to adapt and that adaptation can be facilitated by innovation. This fusion of opposites we call Innovation II.

Is the creative individual the basis for innovation?

It is obviously a good starting point to have some creative talent in your organisation, but this is far from being the guarantee of an innovative team. It is a necessary but not a sufficient condition.

Research has demonstrated that individuals of various styles possess different creative strengths and weaknesses (Bloomberg, 1967; Kirton, 1976; Spotts and Mackler, 1967; and Zilewicz, 1986). Utilising the styles and strengths which various individuals bring to a group will empower the group to function more effectively and efficiently. Kirton (1977) believes that a team that is heterogeneous (in terms of styles) will be better prepared to meet all contingencies than a team that is homogeneous. Understanding and appreciating individual differences can be very beneficial for organisations. Instead of valuing one style, the organisation should respect and value the adaptive and innovative styles of creativity. Individuals within an organisation can work more effectively together by capitalising on each other's strengths, rather than punishing each other because of individual differences. If an atmosphere of openness and trust prevails in the organisation, the adaptors and innovators will be able to join their creative talents to propel the organisation to success.

Creativity + Business Discipline = Higher Profits Faster from New Product Development

Stevens (et al.) conducted a study among 69 analysts, evaluating 267 early-stage new product development (NPD) projects in a major global chemical company over a 10-year time span. This study found positive correlations between profits resulting from NPD project analyses and the degree of creativity of the analysts evaluating those projects[17].

Analysts with creativity indices above the median for the group identified opportunities that provided 12 to 13 times more profit than those with creativity indices below the median, when both groups were rigorously trained and coached in 'stage-gate' business analysis methods.

NPD requires breakthrough creativity because the first ideas for commercialisation are almost never commercially viable until they have been substantially revised through a particular thought process. It is therefore most productive to preselect innovative, creative people for

---

17 Stevens, Greg, Burley, James and Divine, Richard, 'Creativity + Business Discipline = Higher Profits Faster from New Product Development', *Journal of Product Innovation Management* 16 (5), pp.455–468, 1999

the early stages of NPD, then to teach this group the business discipline required in stage-gate NPD processes.

The results show that, by utilising these principles, both the overall speed and the productivity of typical NPD processes can be increased approximately nine-fold, an order of magnitude when compared to today's typical linear stage-gate processes.

From humour to creativity

Many of us fall into the same trap when we go hunting for brilliant new ideas. We roll up our sleeves and say, 'It's time to get to work'. A look at the creative process, however, suggests the opposite and that instead we should roll up our sleeves and say, 'It's time to go and play'.

As Koestler has shown, humour is built on bi-sociation – the ability to make two different planes of thought suddenly intersect, so that the second changes the whole meaning of the first. The second intersecting plane must take the hearer by surprise and transform the existing line of thought, e.g. 'You have a pet gorilla? But where does a 300lb gorilla *sleep*?' 'Anywhere he wants!' The original line of inquiry has been transformed by the gorilla's undoubted strength. The punchline has the effect of ambushing the hearer. If he's heard it before, it's not funny. Humour is non-linear by definition and represents a collision of discrepant flows of information. 'What did Big Ben say to the Leaning Tower of Pisa?' 'I have the time if you have the inclination.' 'For five years she was a poorly paid secretary, then she discovered she was sitting on a fortune.' Harry Graham published the following poem to tease Britain's jingoism during the First World War:

I was playing golf the day
That the Germans landed
All our troops had run away
All our ships were stranded
And the thought of England's shame
Very nearly spoiled my game!

Here are just some of the reasons why humour plays a role in creative thinking:

1 So many are the mistakes you will make in your early attempts to create that you might as well have a good laugh about it.
2 The sudden switches in mental perspective provided by humour are also present in creativity.
3 Laughing charges you with adrenaline and energises neurons in the brain.
4 Playing is a form of practice, rehearsal and simulation. Unless it is inherently enjoyable you are unlikely to persist.
5 Playing and simulating is a cheap way of making all the mistakes you have to make in order to learn, quickly.
6 Humour encourages spontaneity and is a disarming form of criticism.
7 Humour lowers inhibitions and undermines suppression, hence the Fool in the royal court.
8 Humour draws attention to dilemmas by letting these bounce off each other.
9 Humour, and especially satire, punctures pomposity and subverts conventional wisdom.
10 As the Greeks taught us, those who cannot laugh at themselves will later come to weep. People's conduct is first absurd, then, if still un-modified, it becomes tragic.
11 To act out comedy and tragedy 'on stage' is to learn before it is too late about the human condition.
12 Humour celebrates a novel point of view that interrupts and mocks conventional discourse.

Creativity and humour are similar in some respects. But humour simply allows different perspectives to collide harmlessly and unexpectedly, while creativity forms a permanent and meaningful bond between two matrices of information not previously connected. Humour is 'embryo' creativity with most of the embryos not making it, although the best humour has a moral message as well.

A comic story or narrative only proves popular if it grabs our interest. It does this by lurching from crisis to crisis and enjoying the adventures of the protagonists faced by what we would describe as serial dilemmas. Here we analyse 'The Builders', one episode in the *Fawlty Towers* series, starring John Cleese, Connie Booth and Prunella Scales. The protagonist in this series is Basil Fawlty, co-proprietor with his wife, Sybil, of a Torquay hotel, Fawlty Towers. It is upon poor Basil that our dilemmas bite.

A word should be said about the background to this whole series. Britain is moving from a much more traditional, straight-laced society towards the permissive norms that arose in the late '60s. Hotels in the '50s and '60s barred co-habiting couples from occupying the same room; hotels which allowed this were considered sleazy and not respectable.

Basil has some character defects too. He is a snob, resenting those he regards as 'riff-raff' occupying his hotel. The hotel itself is an extended satire on levels of poor service in the British hotel trade, aided and abetted by underpaid, foreign hotel workers, who rarely understand a word you say.

In *The Act of Creation*, Arthur Koestler points out that there is an unfolding logic which we can all follow, which collides with and is demolished by another line of logic, which cuts across it. Hence a man makes overtures to a young woman, who demurs. 'My heart is not free,' she tells him. 'I wasn't aiming that high,' replies the man. Here the word 'high' refers both to the nobility of the sentiment and the young woman's anatomy. There is a *collision between* these two concepts – a double meaning.

A dilemma analysis of 'The Builders' episode of *Fawlty Towers*

This is a review of 'The Builders' episode from *Fawlty Towers*, considered from the perspective of the core philosophy of this book. This story explores how humour 'works' to hold human conduct up to ridicule and thereby purge us of our misconduct. Comedy is 'first aid' for foolishness. Tragedy is what happens to people who cannot laugh at themselves and who persist in folly. Both on their own and in the extreme are forms of 'negative feedback.'

'The Builders' episode was acted by John Cleese and written in collaboration with his ex-wife, Connie Booth. It relates to those who manage businesses because it deals with the contracting out of services. Although the antics of the principals are hilarious, they deal with serious dilemmas facing most managers. Watching the errors of Basil Fawlty, the chief character, is an entertaining way to learn.

Basil and his wife have the weekend off and have left Polly, their manager, in charge. She is probably the hotel's most stable and competent employee, but she had a bad night and is looking for a much-needed sleep, so that Manuel, the Spanish waiter, is the person who in practice will be left in charge.

Anyone familiar with the series will know that Basil believes in cheap labour, the cheaper the better and he also prefers subservience. Having saved money on their hire, he manages them in a very directive manner, which does not shrink from physical assault if they misunderstand his often agitated orders.

As Basil and his wife are leaving, Polly is warned that some builders are coming around to re-position the door from Reception to the Dining Room and it will *not* be Mr Stubbs, their faithful and reliable contractor, but Mr O'Reilly, a cut-price incompetent, whose only virtue is that he is cheap. He is already two months late erecting a garden wall. Basil has countermanded his wife's orders and aims to make savings behind her back. He swears Polly to secrecy.

This introduces to the audience what is probably the most venerable dilemma in the history of business strategy. Do you go for the Low Cost Solution, pricing your product at a level which will drive your competitors out of business, while still making a profit, or do you offer Premium Service, such an enjoyable stay that your guests gladly pay extra to enjoy it. It is clear that Basil Fawlty is an advocate of the first strategy and his wife is much closer to the second. Manuel and O'Reilly give him a 'cost advantage', or so he hopes!

The dilemma looks like this:

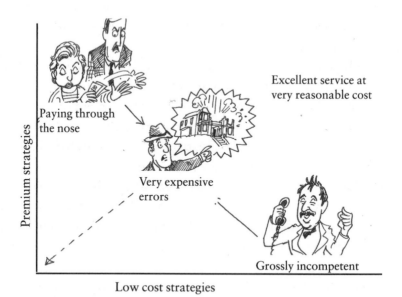

Figure 3.5 Retain excellent service

In the meantime a delivery man has carried a garden gnome into Reception. It is to play its part.

Basil tells Polly to supervise O'Reilly's workers when they arrive. But she wants to take a rest and sleep and tells Manuel to wake her up when the workers arrive. He promises to do so, but when the workmen arrive he cannot wake her and, proud of being left 'in charge', decides to instruct them personally, with disastrous consequences.

'Are you men?' he asks them, and, believing their masculinity is being called into question, they become pugnacious. Basil calls in to make sure they have the right instructions, but when he says he's Basil Fawlty, Manuel tells him Basil is away and hangs up. This happens three times and finally enraged Basil tells Manuel to give a message to one of the workers, the one with a beard, to say that he's 'a hideous orang-utan'. Poor Manuel repeats the message and is duly punched out. A revenged Basil forgets the purpose of his call, an oversight which will prove fatal. The workmen remove the door, completely walling off Reception from the Dining Room. Here the dilemma is one of Diversity–Inclusion.

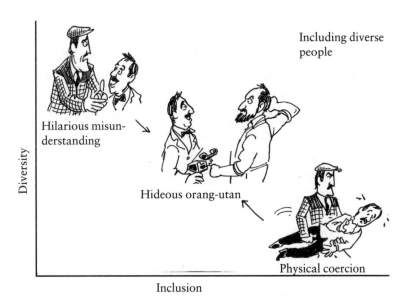

Figure 3.6 Including diverse persons

The world is becoming ever more diverse and Manuel and O'Reilly are just two symptoms of this fact, as are the superior management skills of Mrs Fawlty and Polly, both far more effective managers than Basil, the male proprietor.

Basil's main means of 'including' employees who misunderstand him is to lay his hands on them or curse them. But he cannot have it both ways. If he chooses to employ cut-price foreign labour he needs to invest time and money to help them and train them. He needs to explain himself clearly and patiently, but he does none of these things. It is Polly who speaks a little Spanish who most helps Manuel. Indeed the women are the reconcilers in this episode, while the men are the buffoons, oscillating from top-left to bottom-right on the dilemma charts. Like many contemporary employers, Basil must confront diversity, which includes the Spanish, the Irish, the female and in other episodes, Germans, a deaf woman, an amorous French lady and his *béte noir* guests of working-class origin.

A worried Basil now returns after lunch to make sure everything is all right! He is beside himself with rage at the disappearance of the dining room door and the solid wall confronting him. He picks up Manuel bodily and shouts 'Where is the door?' holding his face to the wallpaper, while Manuel echoes in surprise 'Door gone!'

Basil storms upstairs to where Polly is still sleeping. He blames Manuel. He blames her. He curses and he shouts. Then she reminds him that the mistake was made by O'Reilly's men, which he, Basil chose to do the work. Basil explodes:

'Here I was thinking it was Manuel's fault for giving the wrong instructions. Then I thought perhaps it was *your* fault because I left you in charge and you went to sleep. Now I realise it is MY fault! I must be punished, naughty, naughty, naughty!' And he frenziedly smacks his own behind in a fit of fury.

The dilemma is one of Personal Fault versus Systemic Error. In a sense everything that goes wrong *can* be blamed on somebody, typically the person closest to the mistake when it happened. Yet punishing this person may avail you nothing if the real fault is in how the organisational system has been designed. The series is not called *Fawlty* (i.e faulty) *Towers* for nothing! Among the system's faults is the hiring of diverse persons without adequate supervision. An inability to communicate with Manuel, which is as much management's responsibility as it is his, and a husband-wife conflict over which contractors to hire, has led to outright deception and resulting confusion.

Figure 3.7 Whose fault?

The dilemma is exacerbated by the fact that Basil refuses to take responsibility for the system he has himself designed and then mocks this insight by spanking himself. With employees/contractors like these his vacation is quite unaffordable.

One of the more amusing characteristics of Basil is that he is a *rad-fharen,* literally a (racing) bicyclist, who bows his head to authority and stamps on the people beneath him. The expression is German and is used for supervisors of his type. While blustering and shouting at everyone it becomes clear that what he most dreads is his wife's anger. He is desperate for her not to discover his subversion of her authority. 'We are all dead!' he wails at the prospect of his wife finding him out.

It is not just his wife he defers to. In other episodes it is a con-man pretending to be a lord, two doctors, a suspected hotel inspector and a disgruntled American guest who wants a late dinner and for whose benefit Basil is pretending to lecture a non-existent chef. All these episodes follow the same pattern. He even takes a swing at the peer-turned-villain.

Driven by fear of Mrs Fawlty he gets on the telephone to Mr O'Reilly.

'This is Basil Fawlty, the poor sod you work for.' He goes on to complain that the unfinished garden wall is still not complete, and is taking

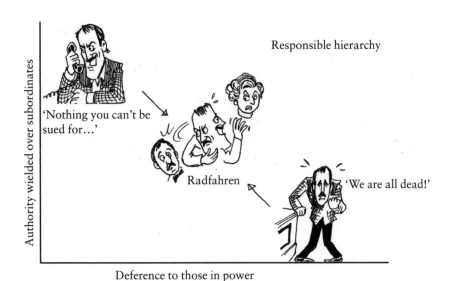

Figure 3.8 Authoritarian conduct vs cringing deference

'longer than Hadrian's Wall', but this is 'Nothing that you can't be sued for.' He wants his dining room door restored forthwith or 'I will insert a large garden gnome into your person... My wife will be back here in four hours!'

In a Responsibility Hierarchy, we both give orders *and* defer to those who know more than we do, see top-right of diagram.

Mr O'Reilly comes around but is in a jocular mood. 'You worry too much Mr Fawlty. The Good Lord intended us to enjoy ourselves.'

'My wife is the one who enjoys herself. I worry!' Basil tells him.

'The Good Lord will see us all through...' O'Reilly is waxing philosophical.

'If the Good Lord is mentioned once more...' snarls Basil, 'I will move you closer to him.' There is humorous counterpoint here between O'Reilly's relaxed and fatalistic attitude and Basil's gnawing panic at Mrs. Fawlty's pending appearance. Basil finds himself incapable of convincing O'Reilly that they are *both* in trouble! The first is too sanguine, the second too agitated and they are not communicating. We can call this panic versus denial (see Figure 3.9).

Doubtless O'Reilly believes he is calming Basil down, soothing him with wise reflections. But then his social skills are on a par with his pro-

Figure 3.9 Panic vs denial

fessional skills and he is making Basil *worse* not better. We are spiralling downwards to disaster. While they might have helped each other to see sense (see top right of diagram) they are instead becoming ever more panicked and ever more self-satisfied, each provoking the other's excesses to greater extreme.

It is at this point that Mrs Fawlty comes back to the hotel having forgotten something she needed for her weekend. Basil orders O'Reilly to hide himself in the bar. Since the door to the dining room has plainly disappeared Basil tries to blame it all on Mr Stubbs.

'There's Stubbs for you,' he exclaims, clicking his tongue, 'a reputable builder!'

'Where is Mr O'Reilly?' demands Mrs Fawlty.

'You never cease to amaze me,' bluffs Basil. 'Just because a mistake has been made, you ASSUME that Mr O'Reilly...'

'His van is in the driveway.'

Basil immediately deepens his deception.

'Well he's here *now*, to clean up the mess...'

But Mrs Fawlty points out that if Mr Stubbs made the mistake then Mr Stubbs should put it right and moves towards the telephone. Basil desperately distracts her before she can reach it. He's just tried Mr Stubbs. He is out.

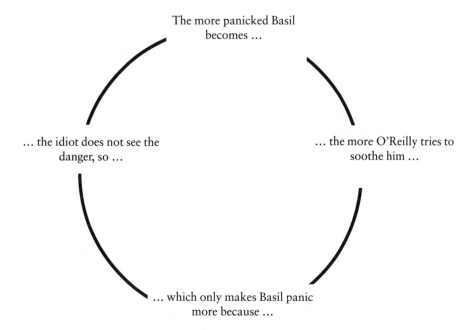

The more panicked Basil becomes ...

... the idiot does not see the danger, so ...

... the more O'Reilly tries to soothe him ...

... which only makes Basil panic more because ...

At that moment the telephone rings. It is Polly, holding her nose to make her voice sound deep and pretending to be Mr Stubbs. But Mrs Fawlty is not fooled. 'You deal with this,' she tells Basil and goes in search of Polly, finding her in the office behind Reception.

'Well done, Polly!' gasps Basil down the telephone. 'Where are you?'

'She's in here with me, Basil,' says Mrs Fawlty ominously. 'I am going to make you *so sorry* for this!'

'Fair enough,' Basil says miserably.

'You thought I'd believe your *pathetic lies* that this was done by a professional builder? Why did I trust you? We've used O'Reilly three times and three times he's failed us. The last time we had no water for a week! You use him because he's CHEAP. But you ignore the fact that he's NO GOOD. He belongs in a zoo! He's a thick Irish joke!'

It is at this moment that O'Reilly decides to cease hiding in the bar and 'calm things down'. He will defuse the situation with a little light banter.

'Oh dear, oh dear', he says cheerfully. 'What have I done *now*?' He decides unwisely to show gallantry towards 'the little woman' and treat her as if they were emotionally intimate.

'I like a woman with *spirit!*' he tells Mrs. Fawlty.

'You do?' she queries, eyes narrowing in rage.

'I do, I do!' he cries sticking out his scrawny chest like a bantam cock. Basil groans with horror. He knows how his wife will react. She picks up the broom and starts to belabour O'Reilly.

'I've seen better things than you crawl out of the garden pond. You're lazy, incompetent, useless...' and she sets about him while he jumps around protesting.

Clearly Mr O'Reilly is a complete stranger to gender equality in the workplace. He has not only infuriated her by doing an incompetent job, he now undermines her authority as the co-owner of the hotel by treating her anger as attractive and sexy, a tactic he clearly believes will 'charm' her. Such conduct puts business women in the bedroom not the board-room and understandably raises their ire. O'Reilly has heaped insult on incompetence.

No one denies that you need more than technical skills to survive in business. Skills of social engagement are vital. But trying to 'charm'

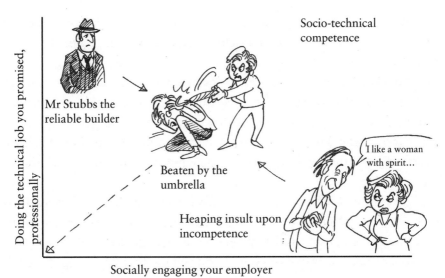

Figure 3.10 Technical and social skills

a female boss when you have been utterly incompetent is a recipe for disaster. Mr O'Reilly is not just making light of his errors, he is trying to substitute for his incompetence with seductive overtures. The vicious circle reads as follows.

We have another downward spiral to disaster which happens to be very funny since those involved richly deserve their fate. Comedy has to be fair for us to laugh.

Mrs Fawlty now goes over to the telephone and arranges for Mr Stubbs to put things right first thing Monday morning. She then leaves to return to her vacation. The garden gnome delivered earlier is still in Reception. After instructing Basil she says, 'On second thoughts why don't we leave this in charge (the garden gnome). He'd do a better job.' Basil seethes.

An extremely chastised Mr O'Reilly is packing up his things ready to go home, but with his wife gone Basil is once more in domineering form. 'Are you going to take that from her?' He demands 'We'll show her! You are going to do the best day's job of your whole life!' Once again we get an insight into the employees Basil prefers, those he can completely make or break. O'Reilly goes to work.

We fade into the next morning. It is 9.00am. The door to the Dining Room has been restored and Basil is looking triumphant as Mrs Fawlty and Mr Stubbs enter the hotel together. There is nothing left for the (expensive) Mr Stubbs to do. Basil's faith in Mr O'Reilly has been vindicated. His money-saving motives *were* astute after all. Mrs Fawlty is clearly perplexed. 'I'm afraid this is rather embarrassing,' she begins. 'I wanted you to do this job but the work appears to have been done already... I can't tell whether it is really a good job...'

'Looks pretty good to me,' says Stubbs.

'You see dear,' it says Basil delightedly. 'The opinion of a professional builder...'

'Of course, you used a jade lintel,' pursued Stubbs. 'Or was it a concrete lintel?' Basil opens and then shuts his mouth in confusion. Stubbs has realised on inspection that there is no lintel at all.

'But this is a supporting wall!' he explains. 'The whole building could come down at any moment... Cowboys!' And he goes hastily to work.

'BASIL!' shrieks Mrs. Fawlty. But Basil is striding down the street the garden gnome under his arm like a battering ram. Its pointed cap is sticking ominously upward. 'I'm on my way to see Mr. O'Reilly!' he announces.

Our final dilemma is about two styles of leadership. Delegating your Authority to responsible persons and Making your own Decisions.

When we lead we need to delegate some decisions to experts. Neither Basil nor O'Reilly know what a lintel is! Mrs Fawlty has delegated wisely to the person who ultimately saves the hotel from collapse. In the meantime Basil, who trusts only himself, hires incompetents and then shouts frenzied orders at them, which only makes things worse, and chases after O'Reilly with the garden gnome.

Humour teaches by indirection. It does not tell you what is right. It tells you what is ridiculous and hence wrong. It points out the Rock on the one side and the Whirlpool on the other and leaves us free to steer somewhere in between the two. In one sense *Fawlty Towers* is 'dated'. It is so full of political incorrectness that it could probably not be made today. We regard this as a pity, because the best way to rid ourselves of stupid prejudices to which Basil is so prone is to LAUGH at them. Condemnation is far less effective. Many people will settle for being considered wrong or immoral but to be laughed at – that is the surest remedy! We can reprove each other without getting nasty.

There are always two opposite ways of messing up. We must just laugh and try again.

Figure 3.11 Two forms of leadership

The use and abuse of creativity techniques

The number of recommended creativity 'techniques' multiply by the year (see our list in Table 3.2, below). These *can* on occasion be useful but can be worse than useless if misapplied. Generally speaking, no set formula can make you creative, especially if all you do is follow it! These techniques depend upon initial diagnoses and are useful or dangerous depending on the accuracy of these diagnoses. Take 'brainstorming', a well-known technique. This could work *provided* members of the culture are shy and inhibited about generating new ideas and speaking out about these. But it is not going to work in cultures where interrupting others is considered rude and if people are *not* shy and there are, accordingly, an excess of half-baked ideas on the table; here, more brainstorming does more harm than good.

Or take 'forced conflict': this could work in a culture of excessive politeness in which disagreements are papered over, but would make things worse in a quarrelsome and abrasive culture. 'Reversal' can be useful because all effects feed back on what caused them, but unless this insight is in short supply little value is added. Role-playing can be so much fun but it risks becoming an end in itself. All these techniques depend for their usefulness *upon this characteristic being in short supply*. It is dangerous to 'play the devil's advocate' if you thereby discourage brainstorming initiatives. All techniques depend on being appropriate to specific situations and upon good judgement. If you have this good judgement about the relative salience of contrasting values then you may not need any techniques! You may find that creative people need no 'guided imagery', no 'purposing' and no 'doodling' and when you suggest they do this you may get a dusty answer.

Table 3.2 Techniques for developing your creativity.[18]

Absence Thinking	Think about what you are thinking about, and then think about what you are not thinking about. When you are looking at something (or otherwise sensing), notice what is not there. Watch people and notice what they do not do.
Assumption Busting.	Surfacing and challenging unconscious assumptions.
Attribute Listing	Listing attributes of objects and then challenging them.
Brainstorming	The classic creative method.
Breakdown	Careful decomposition to explore the whole system.
Challenge	Challenge any part of a problem.
Chunking	Take a higher or more detailed view.
Crawford Slip Method	Getting ideas from a large audience.
Doodling	Let your subconscious do the drawing.
Essence	Look elsewhere whilst retaining essential qualities.
Forced Conflict	Using conflict to stimulate the subconscious.
Force-field Analysis	Exploring forces for and against an idea.
Guided Imagery	Letting your subconscious give you a message.
Head, Heart and Hands	Get all three systems of motivation engaged.
How-How Diagram	Break down problem by asking 'how'
How to	Frame statements as 'How to' to trigger focused thinking.
Incubation	Letting the subconscious do the work.
Is – Is Not	To scope out the boundary of problems.
Lateral Thinking	Thinking sideways to create new ideas.
Lotus Blossom	Unfold the flower of extended ideas.
Morphological Analysis	Forcing combinations of attribute values.
Negative Selection	Sort out the 'definitely nots' first.
Pause	Think more deeply for a minute.
Positives, Negatives	Look at both problems and benefits.
Problem Statement	Getting a clear statement of what you are trying to achieve.
Provocation	Shake up the session by going off-piste.
PSI	Problem + Stimulus = Idea!
Purposing	Finding the real purpose of what you are doing.
Random Words	Using a random word as a stimulus.
Remembrance	Remembering solutions not yet discovered.
Reversal	Looking at the problem backwards.
Reverse Brainstorming	Seek first to prevent your problem from happening.
Reverse Planning	Working backwards from a perfect future.
Role-play	Become other people. Let them solve the problem.
Rubber-ducking	Get someone else to listen to your talk.

(Continued.)

18 Adapted from www.creatingminds.org

Six Thinking Hats	Think in different ways about the problem.	

Hat	Headline	Usage
White	Information	Asking for information from others.
Black	Judgement	Playing devil's advocate. Explaining why something won't work.
Green	Creativity	Offering possibilities, ideas.
Red	Intuition	Explaining hunches, feelings, gut senses.
Yellow	Optimism	Being positive, enthusiastic, supportive.
Blue	Thinking	Using rationalism, logic, intellect.

Storyboarding	Creating a visual story to explore or explain.
Swap Sort	Sorting a short list by priority swapping.
Take a Break	When creativity is fading.
Talk Streaming	Just talk and talk and talk until you unblock.
Unfolding	Gradually unfolding the real problem from the outside.
Visioning	Creating a motivating view of the future.
Why Not?	Challenge objections and assumptions.
Wishing	State ideas as wishes to expand thinking.
Write Streaming	Write and write and write until you unblock.

Concluding comment:

We have shown in this chapter that creativity is embedded in learning processes. The plethora of models and different logics still put too much stress on division into either/or and are too technical, unilateral, dualistic and specific characteristics of Anglo-Saxon culture. The creative process is inclusive, connecting, configured, systemic and whole. It joins differing viewpoints into a larger pattern of understanding in which one value is achieved through another and both are fused or reconciled. To be innovative creativity must be successfully implemented, must adapt itself to the real challenge. To define creativity as exclusive of practical application is to sell it short. Yes, creative persons are disorderly but they have a strong urge to reorder. They should not be underestimated.

ELEMENTS AND PROCESSES IN SUCCESSFUL CREATIVE TEAMS

Creative individuals in teams

The first part of this book was concerned with offering insights to help you understand the fundamentals of individual creativity and how it might be developed. But does this individual creativity guarantee teams and organisations that are more innovative, when these individuals work together?

The answer is very open to interpretation, but research consistently shows that, for a team to be innovative, diversity is crucial. Unfortunately, for many reasons, team leaders often don't start with an innate belief in the importance of this diversity.

The top reasons cited by Human Resources executives for increased diversity in the workplace include not just better utilisation of talent and understanding of the marketplace, but also enhanced creativity and problem-solving ability[1].

However, if you review almost 50 years of social science research on diversity in teams, the reality appears much less clear cut. Elizabeth Mannix and Margaret Lean[2] have attempted to disentangle what researchers have learned over the last 50 years and conclude that visible differences – such as those of race/ethnicity, gender or age, characteristics which mem-

---

1   Robinson and Dechant, 1997 *Building a business case for diversity* G Robinson, K Dechant – Academy of Management Executive, 1997 – faculty.washington.edu

2   Mannix, E. and Lean, M., 'Diverse Teams in Organizations', *Psychological Science in the Public Interest*, Volume 6 - Number 2, American Psychological Society, 2005

bers cannot help – are more likely to have negative effects on a group's ability to function effectively. By contrast, underlying differences – such as voluntary differences of conviction, education or personality – tend to lead to performance improvement. In particular, underlying differences can facilitate creativity or group problem solving – but again, only when the group process is carefully supported.

In some early studies, Hoffman indicated that, for complex decision-making problems, heterogeneous groups produced higher-quality solutions than homogeneous groups. He suggested that diverse groups of individuals should be expected to have a broader range of knowledge, expertise and perspectives than homogeneous groups of like-minded individuals. These factors should facilitate more effective group performance, especially when the task is cognitively complex or requires multiple perspectives[3]. Conversely, other studies conclude that the business case for diversity (in terms of demonstrable 'black and white' financial results) remains hard to support[4]. However, these latter studies have all been based on generic research, without taking a holistic or medium- to longer-term perspective. Of course, many of those with involuntary difference, often migrants in a strange land, decide that they might as well volunteer authentically the difference they experience, which helps to explain the entrepreneurial contributions by such groups. Here involuntary and voluntary differences fuse, which is where their true value lies.

So what conclusions can we draw about how to make a team innovative?

Innovation and teams

In short, successfully innovative teams combine three main factors:

---

3 Hoffman, L. Richard, and Maier, Norman R. F., 'Quality and Acceptance of Problem Solutions by Members of Homogeneous and Heterogeneous Groups', *Journal of Abnormal and Social Psychology* 62 (2), pp.401–7, 1961

4 Kochan, T., Bezrukova, K., Ely, R., Jackson, S., Joshi, A., Jehn, K., Leonard, J., Levine, D. and Thomas, D., 'The Effects of Diversity on Business Performance: Report of the Diversity Research Network', *Human resource management*, vol. 42, no. 1, p. 3, 2003

1   They are diverse.
2   They are inclusive and share knowledge and experience.
3   They take care of the basic enabling processes, especially leadership.

An early stream of research into diversity and problem solving was carried out by Triandis and colleagues. They argued specifically that heterogeneity was most beneficial for challenging tasks requiring creativity[5]. Indeed, as in Hoffman's findings, teams with heterogeneous attitudes generated more creative solutions to problems than teams with more homogeneous attitudes. According to Singh (et al.)[6], such diversity can represent a fundamental strategic lever to improve business performance and support the process of continuous innovation. Implementing a diversity strategy will provide employees with new skills and contrasting perspectives, and thereby both promote a more flexible working environment and enhance innovations. It gives the organisation a better understanding of its customers' needs. A well-managed, diverse workforce offers a more efficient working environment through increased flexibility, because diversity promotes relationships between people with different sets of contacts, skills, information and experiences.

When you look more closely at what type of diversity leads to creativity in teams, you find that the invisible, voluntary characteristics dominate. In particular, functional differences in skills, information, creativity and expertise have been shown to improve performance because they give rise to a stimulating debate, and this leads to creativity and improved problem solving. These findings fuel the view that diversity in teams creates a positive environment of constructive conflict – an environment in which ideas synergistically resolve into higher-level outcomes than would be achievable in more homogeneous teams. In the conceptual framework of this book, we describe this phenomenon as the reconciliation of dilemmas created by different points of view. The tensions deriving from

5   Triandis, HC, Hall, ER and Ewen, RB, Human Relations, 1965 Member heterogeneity and dyadic creativity.

6   Singh, V., Vinnicombe, S., Schiuma, G., Kennerley, M., Neely, A., *Diversity Management: Practices, Strategy and Measurement*, Cranfield School of Management, Cranfield University, 2002

these dilemmas is the main source of creativity; the reconciliation of these dilemmas is the essential challenge and is thus the competence required of a team leader[7].

So, diverse teams should be more creative and perform better than homogeneous teams, right? After all, it's intuitively obvious that diverse teams can exploit a variety of perspectives and skills. On the other hand, it's also obvious that 'birds of a feather flock together', for many reasons. They get along well, there will be less tension (and therefore less time wasted on arguments), and the like-minded team can come to a decision more quickly.

So should a leader assemble a diverse team or a homogeneous team? And then what can s/he do to maximise its performance?

Mannix and Lean[8] offer three suggestions.

- First they indicate that diverse teams are especially appropriate for tasks requiring innovation and the exploration of new opportunities, whereas homogeneous teams are better for exploitation and implementation of what is already known. Thus adapters (who we met in Chapter 3) thrive better in homogeneous groups and innovators better in diverse groups.
- Second, you must make a special effort to reduce any innate process-problems in diverse teams, particularly by helping the team develop a super-ordinate identity, shared goals and values.
- Third, you should take steps to ensure that minority opinions are heard and not suppressed.

A broader point is that organisational leaders should develop open organisational cultures that encourage and reward learning and change. Team leaders play a key role in implementing such cultures, or at least creating them within the team.

---

7   Bunderson, JS, and Sutcliffe, KM, Research on Managing Groups and Teams, 2002
    See also Bunderson and Sutcliffe, 2002; Carpenter, 2002; Pitcher and Smith, 2000
    Why some teams emphasize learning more than others: Evidence from business unit
    management teams.
8   Mannix, E. and Lean, M., 'Diverse Teams in Organizations', *Psychological Science in
    the Public Interest*, Volume 6 – No.2, p.35, American Psychological Society, 2005

In conclusion, the creative output of a team *can* be increased by making that team more diverse. However, the raw materials of diversity are not sufficient; as much attention should be given to what the team members share through the elicitation of common goals, values and corporate identity. And, ultimately, it is the leader who is responsible for the process that reconciles these differences. Human resources should be heterogeneous, while the superordinate goal and norms of fair dealing should be homogeneous and shared. In our view diversity is yet another risk of doing business with rewards for good management and losses for poor management.

In the next section, we focus first on how the diversity of team roles and cultural values can lead to more creative teams, if the differences are reconciled in practice.

Team role diversity and innovation

This section explores how teams can advance, support and facilitate innovation. We focus on how important it is to engage and resolve some important tensions between fundamental team roles.

Margaret Mead once said: 'Small groups have changed the world. Indeed nothing else ever has.' The qualities of the leader and of the team, and the interaction between all team members, are the most important factors in an organisation's success.

One of the most original thinkers on management teams is, of course, the British author and consultant, Meredith Belbin. In his first book[9], he describes administering IQ tests to managers visiting Henley Management College. He noticed that half a dozen of these had unusually high IQs. He put them all in one team, which he called the 'Apollo Team' in honour of the recent moon landing, and had them compete with other teams in a business simulation requiring creative intelligence. He expected them to come first but they came last, beaten by less intelligent colleagues. One reason for this was that very clever people like to display their intelligence and how better to do this than finding fault with embry-

---

9 Belbin, Meredith, *Management Teams – Why they succeed or fail*, Butterworth Heinemann, 1981 (2nd ed. 1993)

onic ideas. The Apollo Team savaged each other into sterility! What is needed is a diversity of roles of which being critical is but one.

In this section, we take an unconventional view of Belbin's work. We try to build a general theory that team innovation comes from the tensions between the key roles. If any of these roles is missing or is poorly served, this hampers the process of moving from ideas to finished projects or products. We go beyond the focus on one particular role – that of 'the Plant' or creative ideas generator – within the group, as we did in our previous work. Here we focus on situations where the Plant's ideas receive broad support from other roles – and as a result we expect the team to be highly effective in its innovation[10].

In the case of entrepreneurship, the single founder of a company must either play all necessary roles him/herself or find colleagues to play these roles. In any event, the founder has to take responsibility for ensuring that these roles are played, or risk the failure of the entire enterprise.

Belbin's original team role model

Subjects complete a diagnostic questionnaire about their most favourite and second favourite roles. The different types have been pictured by us in consultation with Belbin as follows.

The Plant

This is the ideas-generator and originator of the team's creative potential. S/he "thinks out of the box", is creative, imaginative, and unorthodox. Solves difficult problems. The vital spark! The Plant tends to ignore incidentals and is often too pre-occupied to communicate effectively.

---

10 Trompenaars, Fons and Woolliams, Peter, *Business Across Cultures*, London: Wiley, 2005

The Shaper

The Shaper gets people to shape up around the new idea and drives the idea through. S/he is sometimes called the Product Champion and puts momentum behind the idea. S/he is challenging, dynamic, thrives on pressure, with the drive and courage to overcome obstacles.
The Shaper is prone to provocation and tends to offend people's feelings.

Resource investigator

This is a person whose role is to spot opportunities, as well as mobilise the resources necessary to carrying through the project. The Resource Investigator is the networker for the group. Being highly driven to make connections with people, the Resource Investigator may appear to be flighty and inconstant, but the ability to call on connections is highly useful to the team.

Co-ordinator

The responsibility of this role is to "open the gate" allowing the ideas into the team, co-ordinating and repairing the team as it digests the new ideas. New ideas are potentially disintegrative so restoring team cohesion can be vital. The Chairman/Co-ordinator ensures that all members of the team are able to contribute to discussions and decisions of the team. Their concern is for fairness and equity among team members.

The Specialist

This is the expert in some key discipline essential to the project/product e.g. the electronics engineer or tool-maker. The Specialist tends to be single-minded, self-starting and dedicated, providing knowledge and skills in rare supply. The Specialist tends to contribute only on a narrow front and dwells on technicalities.

Monitor–Evaluator

This is the role of critic, who kills ideas that are wasting the team's time, but constructively improves ideas and implementations which require further work and elaboration.

The Monitor-Evaluator tends to be sober, strategic and often discerning. Sees all options and judges accurately. Often lacks drive and ability to inspire others.

The Implementer

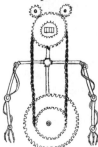

The Implementer is the person who gives the idea its embodiment as a product or services, who makes an ideal real and gives to some vision a practical utility. Being strongly rooted in the real world, they may frustrate other team members by their perceived lack of enthusiasm for inspiring visions and radical thinking, but their ability to turn those radical ideas into workable solutions is important.

The Completer–Finisher

This role "edits" the finished project/product and refines it for customer use. The C/F is a "detail person" and takes infinite pains to get the whole system user friendly. Team members who have less preference for detail work may be frustrated by their analytical and meticulous approach, but the work of the Completer-Finisher ensures the quality and timeliness of the output of the team.

The Teamworker

This role is for the socio-emotional specialist who maintains the morale and the cohesion of the team by healing any hurts. S/he encourages participation, facilitates team processes and may even do running repairs on gaps or splits in the team. They are sensitive to atmospheres and may be the first to approach another team member who feels slighted, excluded or otherwise attacked but has not expressed their discomfort. The Team Worker's concern with people factors can frustrate those who are keen to move quickly, but their skills ensure long-term cohesion within the team.

Figure 4.1 Belbin's main role types

Exploring the link between dilemma theory and team roles

Dilemma theory is distinctly different from role theory. Dilemma theory sees the world as essentially uncertain and paradoxical, and focuses on values not as objects, but as *differences*. For example, the value of a traffic light signal lies in neither its greenness nor its redness. If it were to lock on to either colour, the traffic would come to a halt, accidents would happen and the whole system would be rendered worse than useless! The value of the traffic signal is in the *difference* between red and green, between stop and go.

Table 4.1

Role theory	Dilemma theory
A cluster of traits	Differences among components
Resembles an object	Resembles a relationship
Is unitary	Is binary
Relatively stable	Relatively dynamic
Providing continuity	Providing variability
Strengthening human identity	Expanding human identity

Role theories like Belbin's are neither better nor worse than our theory, but simply different. We've observed that most of the models that describe the characteristics of different roles in a team focus on complementary differences, and they are not wrong. But we argue that, to become creative as a team, you have to take advantage of the tensions *between* the roles – and this is where things can often go wrong.

Although dilemma theory provides new ways of elucidating role theory, it in no sense negates or invalidates it; rather it builds upon it and tries to enrich its meaning and significance.

Since a multiplicity of roles is vital to any and all innovative team working, we can understand why a team is, or is not, effective at innovation by studying *the tensions between team roles*. We can also 'map' these tensions so that teams can diagnose where they stand and, if stuck, take corrective action by strengthening the roles that are underperforming.

Team role tensions and phases of innovation

There has never been a greater need for lean, rapid and profitable new product development. Product life cycles are shorter, competition is more intense and customers are more demanding. Companies that fail to innovate face a grim future[11].

Some leading companies have overhauled their new product processes, incorporating what they have discovered through best-practice research in the form of a 'stage-gate' process for new products.

Figure 4.2 The stage-gate process

A stage-gate system is a conceptual and operational 'road map', used for moving a new-product project from idea to launch. It segments the effort into distinct stages separated by critical management-decision points, called 'gates'. Teams must successfully complete a prescribed set of related activities in each stage before getting management approval to proceed through the gate.

According to a Product Development and Management Association (PDMA) study of best practice, almost 70% of leading American product developers now use some type of stage-gate process[12].

To manage innovation in a team, it is not sufficient just to have the roles played in different intensities at different stages, but you also need to reconcile the dilemmas between the team roles. Below we take you through five typical key stages of a new-product project, and the dilemmas between different roles that these raise. Obviously, there are many other combinations of crucial encounters between roles in the total process, but these give some examples of the way such dilemmas can be addressed, stage by stage and gate by gate.

---

11 www.stage-gate.com
12 ibid.

Five key stages

- **Stage 1: Scoping** A quick and inexpensive assessment of the technical merits of the project and its market prospects.
- **Stage 2: Build business case** This is the critical homework stage – the one that makes or breaks the project. Technical marketing and business feasibility are accessed resulting in a business case with three main components: product and project definition; project justification; and project plan.
- **Stage 3: Development** Business case plans are translated into concrete deliverables. The product is developed, the manufacturing or operations plan is mapped out, the marketing launch and operating plans are developed, and the test plans for the next stage are defined.
- **Stage 4: Testing and validation** This validates the entire project: the product itself, the production process, customer acceptance, and the economics of the project.
- **Stage 5: Launch** Full commercialisation of the product – the beginning of full production and commercial launch.

Here we draw attention to just five of the most common dilemmas or tensions between the roles that are crucial to getting what has been 'sown' to the point of 'harvesting'. While there are other crucial tensions, these five illustrate our main point.

Five common tensions or dilemmas

1. *Scoping*	Plant ——————— Monitor/Evaluator	
	(or Creative Ideas versus Critical Appraisal)	
2. *Build business case*	Shaper ——————— Resource Investigator	
	(or Realised Idea versus Window of Opportunity)	
3. *Development*	Specialist ——————— Co-ordinator	
	(or Disciplines versus Final Alignment)	
4. *Testing and validation*	Team Worker ——————— Completer-Finisher	
	(or Team Process Orientation versus the Finished Product Result)	
5. *Launch*	Resource Investigator ——————— Implementer	
	(or Converging Embodiment versus Diverging Opportunities)	

These five 'crises' are crucial tensions at the gates involved in the innovative process. The challenge is to ensure that each role engages successfully with its opposing role. When all these crises are resolved, successful innovation will follow.

We will now explore these dilemmas, describing:

a) the issue,
b) mapping three forms of failure, and
c) mapping the (successful) reconciliation.

Stage 1 Scoping: Creative Ideas versus Critical Appraisal

A quick and inexpensive assessment of the technical merits of the project and its market prospects.

The Plant or creative person must be present within the team, although there is scant evidence that several Plants are better than one or two. As with all roles, the team needs diversity. It needs all or most of the roles to be covered, otherwise major weaknesses occur. To have three, four or five persons spouting ideas with no one listening or taking them on board is a recipe for team sterility, however imaginative its talk. But having only Plants will lead to ideas that don't get tested: they need to be evaluated so that the merits of the project can be assessed.

The issue
Almost nothing is more crucial to innovation than the relationship between creation and criticism. Criticism can improve creativity, so that excellence emerges from the 'purging fires'. Yet the critic gets a bad press: 'No statue was ever erected to a critic.' Brilliant artists are depicted as starving in garrets because critics can't or won't acknowledge their genius.

Mapping the three forms of failure
Take a look at Figure 4.3. On the horizontal axis, we have Creative Ideas, without which innovation is impossible. On the vertical axis, we have

Critical Appraisal, without which endless time would be wasted on half-baked notions. Creativity that resists or escapes criticism is mostly Blue Sky (grid reference 10/1) – so speculative, so long-term, so pie-in-the-sky that no one is tempted to engage critically with it. If it is *only* an idea, why bother?

But when critics go on the rampage, or the team is full of Monitor-Evaluators, many ideas are Strangled at Birth (1/10). The Monitor-Evaluator is often very intelligent, and what better way to display your critical faculties than to take an embryonic idea and shred it? Simply enumerating all the barriers to its realisation should be enough. It has barely popped out of the ground and you throttle it.

Grudging Acceptance (5/5) is unsatisfactory too.

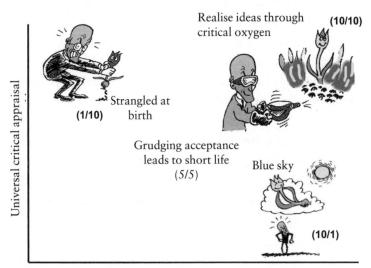

Figure 4.3 Dilemma Grid 1: Realise ideas through critical oxygen

Mapping the reconciliation
The supply of ideas soon dries up. Even when critics are less destructive, ideas may still have a Short Life (5/5). If they do not succumb at once, they may die in development, manufacturing, marketing, etc., especially if saddled with all the costs of distribution through new channels. EMI won a Nobel Prize for its Magnetic Resonance Scanner, but lost £300 million marketing it to hospitals, instead of music shops. Less than 10%

of registered patents actually make money. Perhaps there is too little criticism (not too much!). What is new to science may not interest customers; what is new to customers may use only routine science.

The way to achieve innovation is to improve ideas without destroying them (although some ideas *are* non-viable, for unforeseeable reasons). Criticism must be constructive, offered in the spirit of improving something or someone you admire. The Plant makes errors and needs corrective feedback just like anyone else. In fact, doing something new is *more* prone to error, and negative feedback from a friendly source is invaluable. Great ages of creativity have seen the *interstimulation of like minds*, with artists, patrons, critics, sponsors and sophisticated audiences all involved. The Dada artists not only challenged the conventional art of their predecessors, but criticised members of their own movement even more – usually with the intent to improve.

On the 'map', we follow the path of the Creative Idea from an initial point (2/8), through a period of Critical Appraisal, back to an improved product, then as it is plunged once again into Critical Appraisal, until it emerges from the Refiner's Fire as a realised idea.

Making it part of the team process
The logic and power of positive criticism is beyond doubt, as it increases the chances that bad ideas will eventually be killed and potentially good ideas will be supported. But how can we implant such a spirit into the team?

Synetics developed a very powerful approach. When someone comes up with an idea, anyone who wants to react must start by mentioning at least three good aspects of the idea, before any possible criticism. Criticisms then have to be formulated as follows: 'How can we overcome the handicap I see in achieving this innovation?' So instead of an idea being raised and immediately killed by the Monitor-Evaluator, the response might be:

> 'I like the idea a lot because it has the potential to open our market to a new segment of clients. It also shows that we have another high-quality product, and it would work in our existing distribution channel. How can we find the additional resources and budget to sponsor the market research, and how

can we test the reliability of this potential new product as economically as possible?'

And not:

'Interesting idea, but I think it will overstretch our budget and drain our scarce resources, plus I doubt that the product is reliable enough.'

End of idea.

In fact, positive criticism lifts the idea's potential and sharpens your response to its potential weaknesses. As a result, the idea gains focus. Criticism acts as oxygen to the fire of the team's innovative spirit. It is important to support the Plant as a *person* while critiquing and seeking to improve his/her *performance*.

Stage 2 Build business case: The Real versus Windows of Opportunity

This is the critical homework stage – and one that makes or breaks the project. Technical marketing and business feasibility are accessed resulting in a business case that has three main components: product and project definition; project justification; and project plan.

Now that the initial idea has survived the first criticisms, it is time to create a solid business case. All roles need to contribute, but it is imperative that there are sufficient resources. Here the Resource Investigator and the Shaper come into the picture. They can make or break the project by securing the various type of resource available.

The issue

Ideas have already been generated and provisionally accepted within the team. What's needed now is an exploration of the extent to which these ideas can be shaped and pushed through the organisation, to become realities. In this second stage, business feasibility is checked and project plans are shaped. The Shaper and the Resource Investigator need to reconcile the tension between the Shaper's realism and the Resource Investigator's recognition of opportunities, to create a solid business case.

Mapping three forms of failures

Have a look at Figure 4.4. The Opportunity is shown on the vertical axis and Shaping the business case on the horizontal. The team fails when its opportunities prove unrealisable (10/1): perhaps they were never practicable. The resources needed to carry through the project are mobilised. Windows of Opportunity may only open briefly and you must dart through them. As the group's networker, the Resource Investigator can provide physical, financial or human resources, along with political support, the 'external innovation' of other companies that might be acquired, crucial intelligence and ideas.

The Shaper gets people to 'shape up' around the new idea and drives the idea through by making a business case. This Product Champion puts momentum behind the team and tries to overcome obstacles.

But beware: the Shaper is easily provoked and tends to offend people's feelings, and so often closes the Windows of Opportunity that have been opened by the Resource Investigator.

The team fails when the Window is Closed at 10/1 and when there is No Response to the Opportunity (1/10). It also fails when Trying to Squeeze Through (5/5) with difficulty and pain: too little, too late.

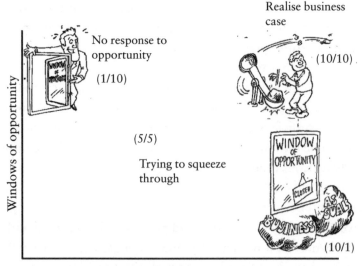

Figure 4.4 Dilemma Grid 2

Mapping the reconciliation
Only the top-right corner of the map shows the two values reconciled. Here the team's *opportunities are fulfilled in action*. Team members have not just generated opportunities, but turned them into a product/project that makes a real difference to real people. Resources are assembled to give the project a realised business case.

Stage 3 Development: Rival Disciplines versus Final Alignment into Business Plan

> Business case plans are translated into concrete deliverables. The product development activities occur, the manufacturing or operations plan is mapped out, the marketing launch and operating plans are developed, and the test plans for the next stage are defined.

Now that the initial idea has passed the first tests, and the general business idea has been realised, it is time to translate this into a business plan with concrete deliverables. Again, every role makes a contribution, but the reconciliation of one key dilemma is vital at this stage. This dilemma demands the integration of the deliverables of the product with the deliverables of the project surrounding the product. This dilemma involves the roles of the Specialist and the Co-ordinator.

Specialist ———————————————— Co-ordinator

The Specialist is the expert in some key discipline that is essential to the project/product. However, the Specialist tends to contribute only on a narrow front and dwells on technicalities, often unhindered by the need for practical utility. The Co-ordinator however is responsible for 'opening the gate', allowing ideas into the team, co-ordinating and integrating the diverse specialisms into one project. The challenge is to reconcile these different orientations so that the strengths from both roles contribute and synergise without frustrating team members.

The issue
Can the team ensure that there are creative inter-connections *between* disciplines or intra-connections between a discipline *and* what business and customers desire?

Most creative breakthroughs occur *between* disciplines, like biology and medicine ('biomed') or mechanical engineering and electronics ('mechatronics'). Yet the Specialist is typically beholden to his/her professional discipline and is reluctant to stray beyond its boundaries, where his/her expertise is no longer acknowledged. When faced with creative ideas, it is not simply the structure of the organisation and team which can feel subverted, but the structure of the profession itself. Specialists have to be persuaded to listen to *other* specialists and/or to people who wish to make the product saleable and profitable, all of which transcends the specialism itself.

What is needed is a Co-ordinator, who can help specialisms to connect and can rebuild the team around the new idea, adding new members and specialisms and dropping others as required. The Co-ordinator creates an open-minded spirit, to give the idea a full hearing and makes it into a cross-disciplinary catalyst.

Mapping the three forms of failure
Look at Figure 4.5. Creative Connections are shown on the vertical axis with Specialist Disciplines on the horizontal. It was George Bernard Shaw who said: 'All professions are a conspiracy against the laity.' The Co-ordinator's main responsibility at this stage of the project is to breach the walls of the specialist professions, by joining them to other professions or to 'commerce', where professionals sell their souls for money.

Most Specialists do not *wish* to be joined to other Specialists by means of a creative idea or product. The mastery of one specialism is difficult enough! What is the point of specialisation if you don't stick to it?

So the relationship between Co-ordinator and Specialist is typically a troubled one. Even if most creative breakthroughs are between disciplines, such work is usually 'applied' science – less prestigious than the individual disciplines, and with less pure motives than those of each Specialist.

If Co-ordinators have their way, won't Interdisciplinary Studies meet their usual fate (10/1)? If the Specialists have *their* way, won't we be faced with Containerised Cargo kills Creativity (1/10)? Here all individual ideas and initiatives are in separate 'boxes' separated from all others, killing connecitons between them.

Even if the discipline is not utterly disgraced, its relationship with another discipline, or with commercialisation, may result in a Horrid Hybrid (5/5).

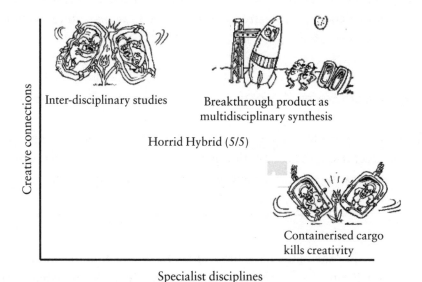

Figure 4.5 Dilemma Grid 3: Multidisciplinary synthesis

Mapping the reconciliation

Reconciliation accepts the need to break down the structures supporting the older system of ideas, but quickly builds up team support for the newer system of ideas. At the same time, it recognises that the organisation may have to change, just as the team microcosm of that organisation is changing.

The Co-ordinator fulfils his/her function by reorganising people and resources to create a structural rebuilding around the new idea, where disciplines are joined and functions integrated. This results in a Breakthrough Product as Multi-disciplinary Synthesis (10/10). Here, at least two disciplines (and hence two Specialists) have, by concerted efforts, joined with a Co-ordinator to create a novel synthesis and a break-through product or project – perhaps a lunar landing craft of the kind NASA designed, a feat that required more than one hundred engineering specialisms.

If we assume that the Co-ordinator has upset the Specialists by threatening to dissolve their disciplines, then the team needs to reassure both Specialists that their professional skills are needed, but that they can contribute their respective strengths without weakening either. Technical skill is indispensable.

Stage 4 Team Process Orientation versus the Finished Product Result

The purpose of this stage is to provide validation of the entire process: the product itself, the production process, customer acceptance, and the economics of the project as reflected in the team process.

Team Worker ——————————————— Completer–Finisher

Now that the plans have been made by connecting disciplines, it is time to validate the entire process which the Team Worker has main-tained and strengthened. For the team, despite the heady excitement it may have enjoyed, exists for the finished product and superlative result. It must now yield up what it has wrought and turn social engagement into physical excellence. The Completer-Finisher is the gatekeeper de-manding that excellence.

The Completer-Finisher brings conscientiousness to the project/product and refines it for customer use. The Completer-Finisher is a 'de-tails person' and takes infinite pains to get the whole system user friendly. S/he has a great eye for spotting flaws and gaps and for knowing exactly where the team is in relation to its schedule. The work of the Completer-Finisher ensures the quality and timeliness of the output of the team.

While process is metamorphosing into product, the role of the Team Worker is not redundant to this shift. Every team member should take on the characteristics of a quality circle and see that every detail is in place, every blemish removed, every refinement considered. If the Completer-Finisher turns into an Inspector General rejecting earlier work then tensions could become unbearable. Perfectibility is a job for everyone with the Completer-Finisher in the lead. The best Team Workers sense what is missing in this particular phase and make sure it is supplied. Negotiating gate after gate can ruffle the nerves of team members and Team Workers excel in smoothing the transitions from one gate to the next.

The issue
The team is inspired by the fact that they are developing an innovative idea, but for innovation to occur, this idea must culminate in a Mature Product. What the Plant, Monitor/Evaluator, Specialist, Resource Investigator and Shaper have begun, the Completer-Finisher in the team must complete. S/he must make sure that the team's product (which could be just a feasibility study) is properly prepared, proof-read and bound for presentation, in a way that will gain the customer's acceptance.

As we saw earlier, this process is full of frustrations and irritations, so there is a risk that the team will dissolve into chaos. Can teams and those working divergently within teams support the converging contributions of Completer-Finishers? Can the team reorganise itself around new ideas, to propel and promote them? For this, the Team Worker is essential.

Mapping three forms of failure
Now look at Figure 4.6. On the horizontal axis we have the ambition of the Completer-Finisher for absolute perfection of result. This can be taken too far and end up gilding the lily or painting the flowers (10/1). The Team Workers will be angry and frustrated at needless elaborations of what they have already accomplished. On the vertical axis the Team Workers have resisted the 'obsessions' of the Completer-Finisher, insisting on the continuation of their careless rapture and smooth processes. The consequence is a 'half-baked product' (1/10), which everyone disowns.

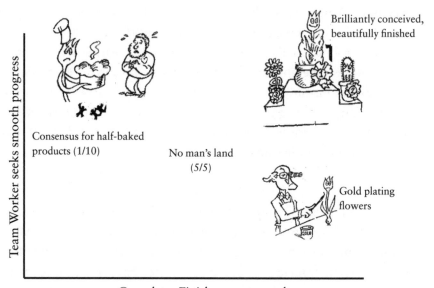

Figure 4.6 Dilemma Grid 4: Brilliantly conceived, beautifully finished

Mapping the reconciliation

This tension resolves itself in Brilliantly Conceived, Beautifully Finished (10/10).

What actually delights the customer is the finished product, not the agreed conception and harmonious co-operation behind the product! What makes an organisation accept the unanimous recommendation of a team is the final, polished presentation of its solution, which describes the route from developing process to outstanding result. Many people decry this 'finishing' of a product or project as mere window dressing. It is nothing of the sort.

The Completer-Finisher makes the strange familiar and the familiar strange and imparts 'the shock of recognition' that surprises people with something somehow reassuring, making them nostalgic for novelty. Perhaps it is a wonderful new present in the familiar packaging. He is carrying the torch that Team Worker has passed.

Stage 5 Launch: Converging Embodiment versus Diverging Opportunities

> Full commercialisation of the product – the beginning of full production and commercial launch.

When all the earlier dilemmas have been reconciled, the team is ready to pass through the last gate. The idea has been tested, given a business case, validated and transformed into deliverables. Now it is time to commercialise the product fully, produce it and launch it commercially.

All previous efforts, all stages and all roles are coming to a head, in other words they are *converging upon the embodiment of the distributed product or service*. One major disjunction remains: while everything to do with the product and its dissemination has converged at one point, the markets out there are still diverging! Customers are changing their minds by the day. Fresh opportunities pop up here and there before promptly disappearing again. This is yet another exercise in alignment in this case between:

Resource Investigator ———————————— Implementer

The issue

By now it is too late to make any changes in what is being supplied. The Implementer has the product or service upon which months of care and improvement has been lavished. He has to get it out there on time and well displayed. The day of the launch has arrived. The Resource Investigator is on the phone checking whether the customers he thought he had are still there and what else has happened in the meantime and who else might be interested. Is there anyone out there that might want to help? All this is very much a moving target, diverging in every direction and therefore more or less suitable for what has been fashioned. Will the bundle of resources the Implementer has put together match the frenetic coming and going of the markets out there? Every potential customer is now a 'resource' to be convinced that what the five stages of development have wrought is just what they need.

In some cases companies have a '70% solution'. The product is not right for everyone and needs customisation at the far reaches of the distribution chain. In this event it is more important to be first innovatively than 100% right for customers, who may appreciate the chance of tweaking the product. But whether this is true or not, it very much falls to the Resource Investigator as to how much co-creation is called for and whether customers wish to fate-share or not. What has been happening of late is that the network of suppliers and customers has grown more and more important and it is the larger ecosystem that succeeds or fails. It is the responsibility of the Resource Investigator to mobilise potential allies and get their efforts aligned.

Mapping three forms of failure

If we examine Figure 4.7 we see on the horizontal axis that all efforts have converged upon the Implementer, but perhaps because of poor timing and/or quickly changing market conditions we now have something that relatively few will want (see 'Brilliant' convergence but too few takers at 10/1). We have converged on a target that has moved and the Resource Investigator is finding scarce interest. At top-right we have 'Busily diverging customers' whose needs have escaped our provision. Our beautifully

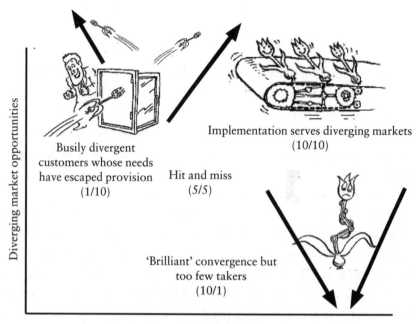

Figure 4.7 Dilemma Grid 5: Divergence implemented

finished product is either not suitable or costs far too much at 1/10. In the centre at 5/5 we have 'Hit and miss'. Our product reaches some of the market but not as much as we hoped since many events have moved on while we were deliberating in our team. We have to settle for a compromise between diverging and converging. We have too little too late. The Implementer and the Resource Investigator are only partly responsible.

Mapping the reconciliation
Where the Implementer and the Resource Investigator have aligned their efforts, the 'Implementation Serves Diverging Markets' (10/10) is realised. We have something basic that everyone wants and the customising can come later. Converging developments carried out by the team have met and fulfilled diverging customer interests. Note that the Plant, our frail flower, is still with us having survived all five stages. The initial, brilliant ideal has been retained and realised, albeit in multiple variations.

Research evidence: our web-based investigative model

We have used this team-role model with many client companies, using a web-based system that captures the dynamics between the roles. From this we have built a team-role database that reveals that more generic dilemmas, facing the whole organisation, are wrestled with by teams seeking to resolve issues. Improved team working leads many of these dilemmas to be reconciled, which in turn improves business performance. This can be captured and assessed on extended versions of the MBTI discussed in Chapter 3 and on the Integrated Type Indicator to be introduced later.

The Chair: the Chief as Reconciler

Belbin's original name for the Coordinator was 'The Chairman'. Pressures for political correctness led to the modification of his term, but this should remind us that leaders of companies or leaders of teams or leaders sponsoring teams have major responsibilities for ensuring that all the roles are present and all are put into optimal configurations. For example, in this chapter we have suggested a possible configuration but this is just one of many. Here it is in summary.

The Plant's idea was criticised and improved by the Monitor-Evaluator before being turned into a viable business plan by the Shaper, informed by the Resource Investigator, searching for opportunities. The plan was then developed by the Coordinator (or Chairperson) joining Specialists from required disciplines. The testing and validation was done by Team Workers needing to satisfy the Completer-Finisher, so the product could be launched by the Implementer, guided once more by the Resource Investigator keeping tabs on diverging customer demand. All five stages were traversed.

Yet in truth all roles need to be coordinated nearly all of the time and all roles can be traced through all stages even if their influences are residual. Since the leader is above all these roles, her judgement is vital. In fact the leader has *all these roles within her* (see Figure 4.8). She is able, after a fashion, to play all these parts herself but for practical purposes delegates most of these to others, while retaining the role of Chief Coordinator or Chairperson. The leader remains responsible for *those to whom she has chosen to delegate particular roles* and for seeing that such performances are mastered.

Figure 4.8 Nine roles, one personality

CROSS-CULTURAL TEAMS AND GLOBAL DIALOGUE I

In this chapter we will inquire as to whether teams can materially assist in cross-cultural dialogues and whether we might reasonably expect such dialogues to lead to innovative outcomes. We saw in Chapter 2 that innovation was in part an association between ideas and pieces of information previously *remote*, so remote that no one had thought of *associating* these before, or so *diverse* that no one had thought of *including* them. While there are many sources of remoteness and diversity, belonging to different cultures and national groups are certainly two of these. It follows that combining the ideas arising from different cultures is more likely to lead to innovation than sharing ideas with your neighbour.

Four crucial characteristics of effective teams

We need to know what we mean by 'effective team'. Is it more than a small group and different from a committee? The first characteristic is that its *membership is shaped by its mission*. The team is not an end in itself. It exists to fulfil a task or solve a problem and its members are selected for their relevance to this task and their possession of the requisite knowledge. The second characteristic is that the team's life is *temporary*. It breaks up once its mission is accomplished and its members may then join other teams with other purposes. For this reason, and thirdly, it consists of *strangers that become intimates*. This means that every team develops over time. You discover perhaps for the first time what every member knows and contributes and the team often becomes 'hot' as it puts these ideas together in new, exciting solutions. Finally, fourth and most important from our point of view, a team is often a *microcosm of the problem it has to solve.* If the problem lies with the way a Chinese subcontractor is manufacturing components then the team will include Chinese members, component manufacturers and those making the specifications that are not satisfied. If teams lasted as long as committees they would probably have the same dismal reputations but they do not. When members stop learning from each other they cease meeting. Teams are non-bureaucratic because they dissolve when the issue is resolved only to reform and tackle another issue.

This chapter will demonstrate that cultures do not simply have different values from each other; they have values in many ways *opposed* to each other. This is probably the last place that people trying to establish common ground would look, but it is also here that innovative connections are to be found, as we have seen in earlier chapters. There has to be a reason no one thought of this combination before and one good reason is that the two points of view are generally seen as antagonistic. There are especially strong tensions between Europe and North America on the one hand and Asia on the other, so much so that Kipling famously said, 'East is East and West is West and never the twain shall meet'. We agree that any meeting is difficult, rare and fraught with tension but it is all the more fruitful as a consequence. Kipling's own career as a writer showed this.

Seven intercultural dimensions of innovation

In approaching a model of competence for teams to become innovative by taking advantage of their diversity, we have applied our seven dimensional model of culture, which we've described more generically in earlier works. Each has contrasting value poles. These are selected because we have found that they best account for the major differences between national cultures.

We have previously published exhaustive data mining our cross-culture database, using principal component and factor analysis that validates this framework. In the following pages, we give selected examples of 'scores' on these cultural dimensions. These should be seen as indicative and relative as, without a full consideration of matters of cultural convergence, multicultural societies, acculturation and generational differences, they do not embrace the full richness of this model.

The reader is referred to our research monographs and other publications that give further detail[1]. Further information is available from www.creatingacultureofinnovation.com.

The seven dimensions are as follows:

1.	Rule making versus … (universalism)	Exception finding (particularism)
2.	Self-interest and personal fulfilment (individualism)	Group interest and social concern (communitarianism)
3.	Emotions Inhibited (neutral)	Emotions expressed (affective)
4.	Preference for precise, singular 'hard' standards (specificity)	Preference for pervasive, patterned and 'soft' processes (diffusion)
5.	Control and effective direction comes from within (inner-directed)	Control and effective direction comes from outside (outer-directed)
6.	Status earned through success and track record (achievement)	Status ascribed to person's potential, e.g. age, family, education (ascription)
7.	Time is conceived of as a 'race' with passing increments (sequential)	Time is conceived of as a 'dance' with circular iterations (synchronous)

Each of these seven dimensions can be polarised with each other, producing spectacular, amusing, and sometimes tragic contrasts; alternatively, all seven can be integrated and synergised, in which case we achieve team innovation.

---

1   Trompenaars, Fons and Woolliams, Peter, *The Measurement of Meaning*, Earlybrave Publications Ltd, June 1998

We will now explore these seven dimensions in turn and consider their relevance to innovation.

For each we need to consider:

a) the sophisticated stereotypes,
b) some typical misunderstandings,
c) what innovative leaders know and have learned, and
d) how we measured transcultural competence.

Let us explain what is meant by 'sophisticated stereotypes'. We use this term to describe the stereotypes (or socio-types) of a culture that we have carefully researched and found to be valid and reliable. They are therefore not the product of prejudice or denigration, but remain nonetheless surface manifestations. We can't avoid stereotypes for several reasons, because cultures stereotype themselves – to sell popular culture, to sell tourism, to idealise themselves and to contrast themselves favourably with perceived enemies.

For twenty years or more, Geert Hofstede with his IBM samples, and Charles Hampden-Turner and Fons Trompenaars with their dilemma methodology, have classified respondents as belonging at one or the other end of various continua. Americans, for example, were individualist, not collectivist. The problem with sophisticated stereotypes is what they miss. How do Americans use groups, teams, communities? How do the Japanese create? Hiding beneath the stereotype there is a lot of crucial information.

We must therefore note the sophisticated stereotype, observe the trouble it causes and move beyond it. We will try to do this by delineating the competence of a team to become creative.

Dimension 1: Rule making versus exception finding (universalism versus particularism)

The sophisticated stereotype

Here the contrast is between the desire to make/discover/enforce rules of wide applicability – be they scientific, legal, moral, or industrial standards – and the desire to find what is, or is to be, exceptional, unique, unprecedented, particular and one-of-a-kind.

As Figure 5.12 (p.122) shows, the USA, Finland, Canada, Denmark, and the UK are all high in their desire for universal rule making. In contrast, South Korea, China, Japan, Singapore and France are all relatively particularistic. One theme in universalism is Protestantism, which sees the Word of God encoded in the bible; a second is the common law tradition; a third is the whole concept of America as The New World, with rules designed to attract immigrants. That America has 22 times as many lawyers per capita as Japan is one consequence of the universalistic preference.

Is the USA an 'obvious' culture because it makes highly standardised 'universal' goods, e.g. Levi's, Big Macs and Coca Cola; or is France a 'snobbish' culture because it prefers products of high particularity, haute couture, haute cuisine and fine wines? Such arguments may entertain, but they are unfruitful[2].

Well-known manifestations of high universalism are scientific management, Fordism, formula fast foods, benchmarking, MBA education and platforms: '100% American', How to Win Friends and Influence People, and similar moral commandments. In contrast, a culture much higher in particularism is China with its great artistic – at times antiscientific – heritage, its family-based Confucian ethics and dynastic splendours.

Some typical misunderstandings

In her dealings with the world, America tends to see herself as the rule maker and global policeman. In her trade disputes with Japan, America tries to personify the rules of capitalism. 'Rice is a commodity. It must be freely traded.' The Japanese say: 'But we are different. Rice is the sacred symbol of our culture. Something very particular.'

---

2 Foucault, Michel, *The Order of Things,* Editions Gallimard, 1966

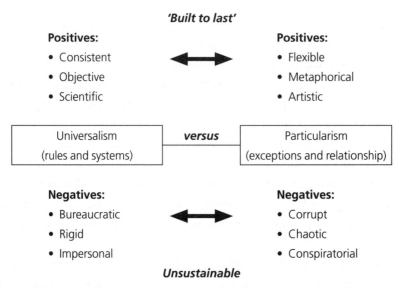

Figure 5.1 The sophisticated stereotype of Universalism and Particularism

A famous dispute about sugar prices broke out between Australia and Japan in the mid 70s. Japan signed a long-term contract to buy Australian sugar at below the world market price. Weeks later, the bottom fell out of the market. Japan wanted to renegotiate a new contract on the basis that their particular relationship with sugar exporters preceded contract terms. Australia wanted the original contract honoured as a universal obligation to keep one's word. Does particular partnership override the law? Or is legal conduct to be expected from true partners, however inconvenient?

But if we are interested in what creates wealth and what is innovative then we find it in the reconciliation of the polarities above. Pizza combines American mass production with Italian toppings of great variety and culinary flair. LEGO produced a standardised box of plastic bricks that just happen to be the components a huge variety of particular structures created by the child in front of a fond parental audience. It was voted the toy of the millennium. It briefly dropped this model and had children work to a universal model it has pre-designed and sales plummeted. Dell Computers uses the same principle with the components of their computers standardised and mass produced, but every configuration tailor-made for particular customers. Toyota, the world's leading automobile manufacturer, has a standard universal chassis and wheelbase to force down costs and a customised superstructure to force up value. The reconciliation of the universal with the particular was in these cases, and many others, essential to the innovative process.

What innovative teams know and have learned

Teams can organise themselves around the problem to be solved, taking their membership from, say, lawyers who uphold rules and from those who most desire flexibility, say designers. Because team members become close colleagues, even firm friends who trust each other, the problem can be solved amid 'intimate strangers', each bringing opposed values to the table.

The dynamic works like this:

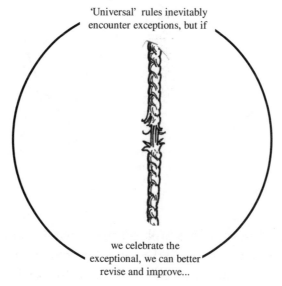

'Universal' rules inevitably encounter exceptions, but if

we celebrate the exceptional, we can better revise and improve...

Figure 5.2 Virtuous circle

In truth, laws are designed and when there are too many exceptions they must be redesigned.

Among famous examples of particularism integrated into universalism are Anglo-American case law, and even the case method at the Harvard Business School, which begins with particular cases before generalising.

Such virtuous circles are much easier to conceptualise than to put into effect. The fact is, it is often infuriating to promulgate a rule and then discover an exception. If you are a boss, you feel defied. If you are a scientist, you believe you have failed. If you are a moralist, you are aghast at such sinfulness. All too common, therefore, is the vicious circle.

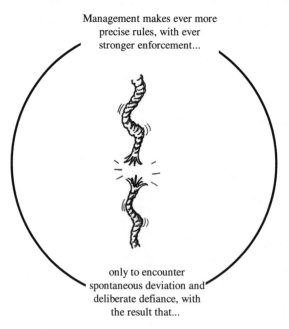

Management makes ever more precise rules, with ever stronger enforcement...

only to encounter spontaneous deviation and deliberate defiance, with the result that...

Figure 5.3 Vicious circle

Once again, 'the string has broken'; the system has run away. Attempts to enforce rules escalate and escalate, as does deviance and defiance, which only intensifies rule enforcement, as 'the snake devours its own tail'. Case studies at Law School and Business School ensure that uniquely puzzling legal cases and new business ventures are first studied in all their uniqueness and only later codified.

There are several examples of innovative teams who have learned from exceptions how to improve rules. Richard Branson of Virgin, for example, shows how a large organisation, worth over $3 billion, with its own rules of operation, can nonetheless retain its particularistic and entrepreneurial flare. When any company grows above 120 personnel, at which point all faces are not known to each other and bureaucracy creeps in, Branson breaks the organisation in two and has the halves compete with each other.

Philippe Bourguignon and his successor Henri Giscard d'Estaing continue to protect the legacy that every Club Med vacation is a personal dream, a voyage into the discovery of an unfolding selfhood, with an *esprit* and an *ambience* that is unique and unrepeatable. Yet many of the elements going into that holiday can and must be standardised, globalised, systematised and generated in high volumes and at lowered costs – all ingredients of a universal logic. You can create fresh scenarios of satisfaction *out of* standardised inputs. It is their combination that is unique, not the elements themselves.

At Applied Materials, rules have been global and exceptions local as they have set up a system of transcultural learning. In this system, a series of discoveries about local and exceptional circumstances is used to *test generalisations about universally applicable knowledge.* Does this principle apply in all places or only in some? How important are the exceptions? And *might one of these exceptions become a new global rule, replacing existing rules?* 'Global versus local' is transcended by 'Glocalism', the process of modifying global rules through examining local exceptions. And this company of highly innovative products, which makes machines for the semiconductor industry, is thriving on innovative teams making this possible.

How a team solved the sugar dilemma

Let us return to the Australian–Japanese sugar dispute. The price of sugar on world markets had fallen and the Japanese wanted to renegotiate in these particular circumstances with persons they regarded as their particular friends, the Australian sugar growers. The growers, for their part, would have none of this. They expected promises to be met. This law had been negotiated between the parties and both should keep their legal promises. It is all too easy to wax on either side of this moral dilemma. Does friendship mean *nothing* to you? Do you *routinely* break your word? But the team solution was most innovative and combined rules with flexibility and friendship. The Australians agreed to sell sugar to the Japanese confectionary industry at $3 a ton below world market price, *whatever that might be*, if the Japanese would sign a long-term contract and keep to this in all circumstances. (This was down from $6 a ton but with a shifting price.) In other words, the universal rule had been stretched to cover the exceptional circumstances of fluctuating prices.

How a team solved a cheating problem

In a New York school a professor was very happy to be teaching a young Puerto Rican female student from a disadvantaged background. She showed great promise. She came to see him to ask for help on a statistics exam, but he was very preoccupied by illness in his family and asked her to come back. She never did. Two weeks later he was invigilating the statistics exam when a tall Puerto Rican youth handed in a paper. It had her name on! The Dean said the case was simple. She had cheated. She must be failed and dismissed from the school. 'What about those who did *not* cheat?' he asked. 'We have our rules.'

But the professor was devastated. If only he had found time to help her. If only he had called her in. It was worse when her local priest called to beg on behalf of her family. But the Dean agreed that a joint team from the school and the local community should discuss the issue. Their solution was most creative. The student and all others who had failed the exam could retake it six weeks hence, giving time for the professor and the student's young man to coach her. However, the pass mark would be ten points higher! They created a new universal rule for a most exceptional young woman and those falling into the same category.

In the process of innovation, we see that, if the universalistic codifications, standards and platforms are combined with the particularistic exceptions and unique combinations, the team becomes creative. With the pizza, we see that the uniform bottom is combined with the topping of choice and as such it becomes one of the top-selling products in the world. The Japanese car has combined the Japanese strength for customisation with the American talent of sharing standardised platforms, making for worldwide successes. And finally, with Deming's Quality Management, we see it needed the Japanese implementation process to make it popular in the USA. Now we see that errors are made to be corrected, and the result is the worldwide success of the error-correcting system. The crucial element is that the team needs to combine the different cultural orientations to make it a successful innovation.

Can these contrasting values and the fusion between them be measured?

This section tells the story of how we first polarised universal rule orientation with particular exception orientation and then succeeded in putting these together again. For many years we had only the first half of this puzzle. Results were first accumulated through our 'old' questionnaire. In these investigations, managers were given a straight choice between two conflicting values. For example, the issue of universalism versus particularism was measured by posing the following dilemma.

You are riding in a car driven by a close friend. He hits a pedestrian. You know he was going at at least 50 mph in an area of the city where the speed limit is 30 mph. There are no witnesses. His lawyer says that, if you testify under oath that he was only travelling at 30 mph, it may save him from serious consequences.

What right does your friend have to expect you to protect him?

Here the responding manager must either side with his friend or bear truthful witness in a court of law. Because the respondent is limited to these 'forced-choice' options only, there is no possibility of integrating opposites, no opportunity to display transcultural competence by reconciling this dilemma.

In our subsequent conversations with managers who had responded to this questionnaire, we kept encountering attempts to resolve the dilemma and some annoyance that we had pressed so stark a choice on them. So we designed a more discriminating questionnaire with five answers, not two. Two answers were the original polarised alternatives. One option was a compromise between the two values. The last two options were alternative integrations, one of which started with universalism and encompassed particularism, and the second of which started with particularism and encompassed universalism. These are set out below.

1   There is a general obligation to tell the truth as a witness. I will not perjure myself before the court. Nor should any real friend expect this from me.

2   There is a general obligation to tell the truth in court, and I will do so, but I owe my friend an explanation and all the social and financial support I can organise.

3   My friend in trouble always comes first. I am not going to desert him before a court of strangers based on some abstract principle.

4   My friend in trouble gets my support, whatever his testimony, yet I would urge him to find in our friendship the strength that allows us both to tell the truth.

5   I will testify that my friend was going a little faster than allowed and say that it was difficult to read the speedometer.

The logics behind these positions are as follows:

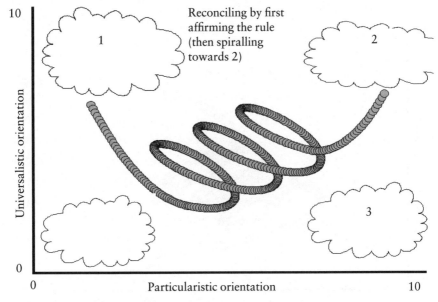

Figure 5.4 From law to friendship

1) (1/10) is a polarised response in which the law is affirmed but the friend is rejected (universalism excludes particularism).

2) (10/10) is an integrated response in which the rule is first affirmed and then everything possible is done for the friend (universalism joined to particularism).

3) (10/1) is a polarised response in which the friend is affirmed as an exception to the rule, which is then rejected (particularism excludes universalism).

4) (10/10) is an integrated response in which exceptional friendship is affirmed and then joined to the rule of law (particularism joined to universalism).

5) (5/5) is a stand-off or fudge, in which both the rule of law and loyalty to friends are blunted (universalism compromised with particularism).

The underlying framework is this.

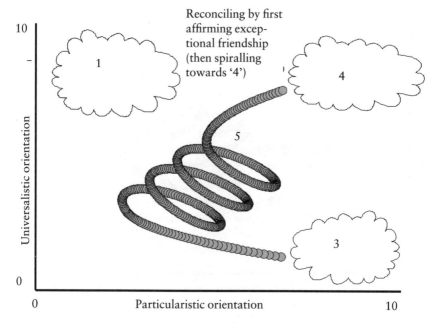

Figure 5.5 From friendship to law

- Integrated responses 2) and 4) show more transcultural competence than polarised responses. Answer 4 is especially creative.
- While American managers will typically put universalism first (adopting the anticlockwise spiral), and East Asian/Southern European managers will typically put particularism first (adopting the clockwise spiral), each can integrate his/her priority with its opposite in a novel combination of values.
- From this it follows that there are at least two paths to integrity, not 'one best way'.
- There are, however, better ways and worse ways.
- Transcultural competence will anticipate and explain success in overseas postings and correlates with 360° feedback ratings.

What we found

We used the questionnaire based on these types of questions with five options extensively. The results have been widely published as they have evolved over the years in the various editions of *Riding the Waves of Culture*. A small selection of the results are shown:

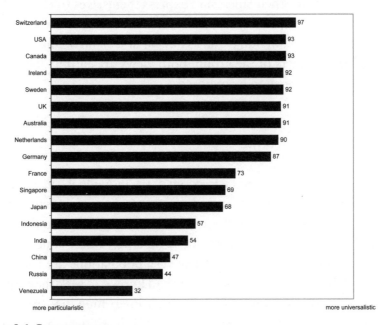

Figure 5.6 Country scores

Universalism versus particularism

Some cultures (such as North Americans and the Swiss) see morality as a matter of standard laws and rules, whereas other cultures (such as Koreans, Venezuelans and Eastern Europeans) see morality as variable, depending on particular loyalties and circumstances. We are currently attempting to establish that integrated answers are better than either extremity in creating wealth and spurring innovation. Early results are most promising.

Dimension 2: Self-interest and personal fulfilment versus group interest and social concern (individualism versus communitarianism)

According to the dominant assumptions of classical economics and most Western cultures, life is all about the happiness and advancement of individuals who vote for their rulers and express themselves freely. Yet large parts of the world, especially in the East, see the family and the community as outliving the individual and as having first claim on the allegiance of individual members of the group. Both views are entirely logical and justifiable. They happen to be opposed.

The sophisticated stereotype

Here the contrast is between the freedom of the individual – in which personal fulfilment, enrichment, expression, competition and self-development are championed above all – and the benefits accruing to the group, community or corporation. There can be no doubt where America, Australia, Israel and Canada stand. Their very populations are formed by those who left the only community they had known to seek their fortune in the New World or promised land. Isn't it interesting that the English language is one of the few languages where 'I' is written with a capital letter, and where people like to be called by their first name? When we go to more communitarian cultures such as the Chinese and Japanese, we find that you introduce yourself with your family name, and then mention your first name. Indeed Figure 5.12 shows that Canada, the USA, Denmark, Switzerland, the Netherlands, Australia and the UK head the national advocates of individualism, while India, Japan, Mexico, China, France, Brazil and Singapore head the advocates of communitarianism.

Did you ever see a Hollywood movie in which group opinion was proved right and the lone protagonist yielded to that view? Yet the superior judgement of he-who-stands-alone has been vindicated a thousand times! It was Hermann Melville who wrote:

'Take a single man alone, and he seems a triumph, a grandeur or a woe. But take mankind in the mass and they seem for the most part a mob of unnecessary duplicates.'

The communitarian attitudes of rice-growing regions should come as no surprise. With fewer than a dozen people co-operating, it is simply impossible to survive. The self-aggrandising schemes of warlords have brought China to starvation again and again. France has progressed historically only when angry groups surged into the streets and manned the barricades. The inspiration may have been individual, but the *force majeur* was communal. History shapes cultures.

American plans to 'motivate' employees in foreign cultures typically fall foul of this crucial cultural difference. How many times has the 'Employee of the Month' called in sick, rather than face an envious peer group at work? Individual incentives can be unfair if other members of the group helped you to succeed or if you believe that your supervisor deserves the credit for briefing and mentoring you so well.

Individualism versus Communitarianism

Individual orientation	Group orientation
• Prime orientation is to 'I'	• Prime orientation is to 'We'
• Sovereign self-interest	• The common good
• Ethics of duty and utility	• Ethics of family and friends
• Self-made persons	• Nurtured members of group

Positive connotation	
• Personal initiative	• Group morale
• Competition	• Cooperation
• Lonely dissent	• Personal sacrifice
• Pioneers capitalism	• Follows very fast

Negative connotation	
• Selfishness	• Conformity
• Egotism	• Group think
• Self-aggrandisement	• Self-annihilation
• Aggressive ego	• Loss of 'face'

Figure 5.7 Cultures differ in putting 'I' or 'we' first

Let us recall that these are stereotypes – what cultures say to themselves and of themselves. The United States has quite a history of imagining itself to be subverted by sinister powers, a belief that allows a defensive sense of community to form. The US is also the home of the lobby, the pressure group, the Town Hall meeting, the T-group, the support group and others.

But, once again, it is the fusion of the values above that leads to innovation and new wealth. A few years ago we might have claimed that individualism had won and communitarianism had lost, but that was before the extraordinary rise of China and the sudden catastrophic collapse of the global financial sector where bankers had helped themselves to rich personal rewards for institutional failure, as when Dick Fuld paid himself $500 million for bankrupting Lehman Brothers. Perhaps individualism *can* go too far! Ironically the rise of China is probably a testament to the *fusion* of individual and community. It was not until China opened up and permitted personal free enterprise that it took off economically. An evaluation of 26 countries by Forrester Research found that too many (Western) countries had identified innovation with personal invention. The report commented:

> 'National empowerment, power, wealth and well-being depend more on deployment of innovation than on the invention itself. The biggest flaw in most innovation agendas is that they look at nations as closed systems, as if nations must have all innovation capabilities in-house. It cannot be done ... Nations must shed their inward-looking innovation attitudes to become successful in the end-to-end global innovation value network.'

Instead, the study sees an emerging global ecosystem of collaborative innovation among countries, companies, universities and other organisations. These 'innovation networks' involve countries identifying and assuming a specific role – inventor, transformer, financier and broker – to match their unique skill set.

As an example of what can be achieved, the USA semiconductor industry achieved global market dominance by fusing teams of creative individuals. Success for one of our clients came from not simply rewarding individuals for their creative ideas or teams for successful projects, but also rewarding the integration of these opposites. The key was to reward creative individuals for giving their findings to their team, and at the same time to reward teams for how they developed the creativity of their individuals.

What innovative teams know and have learned

A team is small enough so that the individual genuinely counts and yet large enough so that social skills are required to be influential and gain group support. We saw in the last chapter that while a new venture might begin with the creativity of the Plant it did not end there. Every role within the group was needed to support the creative idea and work it through the system to final realisation. It is no exaggeration to say that in any team individualism and the group meet and nourish one another.

The team is one of the places the two values fuse. The individual is too socialised to be selfish, while the team is too small and temporary to be coercive.

Richard Branson holds that good service is the outcome of a flight team whose members like one another. You pass on in individual service the way you have been treated by colleagues and by your managers. Studies in a bank of staff most praised by customers found this to be a function of how they were themselves treated by colleagues and supervisors. In BUPA, Britain's largest healthcare provider, training consists almost entirely of members sharing with each other life-threatening episodes encountered within their own families and neighbourhood. When insured members call in to ask for help you have to be 'there' for them, 100%. They have been paying premiums for years now they need you! Are you with them in what might be the biggest crisis of their lives? Taking such calls is very stressful and team members literally hold each other's hands in the aftermath.

Suez Lyonnaise des Eaux, the French water utility company, 'teams' its own national diplomatic service, to reorganise utility systems in developing countries and then *passes these back to the ownership of that country,* having trained teams of local staff how to maintain and repair them. It makes its money from engineering, not from colonial forms of ownership. The business model is clearly communitarian and requires multinational teams at its core. Suez enjoys a 52% share of foreign-run utility systems in the world.

Perhaps the boldest attempt to reconcile individualist and communitarian cultures – one that has been brilliantly successful – is by Jim Morgan, the retired founder and CEO of Applied Materials. Jim turned author to write a groundbreaking book on Japanese business culture in the 80s. The East Asian attitude to electronics, microchips (the rice of industry) and computers was essentially communitarian. These technologies, contributing as they did to the community's industrial infrastructure in general, could not be allowed to fail, and were accordingly nurtured by governments and banks. Jim realised early on that he had to give Applied Materials (Japan) the autonomy to locate itself at the heart of Japanese industrial policy, among the inner circles of industry itself. He has followed this policy in Korea, China, Singapore and other major centres of communitarian consciousness. He has instituted an East-West dialogue at the apex of Applied Materials, in which the new freedoms of the electronic age converse with the priceless communitarian logics of accelerated learning for whole societies.

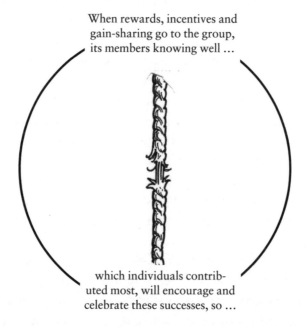

When rewards, incentives and gain-sharing go to the group, its members knowing well …

which individuals contributed most, will encourage and celebrate these successes, so …

Figure 5.8 Virtuous circle

A group can make any one of its members feel like a million dollars. There may be nothing more satisfying in the world than being a heroine or hero to those who know you best. And who would grudge your subsequent promotion or pay rise, once you had steered your group to fame and fortune?

Co-opetition: compete for the best co-operation

The competent innovator knows that individualism-communitarianism is a false dichotomy. The real art is to nurture individuals and then get individuals to serve groups, a process which Adam M. Brandenberger and Barry J. Nalebuff have called co-opetition[3] (see below).

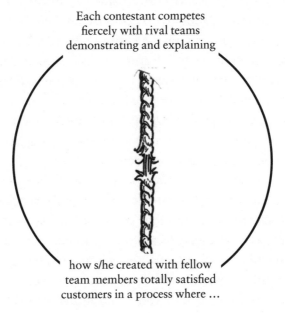

Each contestant competes
fiercely with rival teams
demonstrating and explaining

how s/he created with fellow
team members totally satisfied
customers in a process where ...

Figure 5.9 Virtuous circle

An interesting example is Motorola's Total Customer Satisfaction competition. Teams that have 'totally satisfied' their customers in any part of the world gather together the evidence of their success and enter

3   Brandenburger, Adam, and Nalebuff, Barry, *Co-Opetition: A Revolution Mindset That Combines Competition and Cooperation*, Currency; 1st edition (Dec 1997)

a worldwide competition in which they present their solution on stage, together with the results achieved. The contests teach all members how to compete fiercely – but note that this competition is about co-operating with customers and fellow team members. This is 'collaborative competing' or co-opetition.

Among the advantages of this competition is that 800 or so winning solutions surface, which can be studied and disseminated by Motorola University. Competing differentiates ideas; co-operating integrates them. Innovative executives have finely differentiated, well-integrated strategic maps of their terrains.

In fact it is virtually impossible to compete without cooperating or vice versa. Corporations with the best internal cooperation are likely to compete best in the marketplace. The most engaging and socially effective person in a team is likely to become its informal leader and win personal acclaim and individual promotion. And *who* is it that competes, the individual, the company or the entire network? A new competitor in, say, the airline industry will lower the cost of planes for the whole industry. More competition between companies can lead to better cooperation with consumers at lower prices. The two values are interwoven throughout the economy. Moreover, products increasingly form systems. How can geographical positioning systems work without satellite communications or software without hardware?

The fusion of competing and cooperating is vital to team innovation. The individual creates the sparks of originality but the team has to get behind these, fan them until they combust and then fight to get their new prototype taken seriously by the rest of the company. To have ten to twelve team members rooting for a new venture is a lot more persuasive than just one lonely inventor. While communitarian cultures probably give too much credence to the group, and individualistic cultures give too much credence to heroic individualism defying orthodoxy, they are at their most effective when they mingle, when creative individuals receive the support they crave and the independent criticism they need. It is your friends who wish you well that can most credibly give you the bad news that this project needs more work, that they support you but question your performance.

In the late 80s we tried an experiment in Shell's Amsterdam laboratories. There was a staff of 2000 with teams comprising north-western

Europeans mostly but with some Japanese members. The latter complained that the reward system favoured individuals and did nothing for the teams supporting them. Indeed, there was a rank ordering of 'excellence' that made them most uncomfortable. Many of these persons were simply airing ideas given to them by others. Team spirit was the likely victim of such rewards. Within a year we had changed the system until all approved of it. We first chose the best performing team and gave it an award. We next asked team members within that team and other teams that had distinguished themselves to nominate their chief contributors. We gave 50% of the variable pay to the better teams and 50% of the variable pay to individuals nominated by their teams. Not only were all nations happy but overall performance markedly improved. This process is shown in Figure 5.11.

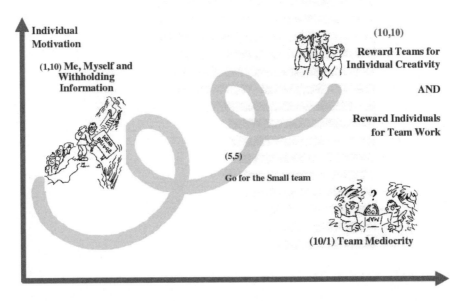

Figure 5.10 Co-opetition

The Shell researchers from Amsterdam competed for the best co-operation in teams and they worked together to compete better. And it made the cross-cultural joint venture into a very creative one.

What we found

A small sample from our database on this dimension is shown below:

Two people were discussing two extreme ways of increasing the quality of one's life. One said: 'It is obvious that if one has as much freedom as possible and the maximum opportunity to develop oneself, the quality of one's life would improve as a result.'

Another said: 'If the individual is continuously taking care of his or her fellows, then the quality of life for us all will improve, even if it obstructs individual freedom and individual development.'

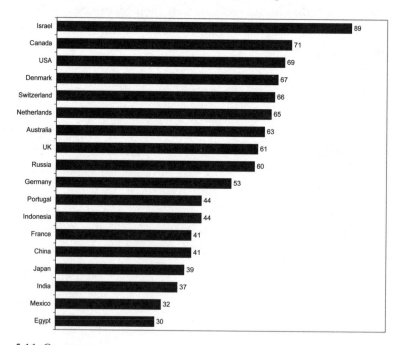

Figure 5.11 Country scores

Individualism versus communitarianism

Americans and Israelis (despite their kibbutz tradition) believe that success stems from individual achievement, while people from Japan, Egypt and India assign primary responsibility to the group. This dilemma often makes it difficult to establish viable performance assessments. An IBM sales team dealt with the problem by awarding bonuses to excellent groups (those that had nurtured individuals) and excellent individual performers (especially those who had been the best team players).

Measuring innovative competence: reconciling the individual and the group

We turn again to the measurement and strategic use of innovation competence and the results achieved so far. In our research, we repeatedly asked leaders to choose between five options. Two of these are unreconciled, one is a compromise, and two are reconciled answers.

Question: jobs in your organisation

Which of the following jobs is found most frequently in your organisation?

    a) A job that is part of an organisation where everybody works together and where you do not get individual credit.

    b) A job that allows everybody to work independently and where individual credit is received on the basis of individual performance.

    c) A job where everybody works together in teams and where the teams are constantly stimulating individual creativity.

    d) A job that allows everybody to work independently and where individual credit is given to the best team player.

    e) A job where there is neither too much individual creativity nor excessive 'groupthink'.

Answers a) and b) are unreconciled answers. Answer e) is a compromise. Answer c) is a reconciliation where we start with communitarianism and answer d) represents a reconciliation that starts with the beauties of individualism. Again, we found that leaders that chose these latter two options were significantly more effective than those who chose any of the others.

Dimension 3: Emotions inhibited versus emotions expressed (neutral versus affective)

Teams are an interesting mixture of neutrality and emotion. A work team of strangers is typically detached in its earlier stages when members are getting to know each other, and typically effective in later stages when it starts to bond and gain success. There are reports of teams that are literally awash with emotion and enthusiasm as they enjoy a *flow experience* while realising their mission.

The sophisticated stereotype

It is well known that cultures display emotions to very varying degrees. The fury of the Frenchman when you nearly collide with his car and the way he uses his whole body to express his rage are legendary. In contrast, you can be forgiven for imagining that Japanese executives may have gone to sleep during your presentation. The posture of 'half-eye', with the eyelid half closed, can be very galling to those who do not understand 'respectful listening'. Equally unnerving are long silences following your statement. This may be read as 'boredom', when it is intended as evidence of thoughtful consideration. These contrasts are set out below (Figure 5.13), with the Japanese highly neutral and the French, Italians and Latin nations more volatile and affective.

But this particular dimension has more subtleties and variations than most others because, of course, there is strong disagreement about what one should be neutral or affective *about*. Americans, for example, show up as moderately affective, despite their Puritan origins of restraint in religious expression. They are perhaps trying to 'break the ice' in a culture whose members are very mobile. They believe in showing enthusiasm for products, visions, missions and projects, but are less expressive to each other. They approve of positive emotion (enthusiasm) but not so much of negative emotion (anger or grief). They will talk *about* emotion

('I'm feeling angry') in a vaguely therapeutic manner, but rarely explode or show physical signs of anger.

The British use humour to release emotions and may begin a speech with a joke to relax the audience; Germans and the Swiss may see this as unserious and frivolous. The Japanese and Koreans reveal desires for intimacy by getting drunk together; Germans prefer to bare their souls and share their philosophies of life. To confuse things further, emotions, although understated, may have great significance in a culture, so that the Japanese will search an impassive face for vital clues and bereaved English heroines will keep their stiff upper lips and ask for cups of tea on hearing of a husband's demise. The patterns are extremely complex.

Emotions: Neutral versus Affective

Neutral orientation	**Expressive orientation**
• Shows emotional control	• Shows emotions openly
• Dispassionate	• Passionate
• Detached	• Attached
• Serious	• Playful

Positive connotation	
• Controlled	• Spontaneous
• Reserved	• Unreserved

Negative connotation	
• Cold	• Impulsive
• Indifferent	• Overwrought

Figure 5.12 The sophisticated stereotype

A major issue is where and when emotions should be shown. Some cultures mix playful humour with serious discussions. Other cultures find this wholly inappropriate. One of this book's authors failed to strike the appropriate note with some Swiss bankers.

The Swiss can be quite serious, especially during work hours. Humour is for relaxing moments before or after the seminar. The Dutch presenter used a cartoon to 'break the ice'. Dead silence. He used a second cartoon. Again silence. Then a Swiss participant raised his hand. 'Can we get on with the seminar please?'

The Dutch presenter tried to make a joke of the intervention.

'You're a serious lot ... Have you ever thought of going into banking?' Silence.

In the coffee break the senior Swiss manager approached the Dutch presenter.

'We didn't like to embarrass you, Dr Trompenaars, but in fact the Swiss have been in banking for some time.'

Note that both parties adhered to their national stereotype and conviction that jokes were appropriate or otherwise. Those who saw humour as inappropriate could not even recognise the attempt!

Often the same word triggers totally different associations. In a recent partnership negotiation, the Japanese and American sides both vowed that they would be 'sincere'. By this the Americans meant outspoken, unreserved, spontaneous – traits the Japanese found insulting. By 'sincere' the Japanese meant making genuine efforts to create a climate of politeness, good etiquette and gracious manners – a habit the Americans saw as 'bullshitting'. The meeting proved a disaster.

What innovative teams know and have learned

Innovative teams, according to research by Michael Shrage, must in the early stages of innovation be *playful*. Unless their work is fun they will never persevere for a sufficiently long time to get it right. Were they to get serious about initial failed attempts they might give up or become discouraged. So long as they are playing they are usually enjoying themselves and following Richard Branson's dictum, 'Have fun!' However, this initial hilarity gives way to seriousness as the day of the launch approaches. While errors were once comedy they could soon become tragedy out there in the cold world of reality. You could lose your shirt. Moreover, when a product is tested you will need all the dispassionate, detached verdicts you can find. It is not going to succeed because you want it to!

It is wise for a team to make the greatest possible use of its emotional range. There are wide variations in the fortunes of a company and it is appropriate to have a mood that fits the occasion. As Robert Whittington wrote of Sir Thomas More:

> 'More is a man of an angel's wit and singular learning. I know not his fellow. For where is the man of that gentleness, lowliness and affability? And as time requireth a man of marvellous mirth and pastimes; and sometimes of as sad gravity: a man for all seasons.'

The innovative team senses its own growing excitement as it nears the solution to its challenge, yet insists on verification of the utmost rigour and dispassion to counterpoint its own zeal. This is too important, too serious to be treated lightly.

Lego put the switch from neutrality to exuberance and excitement to clever use by charging customers *before* they went into Legoland Parks, while the customers were still in a calculative mode. But the entrance fee gave families, and especially children, free access to all the attractions, so that they could let their excitement rip, without clawing desperately at mother's handbag for one more treat. There is a time to seek entrance, and a time to enjoy having done so; the first should be sober, and the second joyful.

BUPA's teams do not just have to sympathise deeply and spontaneously with the 'one life' their customers are trying to protect, they must go into a rapid calculative mode. What is wrong with this customer and is s/he covered for this particular condition? What the insurer can do and cannot do has to be explained over the telephone to a very anxious relative who may be in great distress. This is payback time, yet the insurer may not be able to repay the insured for everything that is needed. No wonder members of the team need each other's support and experience. Another leader, Anders Knutsen of Bang & Olufsen, makers of high-quality audio equipment, used teams to create a symphony of emotional and technical excellence.

Technical excellence and the emotional climate

The last major challenge that Anders Knutsen saw himself as confronting was that of technical excellence and the emotional appeal of products. The latter was a subtle and diffuse concept. Beautiful audiovisual information had to be conveyed on instruments worthy of their content, in the same way that the instruments of an orchestra carry the spirit of the composer and express his or her feeling.

'Time is in our favour,' Knutsen believed. 'The world is flooded with discount junk products which strive to become classics. Products with emotional value will be strongly placed in our "throw away" culture.'

In the history of Bang and Olufsen, both technical excellence and emotional climate had been important – more so than sales or marketing – but even these leading values had not been reconciled or harmonised. First one was dominant and then the other, and their fight for dominance had made the resulting product unaffordable.

So Knutsen extended 'Idealand', a non-localised space where engineers, music lovers, designers and others – both within Research and Development and outside the company in the community of experts – could engage in a dialogue that would stimulate ideas, and balance them. Another balance is between the audio and the visual, which come together in digital sound pictures. Carl Henrik Jeppesen explained:

'We send development teams, usually to the USA, to study what sounds and sights are being made and consumed. They go to concerts, music studies, discotheques. You need someone to champion the original sound pictures and the emotions generated from them, and someone to champion the technologies of recording and playing those sound pictures. It is this creative clash between the artists and engineers that gives you optimal integration.

'In the old days, one competence would dominate the others, but no more. There came a day when Anders Knutsen and his team refused to sponsor a prototype product because the costs were out of line. That was a real shock for all of us. It had never happened here!

'With Break Point, the culture changed dramatically but values were retained and began to strengthen one another. In one sense, the Bang and Olufsen secret is integrated seamlessness – every part of the system has to work with every other part – and now this became true of our values as well.

'We now test our products with our customers and, if they like it, sales start at once with a projected product life of ten years. We position ourselves in the market in such a way that confirms or fails to confirm the hypotheses developed in Idealand. The latter is no private muse, but a test-ing laboratory for viable ideas, a set of hypotheses to which our customers say yes or no.'

We might also pause to consider ways in which emotions are mishandled, and players who are usually neutral may suddenly burst out with inappropriate emotion, uncontrollable anger and self-pity. It was the genius of Maradona that made the Argentinean football team win many matches. But he could also get out of control and was often sent off the field, leaving the team in despair. And who doesn't remember Zidane's head meeting the chest of the Italian provocateur? It left the French with only 10 players and unable to level with or even beat the Italians. This illustrates a vicious circle.

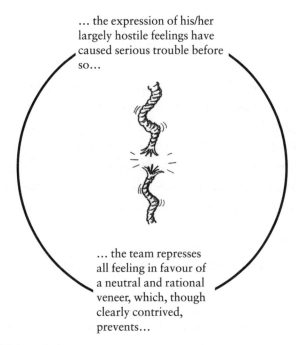

... the expression of his/her largely hostile feelings have caused serious trouble before so...

... the team represses all feeling in favour of a neutral and rational veneer, which, though clearly contrived, prevents...

Figure 5.13 Vicious circle

It is from such a player that one hesitates to buy a second-hand car and such a player is nicknamed 'Cowboy'.

What we found

Our diagnostic instruments include this question:

In retrospect, I quite frequently think that I have given away too much in my enthusiasm.

What is *your* position on this statement?

a) Strongly agree
b) Agree
c) Undecided
d) Disagree
e) Strongly disagree

Neutrality versus emotional temperament

In many countries you lower your status before others by showing emotion. When the English author was made an army officer at the age of 19 he was warned, 'You do not keep a dog and bark yourself.' All I had to say was, 'Rather scruffy belt on that man, Sergeant!' and my sergeant would start abusing him at the top of his voice. 'Filthy 'orrible man!' I was expected to keep my dignity while my sergeant shouted. The platoon was managed by a mixture of my restraint and his expressiveness.

Measuring innovative competence: reconciling neutrality with affectivity

We can measure the extent to which meanings and emotions have been reconciled by distinguishing two polarised strategies, two integrated strategies and a compromise.

Emotions can be so strong that they obliterate thinking. Thoughts can be so calculated that they repress genuine feelings. But to think first and then let out the emotions at the right time, or to feel first and then think hard about how to express this to the best effect, are both pathways to integration set out below. In the following question, we see some very innovative answers and some that make you choose between poles or compromise between them, leaving you with a sub-optimal result.

Question: performance or beauty

When designing a new product (or service), a number of trade-offs are required because of choices of materials, systems, size, strength, technical performance, etc. A group of managers were arguing about whether performance should lead or should follow design appeal.

Which of the following opinions that were expressed is closest to your orientation?

a) Design is always a compromise. In the end, one has to make the best trade-off to balance competing demands.

b) Technical performance must dominate. If the product doesn't work, then the customer has nothing. We can make the product attractive afterwards because of the wide range of shapes, materials and colourings available to us.

c) Unless the product looks attractive, whatever it is, the customer won't buy. We will always have enough technical competence to make sure it works, however it looks.

d) Whilst we start from a technical performance viewpoint, we can consider design and product appeal early.

e) We would start with a range of attractive designs with customer appeal but consider the technical feasibility of performance early.

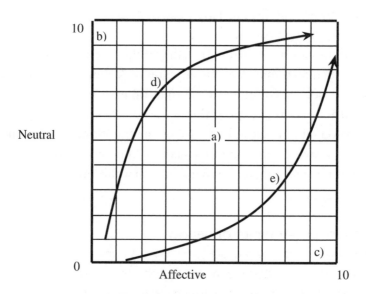

Figure 5.14 Reconciling emotions with reason. Here a curved arc moves from 0 past the letter d) to the top-right corner and from 0 past e) to the top-right corner. This shows movement while b), c) and a) are fixed points.

If you look at all the innovative designs in the world, you see that those designs that reconcile the neutral technical performance and the affective appeal are the most successful. The iPod both is functionally technically brilliant *and* has designer appeal.

There are many ways for a team to position an innovative brand, for example. Censydiam, a leading market research agency, shows one of the better analyses on their internet site. Every year, Censydiam publishes their longitudinal study of the positioning of car brands. They use a two-by-two matrix, where on one axis plots the degree to which emotions are expressed, and the other axis the degree of social integration (see Figure 5.16). It is wonderful to see how the producers of these brands confirm their cultural preference.

Most of the French and Italian brands are represented on the expressive side. On the emotionally more neutral side you'll find British, Swedish and Japanese cars, with Opel and Ford. It will not surprise anybody that, on the side of social differentiation, Alfa-Romeo, BMW, Jaguar, Mercedes and Audi occupy the field, whereas on the social integration side, Fiat, Suzuki, Nissan, Citroën and Daewoo dominate the game.

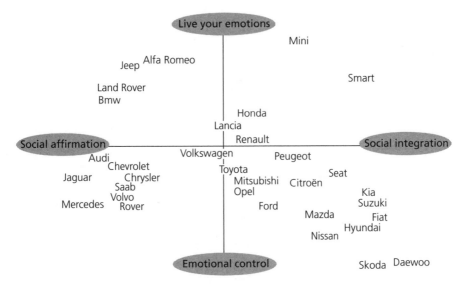

Figure 5.15 Living emotions in cars

Most innovative brands pose a problem, dilemma or anomaly and go on to claim that their product can resolve that dilemma. The more familiar the situation is and the more it engages our cultural archetypes or mental programs, the quicker the consumer will understand and bring his or her cultural ideas to bear on this issue.

For example, Volvo doubled its sales in France by integrating safety, a technical feat, with care of children, an emotionally expressive appeal. Prize-winning advertisements featured a little girl safely strapped into the rear seat with the caption: 'Always take care of the future, especially when the future is behind you.'

It is striking that many successful brands refer to a tension between two values, and that they credibly claim that their product can reconcile this dilemma effectively. When Apple introduced the rainbow logo and a bite out of the apple at the beginning of the 70s, it was a clear reference to the tree of knowledge of good and evil. On the one hand, the computer is the gateway to vast fields of information on the Internet, a cornucopia of objective information. On the other hand, this knowledge may change you forever, lead you into sin and temptation, introduce you to sexual partners and devious practices and impart to you the thrill of what has been forbidden and what you have been warned against. The reconciliation that Apple could offer was that it was possible to do both playfully.

CROSS-CULTURAL TEAMS AND
GLOBAL DIALOGUE II

In this chapter we will examine the final four dimensions of the seven that we have researched. We will be looking in turn at:

4 Specificity v diffusion
5 Achieved v ascribed status
6 Inner-directed v outer-directed
7 Sequential v synchronous orientations to time

For each of these there are significant differences in preferences among different national cultures. Yet in all cases innovative teams integrate both prevailing views.

Dimension 4: Preference for precise, singular 'hard' standards and preference for pervasive, patterned 'soft' processes (specificity versus diffusion)

The sophisticated stereotype

Here the contrast is between cultures that emphasise things, facts, statistics, units, atoms, analysis and 'hard' numbers, and cultures which emphasise relations, patterns, configurations, connectedness, synthesis and 'soft' processes. These contrasting styles have been linked with the left and right brain hemispheres. We call them specificity versus diffusion.

America's exaggerated specificity manifests itself in many forms, such as 'keeping your word' (as if there were only one!), in 'bullet points', piecework incentives, straight-line forecasts, bottom lines, financial ratios and other attempted distillations of virtue. We urge each other 'to get to the point' and 'not beat about the bush'.

Specificity tends to increase when two rival sides 'keep score', when we are bargaining over finite pools of money, when winning and losing can be calculated and when people's relative gains and losses are compared. We may have more than enough provisions to sustain life but still feel resentment because others have more than us.

Analytic/Differentiated	Holistic/Integrated
Positive connotation	
Division of labour	Integration of labour
Market segmentation	Market shifts
Money incentives	Social reciprocity
Forecasting	Scenario planning
Profits	Market share
Small print	Larger context
Reports	Rapport
Bullet points	Dynamics
Quantitative	Qualitative
Job simplification	Job enrichment
Inspected items	Quality circles
Good results	Improved processes

Analytic/Differentiated	Holistic/Integrated
Negative connotation	
Bean counters	Illusionists
Confrontational	Evasive
Blunt	Euphemistic
Obsessive	Hysterical

Figure 6.1 The sophisticated stereotype

Some typical misunderstandings

Alfie Kohn recently compiled a long, sad dossier of what goes wrong with Pay for Performance. Many managers recognise these problems, but are still reluctant to give up on the idea that, just as markets pull money and rewards towards successful enterprise, so should corporations. The problem with Pay for Performance is its exaggerated specificity. It assumes that superiors can know in advance how a task should be done and how difficult it is, and hence what pay should be attached to its performance.

But increasingly this is not possible. Work is too complex, too innovative, too subject to continuous improvement for superiors to know these things, much less construct an elaborate tariff. Markets certainly do pay for success – this is their genius – but they do not tell you in advance what you should do or how much you will gain by doing it! Markets are diffuse, chaotic processes with some very specific and measurable outcomes. Let's count, by all means, but let's not reduce reality only to what can be counted.

Diffuse processes can also be taken too far and lead to self-delusion. Many Japanese banks in the 1990s were unprofitable – even bankrupt – but refused to acknowledge this, so their assets never got redistributed to better-managed companies. Larger contexts can be elaborated to excuse almost everything. Marxism was a doctrine so diffuse it could not be falsified. Beware all-encompassing belief systems!

Some innovative fusions

It is companies that succeed in joining the specific to the diffuse that appeal most to customers. Shell discovered that specific forecasts around the price of oil and the politics of the Middle East were extremely tenuous and wide of the mark. Several had been disastrously wrong and had cost the company millions. It accordingly developed a new planning system with *alternative scenarios of the future*, much more diffuse and inclusive with at least three possible outcomes of current dilemmas. But Shell did not simply replace specific forecasts with wider, more diffuse concepts; it *reinstituted forecasts within each scenario*. It thought out of the box while recognising that 'God is in the detail'.

Jan Carlson of Scandinavian Airline Systems turned round the fortunes of his airline in the 1990s by speaking to staff about 'moments of truth'. Airline passengers had a vague feeling of good- or ill-will towards an airline, but they made up their minds from fragmentary evidence that became specific moments of a more diffuse truth. When your child accidentally spilled something, how did the stewardess react? When the bristles of your 'free' toothbrush come out on the second brushing, what does that tell you about the company's concern for you? Small things add up to big impressions. One of the authors received a travel alarm clock showing the time in dozens of cities, thanks to Singapore Airlines. It occurred to him that this would cost the company *unless he reciprocated and flew again as a consequence*. He did and always has. Reciprocity may be one of Asia's greatest competitive secrets. It is a diffuse reaction to a specific favour which of itself would constitute a cost.

What the innovative teams know and have learned

A good definition of a team is a collection of specific persons with specific skills that over time engage in a *diffuse process of development*. This is no metaphor or figure of speech. A team begins as a bunch of relative strangers; the team then elicits each member's various contributions, which grow to constitute a total solution to the challenge that team faces. Innovative teams make the journey from predominant specifics to diffuse, system-changing wholes. One of the thrills of successful teamwork is that the group grows more intelligent by the hour as each person is mined for what they know. Mihaly Csikszenmihalyi has described this as diffuse *flow process*, as when skills and the challenges these face fuse in a great wave of team excitement.

In his heyday at General Electric, Jack Welch debriefed four or five problem-solving, innovation-creating teams a week *and* implemented 80% of their recommendations unchanged, so well had he briefed them initially on the kinds of solution he wanted. This process not only pushes innovation deep into the corporation, but it also makes sure that leading ideas bubble up from below and keep the leader well informed. Welch called these workout groups, and they remade the company he led.

But perhaps the most remarkable levels of team prowess have been realised in space exploration. The National Aeronautics and Space Administration is credited with having invented the project group organisation, first used in the Apollo Space Mission to the moon. Such organisations consist almost entirely in expert teams working on some part of the overall mission, each having the authority of its own expert knowledge and each needing to be understood if the whole mission is to achieve its goals. Under these circumstances it becomes extremely hazardous for A to 'give orders' to B. B probably knows more than his boss. There is indeed an authority but that authority is science and 'what will work'.

Perhaps the most brilliantly successful space mission of the last decade was the Cassini–Huygens mission to Saturn and its moon Titan, even now ongoing. Its team members were extremely diverse, coming from 18 different nations and initially conceived by a triumvirate of French, American and Chinese space scientists. There were more than two hundred specialists and sub-specialists, everyone from vulcanologists to experts in cosmic dust particles. The mission was studied by Groen and Hampden-Turner (2005). It is a well-known axiom that for a team to be successful it needs a *superordinate goal*, something so large, so momentous, so diffuse that petty rivalries, cultural differences and disputes about money are as nothing compared to the significance of this event.

More was going to be discovered in the first half-hour of this mission than had been discovered in the two thousand years since the first astronomers. The many disciplines would make or break, be famed or forgotten, depending on whether the mission *as a whole* succeeded. This was a lifetime's work, 25 years or more from start to finish. Few would have a second chance. The irony was that one serious error could blight a thousand or more careers and condemn many years of work to futility. It was for this reason that all team members became relentless critics of each other's work, going on and on until some fault was found. All that could prevent the pain of such searching criticism of each other's *reports* was the *rapport* between members. The sterner the specific criticisms, the closer the diffuse bonds had to be to make all this bearable.

The notion that we can somehow choose to be diffuse or specific is fanciful. If we are serious about rolling back the frontiers of space, we need to be *both*. Very early in this mission's preparation there was a ban on voting at meetings. The reason was that one specific person *could well be right about a specific error.* The demand was for consensus, the strongest kind of diffuse bond. The two values develop together.

The whole mission resembled an inverted tree. Every 'leaf' had to be connected to a 'twig', every twig to a 'limb', every limb to a 'branch' and every branch to a 'trunk', which was the launch-ready vehicle. As the assembly converged, every separate element was tested and every connection too. Teams delivered their work to 'integration teams' above them, which delivered to integration teams above them. The entire feat of science was a tribute to the nature of innovative teamwork.

A number of outstanding American pioneers have created diffuse systems that their specific cultures scorned but which diffuse cultures, such as Japan and probably now China, welcomed with open arms. W. Edwards Deming invented the error-correcting system of continuous improvement, but only the Japanese auto industry would at that time listen. He finally agreed to speak to the Big Three in the USA at an industry conference, but only if all three presidents of the companies who had so long ignored him were on the platform to express their regrets. Joseph Scanlon invented a method of 'gain-sharing' between managers representing shareholders and organised workers. He was widely ignored as an ex-trade unionist *until* the Japanese took to his plan by the thousands. When you are sharing ideas rather than money there is no scarcity of contributors.

In highly effective organisations, then, diffuse, 'chaotic', creative teams receive specific feedback on the success or otherwise of initiatives, managing, as it were, 'on the edge of chaos'.

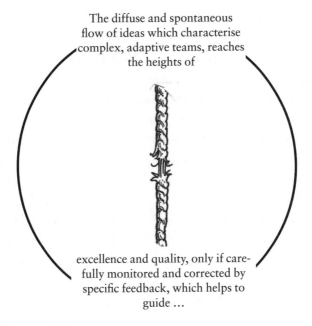

The diffuse and spontaneous
flow of ideas which characterise
complex, adaptive teams, reaches
the heights of

excellence and quality, only if carefully monitored and corrected by
specific feedback, which helps to
guide ...

Figure 6.2 Virtuous circle

Holistische weltanschauungen and analytical bottom lines

An example of teams from different nations working well together arose at Advanced Micro Devices, which set up a fabricating plant for microchips (Fab) in Dresden, former East Germany. This effort was led by Martin Gillo, a German citizen with extensive experience in the USA. American teams liked to brainstorm with jumbles of ideas. Germans preferred to ponder, rationally and privately among themselves, speaking German, not English, and coming up with complete solutions, not fragmentary bits and pieces. Gillo's solution was to call 'time-outs' during which the Germans would write their whole solutions on postcards and pass these to the American team, which was amazed by how much they had accomplished. Each nation used its own specific or diffuse style, and then connected their deliberations. Several of the German 'wholes' connected the American 'pieces'.

By asking Americans to summarise joint meetings this team became more diffuse over time. By asking Germans to work on the agenda for the next meeting their team became more specific. Americans preferred to speak first, off the cuff, and then use the bits and pieces to think with. The

Germans preferred to think first and show how their rational solutions covered all the details. The meetings of the joint teams therefore alternated between the jostling ideas of Americans and the elegant syntheses of the Germans. Each team could use the language in which they thought, having it translated for the benefit of the others.

The effectiveness of a Fab is estimated by its 'yield': the ratio of usable chips to defects. Yields climb in the weeks and months after starting operations. The yield of the Dresden Fab had the steepest, fastest climb in the history of the company. Within two years it was making the most sophisticated chips in the whole of AMD and producing world-class products, a major challenge to Intel. East Germany, originally chosen for its lower cost of skilled labour, now outperformed all concerned.

Measuring innovation competence: reconciling specificity and diffuseness

In our diagnostic instruments, our respondent managers considered five possible answers to the following idea to probe what the best work environment is.

Question: the best work environment

People have different opinions about how the work environment influences job performance.

Which of these alternatives best describes the work environment in your organisation?

a) People you work with know you personally and accept the way you are, both within and outside of the organisation.

b) Colleagues respect the work you do, even if they are not your friends.

c) Colleagues know you personally and use this wider knowledge to improve job performance.

d) Colleagues take some private circumstances into consideration, while disregarding others.

e) The people you work with respect the work you do and are therefore able to offer to help you in private matters.

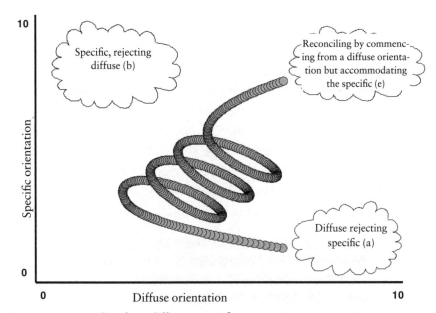

Figure 6.3 Reconciling from diffuse to specific

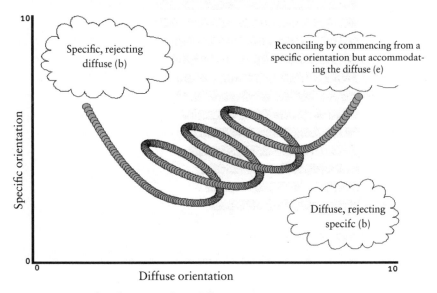

Figure 6.4 Reconciling from specific to diffuse

Here we see that the most effective work environments e) and c) are those in which specific and diffuse sources of knowledge are combined – in either order. In each case, the recognition of dilemmas and their reconciliation helped us and our leaders to create a wider and more inclusive 'integrity of values'.

Formal research investigative studies
More extensive triangulation studies, where we correlated reconciliation with bottom-line results, business unit performance and 360° peer review, have been subject to detailed statistical analysis by our internal research team and several of our university-based PhD students. We have accumulated strong evidence that this integrity or bridging of diverse perspectives is a vital aspect of creating wealth and sustainability.

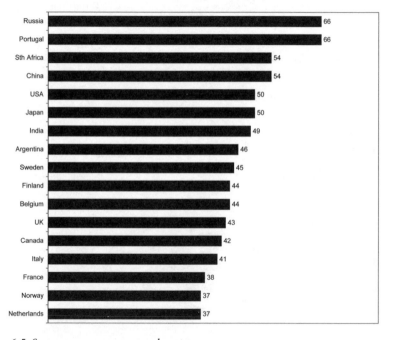

Figure 6.5 Separate versus connected country scenes

What we found

This dimension was probed with the following question.

Question: the essence of an organisation

There are two extreme ways to consider an organisation.

Which of these two ways better represents the way you perceive the essence of an organisation?

a) An organisation is a system designed to perform functions and tasks in an efficient way. People are hired to fulfil these functions with the help of machines and other equipment. They are paid for the tasks they perform.

b) An organisation is a group of people working together. The people have a social relationship with other people and with the organisation. The functioning of the company depends on these relationships.

Dimension 5: Status earned through success and track record versus status ascribed to a person's position or potential, e.g. age, family and background (achievement versus ascription)

The sophisticated stereotype

Here the contrast is between being esteemed for what you do and being esteemed for what you are. Status can be conferred almost exclusively on your achievements. It can also be conferred on your being or potential. So we may expect more of males, of white people, of the college-educated (which includes past achievement), of older people, of well-connected people and of people of good family or class. People assigned to certain roles, e.g. electrical engineer, may have higher status because the business or nation anticipates that such jobs will be crucial to its future.

As we might have expected, Americans, Canadians, New Zealanders, Australians and all immigrant nations have strong preferences for achievement. When you immigrate, you leave class and family associations behind you. Few in the New World care that you came from a 'prominent family in Kent'[1]. But Norway, the Netherlands, Sweden, Ireland and the UK are also high in achievement orientation.

---

1   Kent is a 'county' (small regional unit) in the south-east of the UK

Among those ascribing status are cultures with formidable records of economic growth in the recent past: Japan, Korea, Hong Kong, Taiwan, China, France and Singapore. Are these against achievement? Surely not. They just approach achievement in a different way. They ascribe high status to those entrusted with 'catching up with America', who are given prestigious posts within key innovative projects. The idea is that these people will achieve as a consequence of the trust placed in them.

Achievement orientations assume that what is being tried is *worth achieving*, but this is not always true. Rising to the top of a criminal conspiracy engaged in racketeering is a doubtful achievement.

Status: Achievement versus Ascription

What you do	Who you are
• As good as your most recent performance	• As good as your breeding and lineage
• A self-made person	• Well brought up
• Judged by 'what?'	• Judged by 'how?'

Positive connotation	
• Successful	• Noble spirited
• High-flyer	• Crown prince
• Excellent	• Worthy
• Up or out	• Potential developed

Negative connotation	
• Nouveau riche	• Old money
• Opportunist	• Leisure class
• Go-getter	• Idle rich

Figure 6.6 Sophisticated stereotype

Some typical misunderstandings

Societies that achieve status and societies that ascribe it are often at odds in first encounters. When Americans visit East Asia with a product or proposition, they usually 'put their cards on the table' and behave authentically, as they see it. This is the deal. These are the costs. This is the size of the likely opportunity. With profits on this scale, should we not sink our differences? All this is 'achievement talk'.

And of course, it is deeply offensive to cultures that ascribe status. What these cultures want to know is this: Who are you? With whom are you related and connected? What is your background? What family do you come from?

They also want to know if you are inherently gracious, polite and hospitable. By putting you in relaxed settings, they seek to establish trust. Many hours, even days may be spent on small talk, but the implications are not small. If you were pretending, you would not be able to keep up the pretence. The scattered impressions would not be coherent. What, after all, is five days in a partnership lasting five years or more?

But if we look more closely at this misunderstanding, we see that it is really an issue of priorities. Once Americans have decided to do business with someone and feel that a deal is in the offing, then it is sensible to get to know them, deepen the relationship and check their references. Once a Chinese or Japanese executive has got to know an American and deepened the relationship, then it is time to turn to business. Each accidentally offends the other by getting this sequence wrong.

The reason it is so important to learn from other cultures is that 'pure achievement' or 'pure ascription' are both liable to fail. The British pensions industry faces a pensions mis-selling scandal in which tens of thousands of pensioners were induced to surrender their group pension plan for an individual portable pension, with significantly smaller benefits. The volume of this duplicity is a staggering £2 billion, with companies 'named and shamed' by government watchdogs until they repay the difference.

How could salespeople fan out across the country and talk luckless savers into pensions provisions worse than the ones they currently held? All too easily, we fear, because these sales staffs were being paid on commission only – on what they achieved only. These companies were essentially saying to their sales people: 'We do not care about *you*, only about what you earn for us through achievement.' Not unsurprisingly this attitude was passed on to duped customers.

Most companies in the world, by a very large margin, are still family-owned. Even in publicly owned companies, family concepts survive. One thinks of the Japanese term *amai*, meaning indulgent affection between mentor and subordinate, and *sempae-gohal* (brother–younger brother relationship). Training your workforce and mentoring them is an investment in their potential, a form of ascribed status. That people who care for and respect each other go on to achieve is a natural consequence. The larger training expenses of several East Asian cultures speak for themselves. Japanese auto-assembly plants in the USA give new workers 225 hours of training in their first six months; American plants give just 42 hours.

What innovative teams know and have learned

A team is a self-fulfilling prophecy in action. The team achieves, gets a reputation ascribed to it, which then fulfils itself in further achievement. This results in *esprit de corps* and a winning streak in team contests. Our research findings confirm that cultures putting ascribed status first are still capable of great innovative achievements. Even with East Asia's present troubles, its growth rates are the highest yet recorded in the history of economics. The reason for this is that ascribing status and achieving status are complementary. If you want someone to achieve, then show them initial respect.

In America, we keep stumbling over this fact, but too often 'lean and mean' management ignores it. In the original Hawthorne Experiment, Irish and Polish immigrant female workers were given the status of co-researchers with Elton Mayo and Fritz Roethlisberger from Harvard. Instead of just assembling telephone relays, they were invited to investigate how telephone relays might be better assembled – a totally transformed job description. The fact that they were withdrawn from the factory floor into a small group meant that they could affirm each other's identities.

Many innovative teams also showed great skill in handling the achieved–ascribed dimension and using it to learn with. Richard Branson starts with critiquing those industries in which he has decided to compete – that is, ascribing to them defective status and ascribing to himself the reputation of a reformer of those industries and an underdog in challenging them. Unlike many reformers, he then actually *achieves* superior levels of performance and so proves his original contention, using wide sympathy in the press and among customers to establish his case.

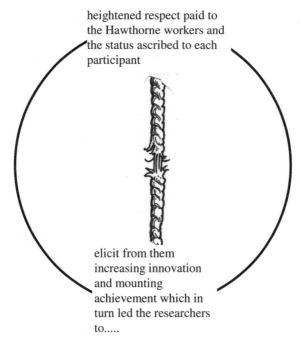

heightened respect paid to
the Hawthorne workers and
the status ascribed to each
participant

elicit from them
increasing innovation
and mounting
achievement which in
turn led the researchers
to.....

Figure 6.7 Virtuous circle

The issue is granting teams sufficient autonomy to *achieve*, without thereby diminishing the *ascribed* status of the senior manager who sponsors that team's efforts. Martin Gillo of AMD struggled with the need to have senior managers risk their senior positions in delegating resources and authority to problem-solving teams. Where these were successful, the sponsor's authority was actually enhanced, and the status ascribed to the team was used by it to achieve and thereby add to the sponsor's reputation.

Stan Shih of Acer had to make sure both that managers and employees achieved *and* that others were prepared to mentor that achievement: to describe, judge and celebrate excellence and in that respect rise above achievement to assure that its ends were worthwhile. You cannot have everyone achieve; some must judge and consecrate the goals of that achievement and some must ascribe status and be seen to symbolise the ends themselves.

Bombardier was another successful family company, which Laurent Beaudoin, son-in-law of the founder, took over some years after the latter's death. Although this might have the appearance of status ascribed by family membership, in fact family members had to work even harder than outsiders to justify their places in the hierarchy, and Beaudoin was not the nearest relative.

The company made very successful acquisitions and in each case the new company became a member of the 'family' and was studied with extraordinary care and respect by Beaudoin, the Scholar-Acquisitor. He took over and managed companies of far greater complexity than the one his father-in-law had founded – hence 'The Ski-mobile which took to the Skies'. By welcoming each new acquisition into the 'family', and giving it great importance, the company laid the groundwork for a succession of extraordinary innovations.

That this was no coincidence has been found many times since. Consultants who use interviews as a method of inquiry often find that executives have seldom had the experience of being listened to, and their morale and competence grows before your eyes. Royale Foote and colleagues tested the proposition that interviewing alone could boost productivity. In the Annheuser Busch's Fairmont plant they trained each level of supervision to interview the level below, from the top of the organisation to the very bottom, which was unionised by a tough Teamsters' local. Interviews were not focused on work issues specifically, but on whatever concerned the interviewee. There was no additional intervention.

In the eight years of the interviewing process, the Fairmont facility climbed from almost the worst plant in the network to by far the best, on a score of hard measures. Something as elementary as brewing, canning and trucking rests squarely on the status and respect ascribed to each member of the organisation.

No less a luminary than Douglas McGregor taught that the respect and confidence we have in one another fulfils itself in subsequent achievement. He called this Theory Y. As Bernard Shaw put it in Pygmalion: 'It's the way she's treated that makes her a lady.' No wonder the Pygmalion Effect has been found in the workplace and the classroom. When teachers are told that a child will 'spurt', the child does, although the 'spurters' were actually picked at random. It was the teacher's belief that spurred the child to achievement.

Measuring innovation competence: reconciling achieved with ascribed status

There are two roads to integrating these values. You could argue that you must first decide *who* you are (ascribed status) if you are to go on to achieve in a way consistent with this. Or you could decide that achieving at this and that is a good way of discovering who you are (ascribed) and what you were meant to stand for.

The five responses below were used to measure reconciliation versus polarisation.

Question: what is important?

Which one of the following best describes your values?

The most important thing in life is:

a) getting things done, because in the long run it serves you best to think and act in a way that is consistent with the way you really are

b) that you are able to do things at times and to relax at others

c) to think and act in a manner that is consistent with the way you really are, because in the long run you will achieve more

d) getting things done, even if it interferes with the way you really are

e) to think and act in a way consistent with the way you really are, even if you don't get things done.

We plot these answers on the grid below.

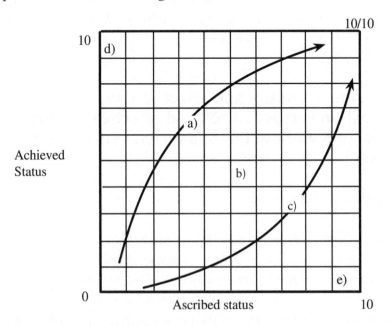

Figure 6.8 Reconciling achievement vs ascription

Combining achievement with ascription

Innovation and creativity are potentials within us and must first be respected, encouraged and elicited if we are to achieve in innovative ways. Too much emphasis on achievement leads to admiration of wealth accumulation without asking how this was achieved – perhaps by doubtful banking practices, by fraud and criminality. In many poor communities *only* the criminals 'achieve'. Too much emphasis on ascription leads to dynasties, to snobbery and to the worship of exclusive circles of gentility:

So this is good old Boston
The home of bean and cod
Where the Lowells speak only to Cabots
And Cabots speak only to God

What leads to higher and higher innovation are groups or teams of innovative persons who incubate and elicit the potentials of their members and encourage achievement, for example the Medici family group of bankers that took Michelangelo, Galileo, Botticelli and others into their homes, the King's Players (which included Shakespeare), the Dutch Masters, the French salons, the Encyclopaedists, the Transcendentalists, the Bloomsbury Group, the French Impressionists, the Cambridge 'Apostles', the Vienna Circle, German Expressionism and so on.

Dimension 6: Control and effective direction comes from within versus control, and effective direction comes from without (inner-directed versus outer-directed)

The sophisticated stereotype

Here the question is about the source of virtue and direction. Is it inside each of us, in our 'soul', conscience, integrity – or outside us in the beauty and harmonies of nature, in the needs of families, friends, customers? Is it virtuous 'to be your own man', or 'to respond to your environment?'

Americans tend to plan and then make those plans work, to rely on ability not luck, and prescribe taking control of their lives. The USA is joined in strong inner direction by Norway, New Zealand, Canada, Australia and France. The latter, we may note, combines communitarianism with inner direction, as in the group of fiercely convinced rebels seizing control of the nation's destiny. While inner direction is advocated by Judeo-Christian values, outer direction is sanctioned by Shintoism and Buddhism. Gods are believed to inhabit mountains, streams, storms, harvests and winds. You mollify the gods by shaping attractive containers they will wish to inhabit.

On this particular bifurcation, we cannot evade the truth that American popular culture celebrates and satirises itself. We have Superman vying with planes and bullets and overwhelming natural forces. We have Frank Sinatra 'doing it my way' and even small children bearing arms against each other in school. *Fortune* magazine celebrates 'America's Ten Toughest Bosses', despite their very brief tenures. Alf Dunlap dresses himself in battle fatigues and ammunition belts to impersonate Rambo. Unfortunately, there are real casualties. When life imitates art, all concerned can escalate to absurd extremes. The flaw in celebrating inner direction is that for every boss 'so tough he tells you when to go to the bathroom', there would have to be several American subordinates waiting to be told! It hardly improves effectiveness overall.

Internal versus External control

Inner drive	Outer response
• Stick to your conscience	• Be sensitive to others
• Mastery of all kinds	• Going with the flow
• Hard sell	• Soft sell
• Internal innovation	• External innovation

Positive connotation	
• Dauntless decision maker	• Chief listener
• Questionnaire	• Interview
• Inventing	• Refining

Negative connotation	
• Manipulative	• Compliant
• Despoils nature	• Hugs trees
• One best away	• Runaway relativism

Figure 6.9 Sophisticated stereotype

Recently international bankers claiming to be Masters of the Universe have collapsed their own system. President Bush, using 'hard power', turned much of the world against America. All these are excesses of inner direction. On the other hand, Japan fell into a cultural depression in the early 1990s and seems to be unable to shake off this gloom, a symptom perhaps of too much outer direction and contagious pessimism. The culture proved very good at 'fast following' but when it struck the front it seemed to lose purpose and direction.

Some typical misunderstandings

No concept has ever taken American management theory by storm as powerfully as strategy. The metaphor is, of course, military and conjures up Alexander the Great's conquest of the known world. No concept better reflects the grip of inner-directedness upon the American imagination. It is the genius and conviction of business leaders that justifies their multimillion dollar salaries.

Now it is true that strategy can make or break innovative business. People Express grew to be a $2 billion corporation when Don Burr slashed the costs of flying. He took out galleys, increased seats, sold tickets on board and had passengers lift their own baggage into larger lockers. This enabled him to slash prices and get loadings (occupancy) above 80%.

Yet this resolute inner direction had blinded him to something happening outside his own industry, in the software sector. Management yield software could tell airlines on the basis of early bookings how full their flights would be and People Express noticed this too late. Its rivals slashed prices on planes destined to be half empty and flexible fare cuts beat fixed fare cuts. With more outer direction he might have survived.

The problem with brilliant inner-directed strategies is that these are not confined to corporate HQ. Intelligence is widely distributed, and the closer you get to the interface with the customer, the better such strategies are informed. In his brilliant *Harvard Business Review* article, Henry Mintzberg argued that strategies typically emerge from the grassroots of the corporation, where market changes begin.

The problem with strategy 'designed at the top' (or inner-directed strategy) is that top managers are typically furthest from the field and from customers.

The danger is that their strategy will be abstract and largely alien from the culture of the corporation. At worst, the strategy will command the impossible; at best, it will command something the grassroots of the organisation have been doing for years without recognition. Top-down strategy says in effect: 'I think, therefore you act.' It reserves for subordinates the role of putting their energies behind the superior thoughts of their leaders. In fact, nearly everyone has a strategy and all of us want to think.

This might help explain why outer-directed Japanese car makers still register 28 implemented suggestions per employee per year, while inner-directed Western corporations register 1.8 at best.

It is prestigious to be outer-directed in Japanese and most East Asian cultures, which is why superiors listen, while subordinates exercise initiatives, as hundreds of suggestions and strategies emerge. If you are really senior in a Japanese corporation, you hardly talk at all!

We are not, of course, claiming that outer direction is better. We do not even agree with Henry Mintzberg that emergent strategy obviates designed strategy or that it is worth holding debates between their respective advocates. We believe that top management can create grand strategies *out of* the initiatives emerging from the grass roots.

Push and pull
This core competence for today's innovative teams is the ability to connect the voice of the market with the technology the company has developed, and vice versa. This is not about technology push or market pull. The innovative team knows that the push of technology finally leads to the ultimate niche market, that part of the market without any clients. If you only choose for the market, your clients will be unsatisfied. Innovative teams are not 'adding value', because only simple values add up. Values are combined by creative groups: a car which is both fast and safe; high-quality food which is also easy to prepare. Nobody claims that combining values is easy; nevertheless, it *is* possible. A computer that is capable of making extremely complex calculations can also be

user friendly. The ever-expanding systems of satisfaction will form the ultimate test for the leaders of this century.

What innovative teams know and have learned

The metaphor which best unites inner with outer direction is the jiu-jitsu artist. He/she carefully observes the outer-directed momentum that is lurching towards him/her and deflects that person in the direction of his/her own choosing. Much of China, Japan, and East Asia tells of the Monkey King who, unlike Superman, is physically weaker than other forces in his environment, but a lot more agile and clever. The trick is to harness your own aims to the external dynamisms and momentum of the market.

Michael Dell was extraordinarily innovative in fusing the distinction between 'inside' and 'outside'. Customers could access the entire history of what Dell had done for them when and why on a protected website, together with ongoing advice on how to proceed. Suppliers could look up Dell's inventory levels for the components they had supplied and ensure that these were re-supplied just in time. Instead of ordering compliance, you share knowledge and the supplier gives you what you need when you need it.

There is much talk of late of 'open innovation'. The phrase refers to opening up internal R&D to external innovative influences and making the team process permeable to the outside. Proctor & Gamble are among the major companies that now have a director of internal innovation, paired with a director of external innovation. P&G's last five major innovations were brought in from the outside by acquiring small companies or by joint venturing.

Towards a 'Big Bang'

We have already seen that teams can provide links between national groups and they can vitally link disciplines. They are also very useful in improving the relationship between departments. Especially vital to innovation is the relationship between research and development (R&D),

which tends to be inner directed, and marketing, which tends to be outer directed, engaging as it must with customers and passing on their requests. R&D typically complains that marketing gives them insufficient time to develop, test and fine-tune products, while marketers complain that R&D is inflexible and slow to react. When Trompenaars–Hampden-Turner tested time horizons they found that marketing had a considerably shorter horizon. R&D was more universalistic, dealing as it must with science, while marketing was more concerned with what particular customers wanted and that special exceptions be made.

A second source of misunderstanding was the use of a precise and specific language by R&D and a diffuse, vague and rather flowery language used by marketing. Finally, researchers suspect that if only marketers looked harder and further they would find many more takers for what they had produced. Marketers, on the other hand, believe that R&D lives in its own private universe with little understanding of what is wanted 'out there' in a rapidly changing world.

Advice on how to handle this comes from the Marketing Science Institute (1994), which conducted research into what goes wrong, and came up with the following recommendations.

MSI's research

The exploration of cross-functional development groups. These so-called 'skunk' groups can achieve many successes when they integrate functions on-site and, further, when they are not too badly hindered by existing bureaucratic processes. In these groups physical, linguistic and cultural borders are very effectively overcome. However, a good deal of attention needs to be given to the quality of management in these groups.

Moving people between functions. Cross-functional moves between R&D and Marketing are not easy because of the specialised nature of their activities. Starting with the recruitment phase, one needs to work at attracting people who can be useful across functions and can be placed in a variety of environments. Moreover, focused internal development programmes need to support the mobility of staff.

The development of informal social systems. This aim is not easily achieved because it cannot be forced upon people, but recreational activities can encourage informal social interaction in a lighthearted way. Here too, much can be achieved by minimising the physical distance between the functions. Fruitful collaboration often occurs unexpectedly around central coffee points.

Changing the organisational design. GE and Philips have many co-ordination groups that bring together specialisations in a balanced way. With good management stimulating cross-fertilisation, many cultural and linguistic barriers can be crossed. Another option is the matrix organisation, in which functional specialists carry on reporting to their particular boss and have a 'dotted line' responsibility toward the project leader.

A more focused reward system. It appears that marketing staff often have a variable reward system linked to market share. Developers frequently receive their bonus on the basis of technological developments. A reward system that depends greatly on how much information is transferred across functions will have a very positive effect on the company's revenues and profitability.

One company that has excelled in this is Bang & Olufsen, the maker of high-quality audio and TV equipment. What is essential to their success is the close relationship with the R&D of music reproduction and the audience for music in the wider world. Time was when R&D was dominant but few in the market could afford the equipment and sales sagged. They were now *so* select that nearly everyone was excluded and the niche market shrank to a hairline crack. Then there came a new leader, Anders Knutsen. He reconciled technology push with market pull. His 'butterfly model' used a team from research and from marketing which jointly piloted the product. There were also dialogues between customers and suppliers. Together they created what Mintzberg calls a 'crafted strategy', which united not simply the departments but also those people the departments served.

Measuring innovation competence: reconciling internal with external loci of control

We measure how inner-directed versus outer-directed a leader is by considering the relative merits of 'push' and 'pull' strategies. Should you allow the customer to *pull* you in an outer-directed fashion towards his or her wishes, even where those wishes change, or should you *push* terms, conditions and deliveries upon a customer in an inner-directed fashion and, having won his or her agreement, carry this through as promised? Below is the dilemma and responses.

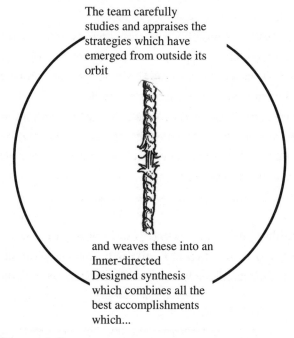

The team carefully studies and appraises the strategies which have emerged from outside its orbit

and weaves these into an Inner-directed Designed synthesis which combines all the best accomplishments which...

Figure 6.10 Virtuous circle

Question: push or pull?
Several consultants were arguing that you achieved greater customer satisfaction and quicker delivery times by using a customer-focused pull strategy, and that push strategies were outmoded. Several consultants disagreed.
Which position is closest to your viewpoint?

a) A pull strategy is best, because it lets the customer reset the deadline and permits resources to converge upon the customer on cue. Remember customers get behind schedule too, and change their minds about the relative advantages of speed, quality, cost, etc.

b) A push strategy is best, because this commits the supplier and customer to a joint schedule with costs, quality and specifications agreed
   in advance. The customer may, of course, change his mind, but then
   the costs for altering the original schedule are calculable.
c) A combination of push and pull strategies is best, so that the customer
   helps us to decide when not to push our products and we tell the clients when we cannot meet their requests.
d) A push strategy is best, because this commits supplier and customer
   to a joint schedule with costs, quality and specifications agreed in advance. If you do as you promised and you do it in time, then you cannot
   be faulted and your record speaks for itself.
e) A pull strategy is best, because it lets the customer reset the deadlines
   and permits resources to converge upon the customer on cue. The
   customer wants it when he wants it and pushing hard may get him
   too early and at needless expense.

The five possible answers are scored as in Figure 6.11. Answers a) and b)
are integrated with outer-directed pull put first in the sequence in the case
of a), and inner-directed push put first in the sequence in the case of b).

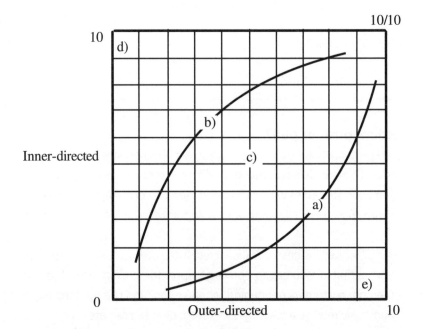

Figure 6.11 Reconciling inner and outer-direction

c) is a compromise, while d) and e) are inner-directed and outer-directed polarities, which brook no opposition from the conflicting principle. Answer d), for example, is concerned with the supplier not being 'faulted', not with satisfying the customer.

What we have found

Though much of our research has focused on national differences, our database allows us to look into functional differences as well. This shows another important source of cultural diversity that could be taken as a source for innovation.

Question: reality

Of the following two statements, which do you believe to be more in line with reality?

a) What happens to me is my own doing.
b) Sometimes I feel that I do not have enough control over the direction my life is taking.

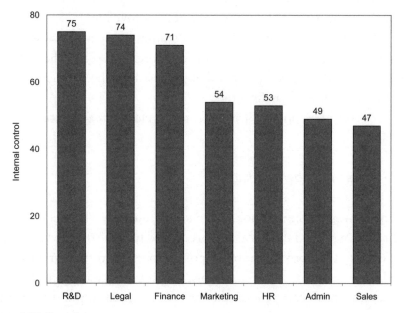

Figure 6.12 Function scores

Dimension 7: Time is conceived of as a 'race' with passing increments versus time is conceived of as a 'dance' with circular iterations (sequential versus synchronous)

The sophisticated stereotype

The contrast is between two alternative concepts of time. Since time cannot really be seen or touched, culture looms large in its definition. 'Time-as-a-race' sees time as a sequence of passing increments; an aim of life becomes doing as much as possible within time limits. 'Time-as-a-dance' concentrates on timing, or synchronisation, so that one moves in time with other people or processes.

Our data shows that American managers take a sequential approach to time, in common with Brazil, Ireland, Belgium, Italy and the Philippines. Japan and China take a mostly synchronous view, as do Hong Kong, Korea, Singapore, Sweden and France. Orientation to time is part of America's self-satire and stereotyped view of itself. There are 'time and motion' studies or 'racing against the clock' as workers sang in *The Pajama Game*. Benjamin Franklin said 'time is money', so no wonder Americans seek 'to make a quick buck'. Andrew Marvel, the Puritan poet, even chided his bashful mistress by saying that 'Time's wing-ed chariot' was overtaking the slow pace of their love life.

While America's time and motion studies made a priceless contribution to the efficiencies of mass-production, so too has the Japanese concept of 'just-in-time' and parallel processing. The former is clearly sequential, the latter synchronous.

Let's consider conflicts arising from the clash of expectations.

Some typical misunderstandings

One of us was buying a book at Singapore airport. The clerk took his credit card, wrapped the book and proceeded to serve the next customer, the card and the book both in her possession. When the purchaser objected, she explained, quite reasonably, that she was saving time. It would take several seconds for the credit card company to respond. When the credit had been cleared, she switched her attention back to the original purchaser.

In practice, few cultures are as well balanced between concepts of time as Singapore. A more usual experience is that sequential cultures regard synchronous cultures as 'rude', because they typically run late and then overstay to 'make it up to you'. Synchronous people dislike waiting in line for service and often form a scrum. They also interrupt your work and are themselves highly distractible, seemingly doing several things at the same time.

Synchronous cultures may regard sequential cultures as 'rude' because they respond not to you, but to some 'inner clock'. They stride hurriedly from one place to the next, occasionally waving at you but never stopping, and are so immersed in their work that they ignore people. They seem to want to stand behind you or in front of you, but never by your side. They refuse to abandon their plans in the face of unexpected meetings. Politeness makes them impatient.

Synchronous cultures have a logic of their own. You 'give time' to people important to you and if these abound, you will be delayed. Top people deserve more scope to synchronise their face-to-face engagements, so they enter the room last, after juniors have assembled. Synchronisation is often symbolised by bowing, nodding or making exclamations of assent. It is as if you were all on the same wavelength, practising the co-ordination of your inputs.

While pure sequentialism leads workers and employees to be machine-timed and dehumanised, purely synchronous cultures seem haphazard and inefficient, episodic and lacking purpose. Sequentialism is typically short-term, since deadlines need to be close by to have much effect. But synchronous cultures may or may not be long term. If they lack direction, there is no long-term goal.

What innovative teams know and have learned

Essentially, doing work fast and doing it in timely fashion are what teams design into the workplace. One worker operates faster than two others, so good timing decrees that he supplies the next two who halve the time they take by working in parallel and more slowly, without making errors.

Indeed, they could afford to work at half the speed of the first and still keep up with him. If they *do* make an error, subsequent work on the same product may be wasted. You can put one worker on five machines, but each must complete the cycle at precise intervals; that way the machine operator can check it and put it back in motion.

Sometimes sequential and synchronous working resembles a relay race with courses that overlap so that runners both follow each other and race side by side. Or a sequence 80 metres long can be shortened to four 20-metre processes done in parallel and then integrated. Historically the USA emphasised speed and sought to keep expensive machines running at all costs. The costs turned out to be the large inventory used to buffer the machines against running out of components. Japanese just-in-time method used quality circle teams to redesign and balance their own workplaces. This revolutionised manufacturing and turned Taichi Ohno's Toyota production system into a world-beater. All this is well known in the West by now, but getting a culture to go against its own grain is not easy.

We can identify innovation competence by giving respondents an opportunity to integrate sequential with synchronous views of time and seeing if they take this opportunity – because, of course, modern innovative practices must combine both concepts; neither is sufficient by itself.

It is self-evident that you will complete a process sooner if you speed it up. The gains from synchronous thinking are less immediately obvious. One source of considerable timesaving is to take a sequence 80 yards long, and divide this into four 20-yard sequences, work on these simultaneously and then assemble the four parallel processes. No wonder the workers at AMD sing 'Doing it Simultaneously'.

Historically, costly sacrifices have been made to continuous process machinery. Such machines symbolised speed. Sequential movement was what it was all about, so cheap workers doing simple operations were hired to keep the machines moving. Other sacrifices were just as serious. The machines had to be buffered by large inventories of supplies and work-in-process. In some plants, 80% of products were not being worked on, but remained in large piles, tied up in such inventories.

Enter Taichi Ohno and the Toyota Production System. If you think synchronously as well as sequentially, the huge inventories and the semi-trained workers doing dumb, repetitive tasks are suddenly seen as limitations. Inventories are cut to a fraction by JIT (Just In Time), and you need multiskilled workers of considerable intelligence to ensure smooth synchronisation among parallel processes. The West has known all this for a decade or more, but cultures are stubborn patterns to change.

Reconciling a sequential concept of time with a synchronous concept of time can give you the advantages of both and the limitations of neither. Each corrects for the potential excesses of the other. Ever-faster sequences with ever-finer synchronisation is what modern manufacturing is all about. The virtuous circle can be seen in Figure 6.13.

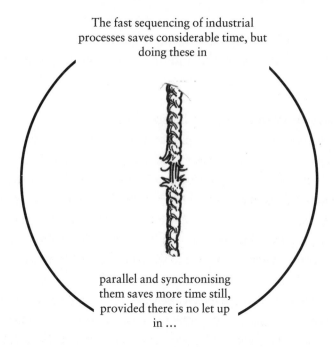

The fast sequencing of industrial processes saves considerable time, but doing these in

parallel and synchronising them saves more time still, provided there is no let up in …

Figure 6.13 Virtuous circle

Roughly the same rules apply to reducing 'time market'. The traditional approach has been sequential, with 'progress chasing' and a push strategy to get projects through faster. Analog Devices even culled projects running behind schedule by more than the permitted margin, so that the remaining projects would 'run for their lives'.

A recent innovation at Motorola University substituted a synchronous 'pull strategy'. This adopts the deadline and the viewpoint of the customer and pulls resources, people and products into the development process in the volumes needed to make the rendezvous with the customer. More resources are needed for late projects, fewer for those ahead of schedule. Since the customer falls behind schedule himself, such delays can release resources needed elsewhere. Here, just-in-time means synchronisation with the customer's latest deadline.

Measuring innovation competence: reconciling sequential with synchronous time

In the dilemma below, a somewhat haphazard and synchronous fashion house is frustrating a sequential and time-conscious wholesaler.

Question: how to speed up latecomers

You, as a manager of a wholesale distributor of a fashion company, are getting very worried about late delivery times to your clients. The summer did not allow you to deliver high-priced goods within a week of the scheduled delivery date that is the accepted norm in the fashion industry. You have tried many ways of solving the problems of late delivery. You still have not made any progress. You are now also in conflict with the transport firm because a contract was signed and the fashion supplier denies any responsibility.

Which of the following most closely describes what you would do?

a) You need to explain your problem to the supplier while appreciating the excellent quality of the goods. This will most probably lead to better adherence to deadlines.

b) You need to order early and ask for the goods two or three weeks before you need to distribute them to the shops.

c) You need to recognise that the fashion business is highly dynamic, artistic and in constant turbulence, and to accept that sometimes goods will be early as well as late. What difference does another week make anyway?

d) Your partners have a flexible time mindset and you will not be able to change that. You need to talk to your clients in order to prepare them

for a possible late delivery and give them a discount if it occurs. Separately you need to negotiate a premium for punctual delivery.
e) You need to know the suppliers personally. You should try to avoid
problematic issues and during the visit emphasise how important it is
for the clients to get on-time deliveries.

We classify the responses d) and a) as integrated, b) and c) as polarised,
and e) as compromise.

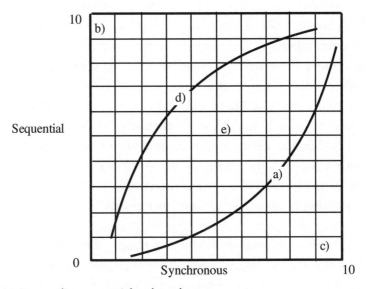

Figure 6.14 Reconciling sequential and synchrony

Clock time versus cyclical time

As well as considering the sequential versus synchronic aspects of time,
we also found cultural differences arising from the relative concern for
the past, present and future. In addition, 'time horizon' is another variable that differentiates the meaning that cultures give to time. How long
ago was your past? Is the future next month's sales figures, your next
financial year or the next stop-go economic cycle?

Innovation, teams and cultural value differences: a summary

Innovation occurs when teams help to reconcile differences in national, disciplinary and departmental cultures. They do this by:

1   Discovering new rules that cover more particulars and by making rule-changing, particular initiatives.
2   Encouraging competition only to cooperate around winning initiatives and cooperating better to be more competitive.
3   Expressing passionate convictions but having enough detachment to discover whether these guided you well or not.
4   Analysing the better to synthesise again by creating whole systems wherein details play a vital part.
5   Ascribing status to the potentials of team members so that they become more likely to achieve excellence.
6   Being directed by internally generated innovation but fusing this with 'external innovations' in the wider world.
7   Accomplishing tasks in the shortest possible time consistent with being able to synchronise these 'just in time'.

These seven integrations represent not simply the innovative capacity of teams but also a capacity we call *trans-cultural competence* or TC. Indeed, these seven reconciliations are a model for valuing in general, which puts the integration or integrity among contrasting values in the first place. All cultures are more than their stereotypes and it is a feature of their finest literature that these latent aspects are exposed; see such classical American writers as Hawthorne and Melville to note what lies beneath the American stereotype. The plea these writers make is to fuse the surface manifestations with deeper yearnings and realities and to cease the Great Repression, which may now have gripped Western economies.

We have experimented with several questionnaires, all seeking to discover whether respondents prefer to polarise or to integrate their values, and the respondents have included several clients and the Intercultural Communications Institute in Portland. The following trends are evident. There seems to be a *generalised tendency to integrate, compro-*

mise or polarise regardless of the particular value dimensions, so that if the subject integrates one pair of contrasting values s/he is very likely to integrate others. Logics of compromise, of polarity or of reconciliation tend to be applied across the board. This capacity to integrate innovatively correlates strongly, consistently and significantly with:

(a) extensive experience with international assignments;
(b) ratings by superiors on 'suitability for' and 'success in' overseas postings;
(c) high positive feedback on '360-degree feedback', an instrument that records verdicts of peers, subordinates and superiors on the value of engagement with particular managers.

We had assumed that managers would nearly always put their own cultural stereotype first and learn to add to this the values of foreign culture, but here we were mistaken. Most managers in cultures foreign to them had learned to put the values of that culture first and then include their own. Perhaps out of courtesy they took 'the road less travelled' and relied on reciprocity. Finally, we believe that being trans-culturally competent is just the tip of the iceberg and that managing diversity of all kinds, cultural, disciplinary, industrial, economic, gender and class-based, is essential to wealth creation in general. Most important especially is bridging the gap between those who are voluntarily innovative and the colleagues and customers they need to convince. Can we bridge the gaps to our own creative minorities?

TEACHING INNOVATION AND ENTREPRENEURSHIP: THE SINGAPORE EXPERIMENT

In 2002 the Economic Development Board of Singapore sponsored a series of four-month experimental programmes in 'technopreneurship'. The word is a hybrid of entrepreneurship and the kind of high-tech development that Singapore has been promoting for decades. The EDB is one of the most creative departments of government in the world. It wanted to discover whether entrepreneurship could be deliberately taught in its universities to its own citizens and whether such programmes would lead to new start-ups. The answer was 'yes we can!' to echo Barak Obama. This chapter tells the story of the last six years of this programme, which we also carefully evaluated. Our methods of capturing this innovation are also potentially important.

The Nanyang Technopreneurship Centre was purpose-built as an interdisciplinary programme, apart from other graduate schools at Nanyang Technological University in Singapore. The course was designed and run by Professor Tan Teng-Kee, a Singaporean-American alumni of NTU, an ex-entrepreneur and corporate executive who obtained his PhD from Cambridge University in 2002, under the supervision of Charles Hampden-Turner. The design of TIP (Technopreneurship and Innovation Programme) was crucially influenced by his thesis and by the ideas set out in this book. Dilemmas methodology is at the heart of this initiative. Recently a second programme in Mandarin for students from the People's Republic of China has been started. This remains to be properly evaluated although early indications are very positive.

The programme was not confined to the classroom. Innovation cannot be enclosed in a specific place. Rather 'Prof. Tan', as he is called, designed an 'innovative ecosystem', stretching from Singapore to China to the USA. The idea was to confront students with an environment that had highly contrasting stimuli, great *hopes* and great *disappointments*, great *riches* and great *poverty*, a *past* heritage that had been invaluable and *future* prospects that must be brighter still, as the torch was passed from the entrepreneur founders of Nanyang to the second and the third generations.

'You will go from zero to millions and back to zero,' Prof. Tan tells his students. Why back to zero? Because they will all end up dead and can take nothing out of this world. Everything they *get* they must *give* and the only legacy they can leave behind is the bestowal of the wealth they have created to enrich the lives of others.

An ecosystem is characterised by a great *variety* within a single *unity*, like the coral reef that plays host to a thousand species of tropical sea creatures. The programme begins with three days on an Outward Bound exercise wherein *individuals* are taught to bond in *teams* as they discover *opportunities* in *crises*. It is also intended to join *minds* with *bodies* and *challenges* with *responses* to these.

The next stop is the Chinese Heritage Centre at the heart of campus, a museum of the struggle of early Chinese immigrants. Nanyang is an authentically Chinese university built not simply by wealthy entrepreneurs but by the pennies of rickshaw drivers who wanted their children to have a better chance than they. The key to *change* is *continuity*, stresses Prof. Tan. You can only transform yourself if you know where you came from and where you want to go; a 'red line' joins your *heritage* to your *legacy*.

Throughout the entire 16 weeks the teams of students engage in a *simulation* of *reality* and *play* at the *serious* task of running their own businesses. The exercise speeds up the process of *trial* and *error,* with *strategies* created and *results* fed back to improve those strategies in a process of *error* and *correction*.

Students are also put 'on stage', there to *imagine* and *dream* a scenario they want to *come true* and to *realise*. Theatre is a mark of higher civilization that allows us to imagine shocking *failures* so that we can avert these to *succeed*. To imagine disaster is to suffer only vicariously while experiencing life vividly, dramatically and memorably. Students exposed to twenty common reasons of business failure, experienced while rehearsing, can avoid such mistakes in their futures.

Students of Chinese ethnicity are raised to be *modest* and *shy*. There is no problem in having such feelings within you, but those seeking to be entrepreneurs must be at least outwardly *bold* and *confident,* even while questioning themselves. After all if they need others to believe in them, they must believe in themselves.

Another strong contrast within the classroom is between having a *competitive arena* in which participants vie to think up better ideas and having a *family atmosphere* in which all have close memberships. 'What are we?' cries Prof. Tan rhetorically. 'A family!' respond the class. One result of everyone being so *different* in their aspirations is that they are the *same* in their need for attention, warmth and support. They need to be *supported* as people yet *critiqued* as innovators and trust that this feedback is authentically intended to help them succeed.

What this programme does is to transcend a zero-sum game in which good grades are inherently scarce and another's brilliance spells your own eclipse. Because success is multidimensional and every success is unique, students no longer win plaudits at each other's expense. There are still failures, a great many, but these are steps in the process of improvement. Better by far to be told that your product is not good enough by a member of your 'family' than by a distant angry customer demanding a refund.

Not only is Nanyang Technopreneurship Centre full of new products, trophies and pictures of successful product launches, but also visitors go there most days. These are entrepreneurs willing to share their secrets, venture capitalists willing to explain their judgements, government representatives with details of incentive programmes and soft loans to the enterprising, 'Angel' investors looking less for personal gain than a noble cause, and experts on the acquisition of small companies by larger ones (a common strategy for start-ups is to get acquired and begin again).

There are visitors from other universities, loan officers specialising in smaller businesses, corporations seeking to renew themselves and hosts of the curious. Students come to realise that this is *their* programme, a new venture in itself and one for which they share responsibility with their mentors. They interview the next intake, choose the speakers they want to hear from and help improve the programme design for next year.

But if the world comes to NTC, NTC also goes out to meet the world. The entire class travels to Shanghai, to the eco-suburb nearby, to incubators near Fudan and other universities there and around Beijing. It travels to Seattle on America's West Coast to visit Google, Starbucks and others. Students discover and champion inventions created by the Bioengineering School at the University of Washington, where the *disciplines* of biology, medicine and engineering meet and *cross* each other. Students write up business plans for the *commercialisation* of these *inventions* and pitch them before real venture capitalists, who are not simply *sharing their knowledge* with students but also *practising* their profession. Some inventions are funded.

The tour moves on to the Bay Area around San Francisco, down the peninsula to Silicon Valley and to Stanford University's innovation courses, while visiting IDEO, the world's best-known consultancy on innovation started by Tom Kelley. The $2 billion Kaufmann Foundation, America's fourth largest foundation, which commits all its funds to innovation, is also part of this extended Learning Journey. Carl Schramm, CEO of Kaufmann, has designated this programme the best in the world outside the USA and among the best even there.

This extensive tour contrasts *developed* with *developing* economies, those calling themselves *capitalist* with those proud of *socialism*, relative *affluence* with relative *poverty*, innovation driven by *self-fulfilment* with innovation driven by *necessity*, a system of *laissez-faire* with a system of *government oversight*, a culture of *individualism* and a culture of *communitarianism*. The contrasts could hardly be stronger.

After their return home the students are exposed to the contrast between *supply* innovation and *demand* innovation. Supply is something novel and valuable to customers, typically a technological development, but demand innovation is more subtle and well suited to tough times. You search out the 'pain-points' in the customer's system and try to relieve these. For example, a hospital's surgery unit was forever running back to the steriliser when an instrument was dropped or mishandled. An innovative company identified the problem and supplied 20-foot rolls of sterilised towelling with the instruments inserted in pockets in the order in which they were used by that particular surgeon. The hospital's problems were solved.

Developing a methodology

Given our belief that innovation consists of being presented with highly contrasting values at powerful levels of intensity and learning to reconcile these, how could the success or otherwise of the programme be measured? We took a single dilemma, *transforming ideals into realities*, and created a questionnaire around this theme.

Despite the risk of doing so, we decided to contrast the pedagogy of the TIP programme with the three-year bachelor degree programme the same students had received earlier. This was risky because students are typically nostalgic about their undergraduate days and grateful for the degrees conferred upon them, which is the gateway to a career. In contrast, the TIP diploma had scant recognition. Any university fundraiser will tell you that alumni funds are more forthcoming for undergraduate than for graduate studies. Comparing TIP to the university at large, and with courses and head teachers the students had selected for themselves, was going to be tough. Below are the kinds of instruction we gave to our respondents.

Question x

Please indicate your judgement of the values attained by NTU (U) and NTC (N) as measured against the following statements.
(a) My education has been realistic. It readies me for the world as it is, not necessarily as it might be. It is practical and effective.

Not at all									**Very much so**
1	2	3	4	5	6	7	8	9	10

(b) My education has been idealistic. It shows me how realities can be changed, so as to create new values. It is inspirational.

Not at all									**Very much so**
1	2	3	4	5	6	7	8	9	10

Suppose, for the sake of argument, that you have judged NTU (U) to be slightly more realistic than NTC (N), so you give (U) a score of 6 and (N) a score of 5. Suppose that you have judged NTC (N) to be slightly more idealistic than NTU (U), so you give (N) a score of 6 and (U) a score of 5. Please place 'N' and 'U' on the scales above. With these scores in mind, please consider transferring them to the grid below. This gives you an opportunity to record whether 'realism' and 'idealism' have been integrated or whether these have been polarised. For example, a score of 8/1, 2/9 or 5/5 would indicate polarisation while 9/9 or thereabouts would indicate integrity. Were you to copy your scores of 5 and 6 straight on to the grid, they would appear as below.

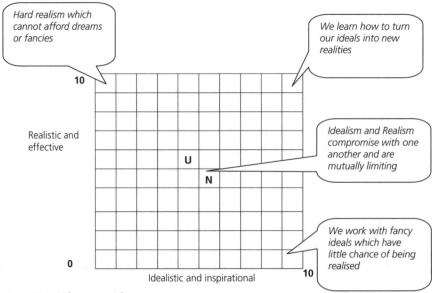

Figure 7.1 Dilemma grid

As you move your cursor across the grid, various pop-ups appear as balloons. These are there to prompt your choices, so that at top-left we have non-idealistic realism and at bottom-right we have idealistic unreality. Do *not* worry if you change your mind. After all, we have changed the question. *We* will count your scores on the grids only. Please make sure there is only one (U) score and one (N) score for each grid. Please place your score inside a square. We now proceed with the questionnaire.

We posed ten sets of dilemmas, but there is space here to report only five. This is not a serious omission because the answers to all ten different questions were remarkably similar. What seems to matter are not the particular values referred to in the questionnaire but whether the respondent experiences the pedagogy received as polarising or integrating. There is a persisting pattern crossing *all* dilemmas posed. As we shall see, NTU's undergraduate pedagogy was largely polarising in its effect on respondents, while TIP's graduate course was largely integrating in its effect. The differences were very large indeed and highly consistent across all questions. Two very different styles of education are being assessed here. The first is quite sterile. The second is highly innovative. No less an authority than the new President of the United States is an advocate of this integrative view. The five pairs of values are summarised below.

Table 7.1

Emphasised by universities (values of realism)	Emphasised by the TIP programme (values of idealism)
1 Training the intellect to master and organise concepts.	Training human experience, including feelings, emotions and ideals.
2 Absorbing information given by instructors.	Thinking for yourself and testing your convictions.
3 Classroom culture resembles a level playing field for competitive efforts.	Classroom culture resembles an extended family willing one to succeed.
4 Work is hard and serious, with long hours and hard challenges.	Work is playful and enjoyable. The hours slip away as we are challenged.
5 Career continuity and mastery are crucial.	Transformation is vital. We reinvent ourselves.

The results

We now turn to the evaluation of TIP as compared to NTU undergraduate courses. We found 153 qualified respondents. Many others had attended other universities. These were omitted. Many qualified respondents were out of the country and preoccupied with business. We received 68 usable replies. All questions were on the theme of Realism v Idealism. We regarded the first as a traditional value, which NTU was pledged to uphold. We regarded the second as a 'progressive' value, as one essential to innovation and acclaimed by TIP and many creativity experts.

We first used the Likert scale to measure (from 1 to 10) how *intellectual* the pedagogy was in the mastery and organisation of key ideas. We next used the same scale to measure how *experiential* the pedagogy was, in working with feelings and emotions. Respondents were then presented with the grid above and asked to locate themselves upon it.

We were looking for those who could experience emotionally what they were thinking about at the top-right of the grid. We were also looking for those who failed in this attempt, at top-left and bottom-right or compromised in the middle. To this end pop-up balloons prompted their choices and nudged them to consider whether these values had been integrated. The results are below.

Dilemma 1: Intellect v Experience
The responses are set out below and we see that Prof. Tan's TIP education has not only exceeded other university courses, but has done so by landslide proportions. This is not on one axis only, as we might have supposed, but on *both*. If you use your intellect to be innovative, you not only have your heart in your mouth but you also strive to be more rigorously intelligent still, since your whole future now depends upon it. Although vivid emotional experiences can detract from intellectual rigour and although intellectual activity at universities often occurs in a moratorium from stressful experiences, intellect and experience can develop together. This is strongly suggested by TIP's scores, recorded below (Figure 7.2).

The different locations on grids 1–5 need to be explained. There are two 'pathology zones', the nine squares at top-left and the nine at

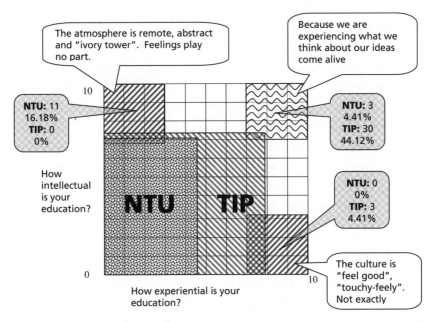

Figure 7.2 Dilemma Grid 1: Intellect v Experience

bottom-right. There is one 'reconciliation zone', the wavy pattern across the nine squares at top-right. The average scores for the NTU pedagogy are clearly marked, as are average scores for the TIP pedagogy taught at NTC. In virtually all cases the number of squares occupied by TIP is substantially larger than those occupied by NTU. We see that the intellectual attainment in the 'Technopreneurship' course was judged to have exceeded the NTU average. The TIP course scored 7.20 out of 10, compared to the university average of 7.06. Yet, as expected, TIP won hands down on the intensity of emotional experience, scoring 7.97 to the university's 4.78. The simplest comparison is to count the number of squares covered in the grid above by NTU and by TIP. When we do this NTU covers 33.26 squares and TIP 57.38; the latter is 74.2% higher (R2 = 34.23%, P<0.01).

We laid two deliberate traps for TIP and the university respectively and these are represented by the 'pathology zones', top-left and bottom-right. We prompted respondents to say that the TIP programme was 'feel good' and 'touchy feely' (see bottom-right of the diagram above). We wanted to smoke out any anti-intellectualism. But only 4.41% agreed with this verdict. We also prompted respondents to say that NTU courses were 'abstract, ivory tower and remote'. Fully 16.18% agreed that this was so. It is important to stress that NTU as a university *does* succeed on its own terms: 42.65% of its students rated their education as 8, 9, or 10 on intellectuality. What it does not do so well is to bring intellectual order to its own personal experiences: only 4.41% of respondents succeeded in scoring their undergraduate learning in the reconciliation zone (see wavy square at top-right) whereas 44.12% of TIP graduates reached this zone, their 'ideas coming alive'. Hence on Question 1, TIP's capacity to combine intellectuality with emotion, the programme scores ten times higher.

Dilemma 2: Learning by absorbing top-down information v Learning by thinking and acting for yourself

Our second dilemma, one that affects all pedagogy, is to consider how learning is communicated. Is it transmitted top-down by educators 'filling up' students with information and knowledge? This was the view of John Locke that educators 'wrote' upon the tabula rasa of the mind. Or are there innate structures of the mind (Platonic forms) that educators elicit so that in a sense we already know? Clearly both visions have some validity. Those who wish to think and act for themselves need information *with* which to think and they might be wise to listen first, or they may jump to a wrong conclusion. Those who only absorb conventional wisdoms filtering down upon them may take on the characteristics of a sponge. Since this accusation had been made against traditional Chinese education, we wished to see if it had lingered. Genuine innovation requires us not just to listen and absorb, but also to select, convince ourselves and act. We obtained the following results, as shown in Figure 7.3.

Once again the pathologies are located at top-left and bottom-right, while the wave-forms characteristic of the reconciliation zone are top-right. Comparing the number of squares covered gives NTU a score of 33.66 and TIP a score of 53.52 squares covered. This is a 60% advantage ($R2 = 25.36\%$, $P<0.01$). As we had anticipated, NTU scored higher on the top-down transmission of knowledge, but the difference was surprisingly small considering how much less time TIP spends lecturing com-

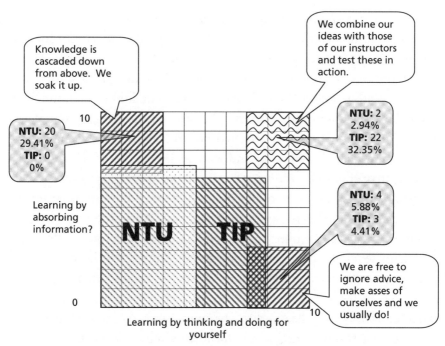

Figure 7.3 Dilemma Grid 2: Absorbing information v Thinking and doing

pared to the university at large. NTU scored 7.24 and TIP 6.74. Anyone wishing to think and act using information would need first to absorb the information. It seems TIP students did this. When it came to 'thinking and acting for oneself', the university scored only 4.66 and was swamped by TIP scoring 7.94, almost three squares higher. Again we tested the authenticity of 'thinking and acting' for oneself. Was it just pretending? We prompted the answer above: 'We are free to ignore advice, make asses of ourselves and we usually do!' Yet only 5.88% taxed TIP with this fault. We prompted respondents to complain of NTU 'Knowledge is cascaded down from above and we soak it up': 29.41% believed this to be the case so the concerns about passive memorisation are upheld.

Yet the university succeeds in its aims with 58.82% testifying that information from above is absorbed in the degrees of 8, 9 and 10, yet only 2.94% felt that they could use that information to think for themselves! In contrast, 32.35% of TIP scored in the reconciliation zone by absorbing information *and* using it to think.

Dilemma 3: Level playing field for competitive efforts. Are we good enough? v Extended family with brothers and sisters who root for you
Whether business enterprise is 'basically' competitive or cooperative is one of the oldest arguments. But no one witnessing the rise of Asian countries with Confucian family-based ethics can doubt that familial relationships play an important part. The case is even stronger for creativity and innovation. Great writers, artists and scientists, for the most part, knew and respected each other and were members of a salon or group.

Creative eras tend to come in bursts of one or two generations. There occurs an inter-stimulation of like minds, a mixing of intimate strangers. There are signs of this today in such places as Amsterdam, Seattle, the Bay Area, Helsinki, Dublin, Taipei and Shanghai. Singapore follows the American 'level playing field' axiom, so faithfully that it may be a purer meritocracy than its mentor. Yet innovation is crucially different because *what* constitutes 'merit' has not been defined beforehand. You need an extended family of colleagues to champion and to give significance to what you are trying to do, which authorities may not recognise. It may be recalled that we wanted to test the proposition that where those in the class wanted something *different* from each other, head-on rivalry would be less and most would wish each other well. We believed a 'family' of innovators might well rejoice at each other's fortune. Players needed coaches. Might programme members willingly coach each other, mixing cold criticism of the work with warm support for the person?

It was, at any rate, our hypothesis that TIP might be more competitive *and* more cooperative and familial than NTU. We believed this to be true of creative communities historically, a crucial blend of personal striving with interpersonal supportiveness, a co-mingling of contrasting minds.

In all, NTU covered 26.80 squares. TIP covered 56.37, or 103% higher ($R2 = 36.23\%$, $P<0.01$). TIP's average score on competitiveness was 7.19, compared to 6.85 for NTU, so that NTC was even more competitive than the mean for the university at large, but on the classroom environment resembling an extended family, the university scored but 4.22 compared with TIP's 7.84, a huge margin of 3.62. Once again the university 'succeeds' in being competitive, 42.65% score the environment 8, 9 or 10 as a 'level playing field' for competition, yet 44.12% of TIP

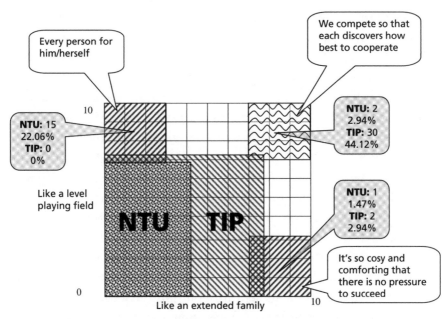

Figure 7.4 Dilemma Grid 3: Level playing field v Extended family

report 'co-opetition', with competition and cooperation in a family-style culture reconciled at top-right. Once again we probed for dysfunctional extremes of too much familial atmosphere and too much 'cut-throat' competition (see squares at top-left and bottom-right). We tempted respondents to admit that the family atmosphere at TIP was 'cosy, comforting and free of pressure' but only 2.94% agreed. We tempted respondents to say that NTU's competitiveness placed 'Every person for him/herself' and 22.06% agreed – a rather worrying proportion. NTU appears to have imported a large dollop of Western-style alienation into its pedagogy. Undergraduates feel apart, absorbing information with their emotions not engaged.

Dilemma 4: Serious hard work v Playful enjoyment
Those who want to succeed in the world of free enterprise and opportunities-for-all had best take such challenges seriously. Few will make it without determination and perseverance. Hard work is the inescapable recipe. Yet countless studies of innovative persons note their playfulness. They have created something that gives them untold pleasure and they

want to share it. They find joy in their work and are guided by secret delights. Moreover, much use is made of simulations, skits, role-plays, prototypes and models, because these can fail inexpensively. Innovators practice with 'toys' as the actual product takes shape.

Michael Shrage has suggested that innovation consists of serious play, i.e. a playful process leading to a serious outcome, light-hearted experimentation in search of a crucial solution. We hypothesised that the university would tend towards seriousness, even to the point of strenuousness. We knew TIP was much more playful but were its participants aware of the serious purpose? The course has a business simulation running its full length. It has practice presentations to venture capitalists and many skits and plays, but were these games more than fun? Could seriousness and playfulness combine in a joyful rendezvous with reality? Could playful prototypes culminate in serious products and services? Could we take the problems seriously but not ourselves? Play inevitably involves error, but because models, simulations and prototypes are cheap, such errors are not 'serious' as much as instructive. Piet Hein calls it 'The Road to Wisdom'.

> The road to wisdom – well it's plain
> And simple to express
> Err and err and err again
> But less and less and less ...

What we are talking about is the 'error-correcting system'.

The university scored 7.54 on seriousness, but interestingly TIP is extremely close behind with 7.50, a non-significant margin. TIP is quite as serious as NTU. But when it comes to playfulness the difference is dramatic. The university scored 4.24 on playfulness and TIP scored 7.97, over three squares above. NTU covered 31.54 squares and TIP 59.78, or 91% higher ($R2 = 34.53\%$, $P<0.01$).

We tested to see whether TIP's playfulness was 'like a non-stop party', a trap it is easy to fall into, but only 4.41% agreed. We asked if the experience of university courses was not 'a bit grim and strenuous' and 22.06% agreed. Once again TIP has demonstrated that playful processes can prepare for serious purposes as the hours slip by because you are

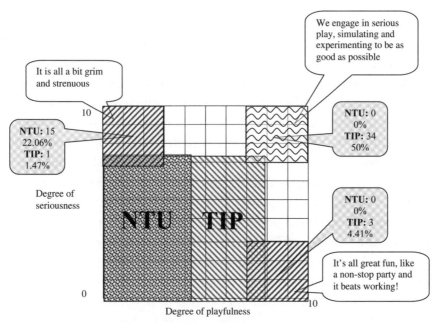

Figure 7.5 Dilemma Grid 4: Seriousness v Playfulness

enjoying yourself: 50.00% of respondents said that TIP reconciled work and play, but none (0%) claimed that the university managed this.

But note that once again the university succeeds on its own terms: 52.94% of its students score the teaching environment 8, 9, or 10 in seriousness, even if fun is scarce. However, this is lower than TIP's score on playfulness.

*Dilemma 5: Career continuity and mastering chosen paths v
Transformation of yourself and reinvention*
Universities still prepare people for careers, although how long certain careers can now last grows ever more problematical. Whole technologies may come to the end of their useful lives. Nevertheless, continuity remains crucial, as does choosing your career path. Even innovations tend to advance certain disciplines and callings, with one innovation forming 'the platform' on which the next is based and so on. The core competence of a company makes no sense without thematic continuities. The greater the whirlwind, the more you must rely on sense of direction so as to ride upon it.

Increasingly those who learn will ride a new technology for perhaps five to ten years and then transform and reinvent themselves jumping from one form of competence to a contiguous one in variations on underlying themes. The TIP course was designed to help students transform themselves, hopefully without losing an underlying sense of continuity. Is it possible to combine the two, changing radically while still retaining a stable identity? We believe it is. Transformation that sacrifices continuity takes you back to square one. In any true development there must be a path, however winding, that brings you to your destination.

We set out to discover how NTU and TIP balanced career continuity with self- transformation of the kind that outstanding entrepreneurs and innovators achieve. We expected NTU to stress continuity and TIP to stress transformation, but we hoped to discover whether TIP retained at least some sense of continuity, without which a sense of growth and the development of core capabilities over time may be lost. Knowledge is to an important extent cumulative. One verified proposition links to another. We generalise as far as we can and then examine the exceptions. Disrupt continuity and you break up knowledge into incoherent fragments. TIP must serve continuity *and* transformation.

What 'technopreneurship' means is that you simultaneously follow relevant technologies in their most advanced states, yet take a stand between these: entre-preneur, 'to stand between'. As we shall see, TIP succeeded in this. You take the most advanced work from at least two disciplines and create a novel synthesis between these. Their scores are shown in Figure 7.6.

NTU covered 34.80 squares; TIP covered 49.45 or 67% higher (R^2 = 24.77%, P<0.01). NTU outscores TIP on career continuity by 7.76 to 6.81 or 0.95. Note how small this difference is and how emphatic is the TIP course on maintaining a sense of continuity. Since innovations often combine two disciplines, the entrepreneur needs to be aware of career trajectories that are converging or running parallel in a way that makes connections possible. The combination of two lines is often transformative, while still retaining the initial continuities.

When we asked how transformative NTU's courses were, the university scored 4.69 but TIP scores 8.35, nearly four squares better. 47.06% of respondents reported that TIP combined continuity with transformation

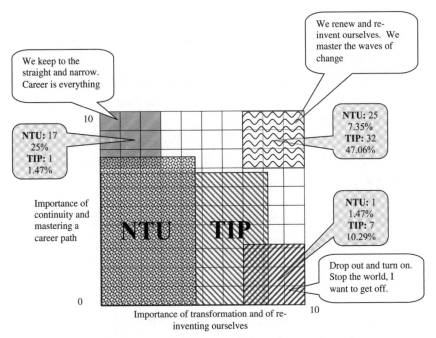

Figure 7.6 Dilemma Grid 5: Career continuity v Periodic transformation

(the reconciliation zone) but only 7.35% made that claim for NTU. We checked that TIP was not cheating in selling transformation as 'dropping out and turning on, hippie fashion' yet 10.29% agreed and there may be a little danger here. We asked whether students 'kept to the straight and narrow' at NTU and 25% agreed. Yet this 'straightness' meant that 63.24% of our respondents rated the university at 8, 9 and 10.

Final proof of success

We have looked at the scores for the five questions and found that TIP scores considerably better on all lateral dimensions, while not being below NTU on the traditional, vertical dimensions by any significant margin, so that TIP may be said to uphold the university standards. However, the most remarkable finding is that nearly 42% of all TIP students scored in the reconciliation zone, eight times more than achieved in undergraduate classes at NTU. This unique capacity to integrate contrasting educational processes would seem to be its greatest virtue. Yet there remains one nagging question. The purpose of this programme was *not* primarily to be well assessed by those who participated in it, encouraging though this is. The programme is not an end in itself but a means to making its members more innovative and entrepreneurial. Is there any evidence that they became so? There is.

By January 2008, out of 154 students 46 had started business ventures, employing about 75 of their number. This had happened despite the fact that ...

(a) Many had not joined the programme to become entrepreneurs.
(b) Twenty or more had gone on to get their MSc degree of which this programme was a module.
(c) Most are in debt when they graduate.
(d) The course advises them to get experience in their selected area of innovation before launching their own ventures.
(e) They have an average of only 2–3 years to launch such a venture.

We contend that 46 surviving start-ups is a very remarkable result. If only 10% of these eventually prosper they will have repaid the cost of the course several times over.

Can we model the innovative process?

By what process do TIP students and innovators in general reach the reconciliation zone at top-right of our grids? In order to understand this we need a three-dimensional model, with the third dimension representing time. One way dilemmas are resolved is by emphasising first one dimension then another in sequence, and by achieving the second dimension *through* the first.

For example, when innovating we first feel excited, doubtful and emotional until such a time that we can intellectually order these fresh insights (see Figure 7.7a). This results in an anticlockwise helix. On the other hand, most students must first absorb top-down information, and only when they have enough of these resources can they think and act for themselves (see Figure 7.7b). This results in a clockwise helix.

It is at least probable that students feel initially that they are competing with all other members, but as the extended family develops around them and team skills develop they start cooperating (see Figure 7.7c). This results in a clockwise helix. There is little doubt, however, that playfulness, experimentation and simulation precede the serious business of creating finished quality and risking everything in the market (see Figure 7.7d). In this event, the helix is anticlockwise once more. Finally, the mastery of your chosen discipline and career path precedes the intersecting and cross-cutting with other disciplines to make new connections (see Figure 7.7e). In this event the helix is clockwise. Note that we have retained our grid pattern on the face of each cube and that helices flirt with pathology by skirting these zones. There is no innovation without danger. It is easy to go too far in either direction, as our results show.

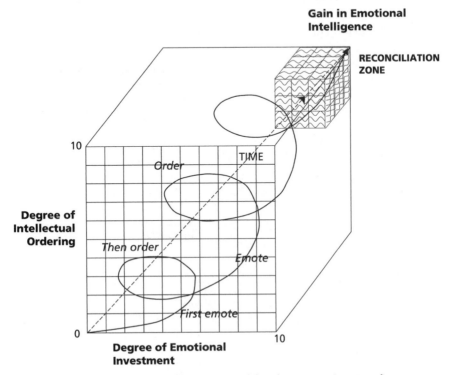

Figure 7.7 (a) Three-dimensional dilemma model: Dilemma 1. (*Continued*)

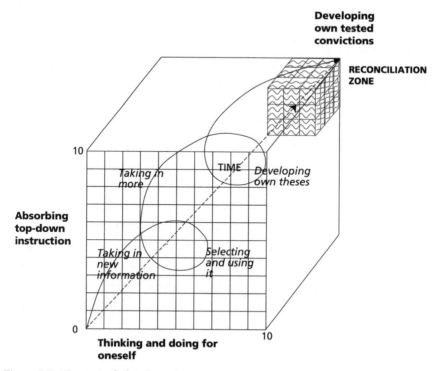

Figure 7.7 (*Continued*) (b) Three-dimensional dilemma model: Dilemma 2

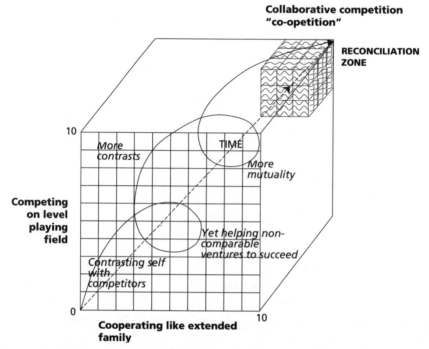

Figure 7.7 (*Continued*) (c) Three-dimensional dilemma model: Dilemma 3

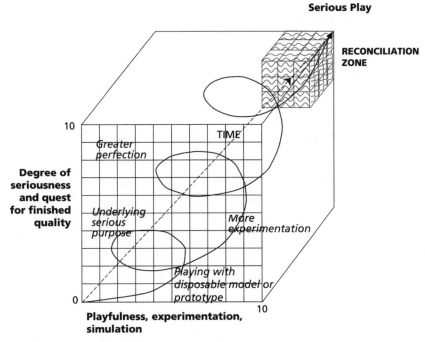

Figure 7.7 (*Continued*) (d) Three-dimensional dilemma model: Dilemma 4

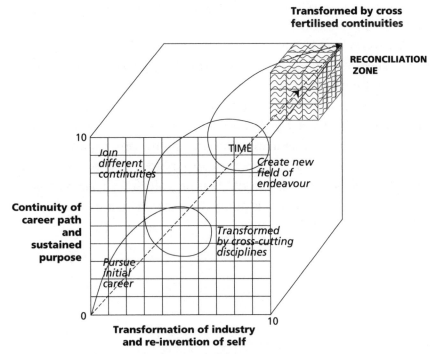

Figure 7.7 (*Continued*) (e) Three-dimensional dilemma model: Dilemma 5

Is this nothing but the 'Hawthorne Effect'?

Before concluding, let us address a likely critique of this chapter. 'Here we have,' critics will say, 'nothing more than the Hawthorne Effect.' This occurs when respondents grow to like their teacher and 'give him what he wants', perhaps because his own enthusiasm is infectious or because they feel they owe him in return for a fun time, or both. What these critics fail to realise is the 'Hawthorne Effect' is a *vital part of life itself*. We create nothing without hope and yearning, nothing without passion and optimism. So *what* if the prophecy is self-fulfilling? You believe in yourself, in part because your teacher does and that belief is vindicated. That is what being innovative is all about and if it breaks taboos on clinical detachment then the fault is with those taboos.

But in any event this was not research that measured a heady optimism at the end of the programme. Students had, on average, been out in the cold, hard world of business reality for two and a half years when this research was conducted. It is more than likely that they had tried and failed at least once since graduating. What is more likely than they would blame this programme for any disappointment? That they do not seem to have done so in any numbers testifies to the lasting legacy of this educational experience.

Are we to have a science of only dead things that cannot respond to the investigator? *You discover innovation by engendering it.* There is no other way. Remain cold and unmoved and the world around you mimics your own demeanour. We hope to have demonstrated that innovation can be elicited, that it builds on what the university already teaches, while qualifying and augmenting this, that innovation requires dilemma-resolving, lateral-type thinking. The capacity to create wealth resembles the ancient alchemists' dream of creating gold from base metals. The world's current predicament is pretty 'base' as we fight the credit crunch and a possible Great Depression.

Conclusion: an answer to world crises?

It is clear that innovation *can* be taught, that this builds upon the university's traditional mission to society by placing this in an innovative context. This is very exciting for students, transformative in its impact upon them, as witnessed by many moving accounts. It is hard to think of a more vital topic in world affairs than generating a capability to innovate spontaneously. This capacity can reconcile and generate abundance out of scarce resources, create satisfactions out of wants, agreements out of discord and realities out of ideals and imaginings.

The very process is joyful and playful, while the consequences are valuable and serious. It is hard to see how societies dedicated to innovation would have the time or the inclination to kill, how a mind that could be generative and thus get its 'highs' could ever want to be befuddled with abusive substances. Teach our children and young people to be innovative and scarcities are transcended, ideas are joined and so are the people who believe in these. Innovation needs not just diversities of ideas but also diversities of people supplying those ideas. From their inclusion comes not only wealth but also our best hope of tolerance and global dialogue. A world where imagination fathers new forms can solve its own problems.

Those who 'give' each other knowledge still retain it within themselves. Romeo's words to Juliet become more nearly true: 'The more I give you, the more I have.' There is a secret world of abundance within us that is widely shareable by those willing to gain-share and fate-share. To create makes of our lives a lasting legacy. The obscenely large salaries of bankers who proved to be incompetent can become things of the past. People who innovate do not need to be bribed to do so by extrinsic rewards. It is simply a better way to live. To have shareholders' money to play with is a privilege.

INNOVATION, LEARNING AND ORGANISATIONAL STRUCTURE

Creative people and teams are necessary but not sufficient

Your staff may follow the advice on becoming creative individuals in Chapter 2. They may self-organise into effective teams, as in Chapter 5. All this is necessary but it is not sufficient. The structure of the entire organisation must be such that individuals and teams are mobilised and the information arising from them is organised into comprehensive knowledge and into strategies about how better to engage the environment. Without this the talents of persons and teams cannot be brought to bear and may trickle into the ground.

All organisations are structured and shaped by the work they have to do. The question becomes what *kind* of structure is required to give innovation its fullest and most effective expression? What does the corporation need to encourage, facilitate, promote and reward in order to remain innovative and bring a string of new products, initiatives and ventures to its customers?

We will look at how organisations need to configure themselves to ensure better innovation. This will take the form of twelve dilemmas that have to be reconciled so that the organisation learns. Indeed, learning has to be the prime purpose of the organisation. That it is profitable, that it is growing, is less vital than *why* this is happening so it can be continued. Among innovative initiatives is the business model used by the organisation. The dilemmas needing to be solved are listed below. The values on the left are the traditional ones. The values on the right need to become part of the equation if innovation is to be achieved. They read as follows:

1	Centralising knowledge	_____	Decentralising activity
2	Functional and technical departments	_____	Project teams with human processes
3	Top-down instruction	_____	Bottom-up participation
4	Answers provided	_____	Questions posed
5	Right-first-time	_____	Error and correction
6	Explicit knowledge	_____	Tacit knowledge
7	Authority of leaders	_____	Delegation to creators and teams
8	Design strategy and business model	_____	Emergent strategy and business model
9	Standards/benchmarks of internal order	_____	Chaos of unpredictable external customer needs
10	Past financial performance	_____	Future learning goals
11	Innovation internal to the company	_____	Innovation external to the company
12	Building a profitable company	_____	Building an innovative network

1 Centralising knowledge _____ Decentralising activity

A company has very little chance of being innovative if it retains a quasi-imperial and colonial structure, with power and prestige at the centre and tributary status in its far-flung regions. This prevents outlying discoveries or information from being taken seriously by the HQ, with the inevitability of imperial decline. Let us recall that innovation consists of new, valuable combinations. If anything 'out there' in the hinterland is deemed inferior, such combinations are much less likely to occur.

A consistently vexed issue is where information originates and where and how it should be captured for greatest effectiveness. If a corporation is to communicate its knowledge, from where and to where should it travel? Should it move bottom-up, top-down, outside-in or from the inside to the outside? Arguments about centralising versus decentralising never seem to end and are rarely settled. For several years the watchword has been 'decentralise!' But those with memories can recall that 'centralise!' was once the cry. Will we ever make up our minds, or is the concertina with us for good? We must conclude that, at their extremes, both centralisation and decentralisation jeopardise the innovation process. Extreme decentralisation leads to unknowable activities in God-forsaken outposts. Extreme centralisation leads to needless rigidity and the imposition of outdated rules. A clue is given to us by the slogan 'Think Global – Act Local', because it suggests that while activities are decentralised, knowledge about these enables us to think about such activities at the centre of the company. Innovative companies need a central nervous system, where information is absorbed.

Figure 8.1 below explains this process. We begin with Centralisation–Decentralisation as a polarity and vexed alternatives. We move from here to creating a dual axis and a culture space, and we finally move to a helix, spiralling to the top-right corner in which we achieve 'Better centralised knowledge of ever more decentralised activities'. It is amidst the flood of information reaching the centre from across the globe that new and exciting combinations can be created.

There is a final, even more mature phase in which Centres of Excellence are themselves decentralised. Ideally, countries of the world should be allowed to specialise in what they do best. Hence Apple Computer's Centre of Excellence for skilled assembly and manufacturing is in Singapore, because this location is best for this function. Motorola's Centre of Excellence for software is in Bangalore. Sony chose to place its software centre in California; AMD's star Fab is in Dresden, East Germany. These 'centres' do not have to be in one place in a system. Different functions may take their own Centre of Excellence to those countries in which such excellence is most admired.

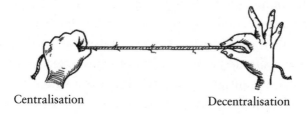

Centralisation   Decentralisation

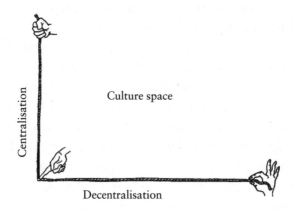

Culture space

Centralisation

Decentralisation

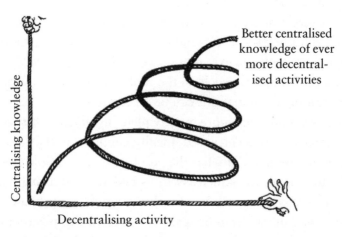

Better centralised
knowledge of ever
more decentral-
ised activities

Centralising knowledge

Decentralising activity

Figure 8.1 De/centralisation

2 Functional and technical departments _____ *Project teams with human processes*

Corporations have a traditional division of labour among their functions, such as R&D, manufacturing, sales, marketing, planning and human resources. This was never intended to reduce innovation but, like all hard and fast classifications, it does so. Anything new will require R&D to create not just a new product but easier manufacturability and distribution, its ready recognition by markets, new sales outlets etc. Functions need to work together but they rarely do so effectively. This is why they are often called 'silos', after grain-silos or pillars. There is a division of labour, but the integration of labour is too often absent.

Even human resources is given a name suggesting that humanity can be stored in the manner of physical resources, but the truth is that human relationships pervade *everything a corporation does*. To turn this into a specialist activity is to place what supposedly binds us all into a discrete compartment. One of the chief casualties of functional specialisation is deterring new combinations of information that departments have divided. What cuts across functions are *the processes within project teams*, so that, say, a new advertising campaign has input from copywriters, visualisers, the customer rep. or account executive, the media-buyer, the commercial production department etc. Each function is represented by a team member and its purpose is to run an effective, seamless advertising launch for the new product.

Innovation within teams cannot occur unless the corporation is at least in part a *project group organisation*, with teams cutting across various functions and combining their expertise to achieve a goal, mission or target. A company with both functions and project teams is sometimes described as a matrix organisation, with twin reporting lines to one's function and to the project being ventured.

To be innovative these teams must be part of the design of the organisation and bringing projects to fulfilment must be a continuous process. Teams are *not* permanent, as we saw in Chapter 5, lasting only as long as their projects take to complete, at which point they break up and reform. A member of the marketing function may have membership in two to three ongoing teams and when one of these breaks up on completion, s/he will join another.

With the exception of HR most functions are *technical*, especially R&D, manufacturing, planning and so on, while team processes are typically *social* and favour those who are more verbally skilled and persuasive. The innovative corporation is a socio-technical system, with the techniques of functions joined together in new ways by those high in social skills. What is required is concern with tasks and concern with people. Where social processes are weak and concern with people is low, you get a sweatshop atmosphere (see Figure 8.2). Where concern with people is high but concern with task is low, you get a country club atmosphere. Where both concerns are high you get concern with productive people; all the technical skills are mobilised by teams working effectively to fulfil their missions.

Figure 8.2 The Guided Missile vs the Family – Concern with tasks versus Concern with people

3 Top-down instruction _____ Bottom-up participation

A company that is run by instruction from its leaders, top-down, is very unlikely to be innovative. It may be successful where the leaders are highly competent, but for a company to be innovative, different points of view must clash and later forge a permanent connection. For this two-way communication, bottom-up and top-down are essential.

Most information enters an organisation at least halfway down the hierarchy. Those with day-to-day contact with customers are rarely very senior. Unless these sales staff and middle managers are enabled to inform top management, requisite information is unlikely to reach the top. In this case the decisions coming top-down are likely to be ill-informed. Bottom-up, top-down is a learning loop and knowledge at the top of the organisation needs to be supplied by information from below.

This becomes even more vital if the leader seeks to make the organisation innovative. Anyone, however junior, may have a winning idea, just as anyone may have one element of a larger synthesis needing to be joined with what leaders already know. Innovation happens at the margins of any system, where it interacts with other systems and, if leaders are not participative, there is no reason to suppose that they will hear of these developments or seize the opportunities provided.

For this reason leaders need to listen long and hard and they need scheduled occasions in which they are briefed and during which information bubbles up from below. There should be both face-to-face and electronic forms of communication with finely detailed information. The whole notion of decision-making is distorted by the origins of the word: _decido_ in Latin means 'I cut off' one alternative from another. The assumption is that the leader has the sword of Alexander the Great, which cuts through knots with a single blow, or is a hero at the crossroads, taking one path and foregoing the other.

This mythology overlooks the principle of innovative decision-making, which is _not_ either-or, but both-and, or through one value to another. The participative leader, having listened, is more confident in making a decision that joins viewpoints. Moreover, the followers who have informed the leader will see their own inputs reflected in that decision and will therefore carry it out with more enthusiasm. It is in part *their* decision. Figure 8.3 clearly shows how decisiveness and participation can combine and the result of doing this.

Figure 8.3 Top-down instruction vs Bottom-up participation

4 Answers provided _____ Questions posed

Answers are put before posed questions because in non-innovative organisations the leaders supposedly have the answers and need only instruct others. Leaders of innovative organisations know that they do not know until they ask. They cannot simply hold meetings or solicit emails in which hoped-for participation will occur. It may not do so, especially if employees are used to top-down communication. One way to assure bottom-up information is to ask questions and throw down challenges to which your employees must find answers and make responses.

There is some good sense to this. The idea that top-management already knows the answers is patently false. If you are innovating, you *cannot* know the answers because no one has done this before and the answer as to whether customers want this or not has never yet been posed. In such circumstances it is reasonable to infer that leaders know the questions and the challenges that the organisation faces but they do *not* know the answers as yet, although they aim to find out.

An innovative organisation is, above all else, an *inquiring system*. This means that top managers are leading an investigation, or are engaged in search behaviour and are *chief inquirers*. They may know what the answer must accomplish and they will recognise it when they see it. They may even have devised a metaphor or symbol that suggests the essence of any solutions, but they are framing questions rather than proclaiming answers. They need the help of all knowledgeable people in the organisation. Typically senior management will have some working hypotheses but these are only confirmed or disconfirmed when the people they question supply the data. The answers will be known first to the 'search teams' seeking a solution.

Some quite humdrum activities can be turned into questions to reveal new meaning. Suppose you must deliver many litres of heating oil to several contractors each day. This is pretty routine work, not enough to keep the mind alive. Yet you can turn this into a question. Which is the quickest delivery route? Which is the most economical? If I use my mobile phone to call ahead will they be ready for me and have the tank opened? The supply of every product is really a series of questions. Do you appreciate this? How much? At what price? What reservations do you have?

One way of using teams in an organisation is to set them the challenge of solving a problem. Is it possible to halve late deliveries? What are the costs and the gains? Can the success of a particular business unit be generalised to other units? Why have they not picked up the better practices of particular units? The dilemma of questions and answers is depicted in Figure 8.4.

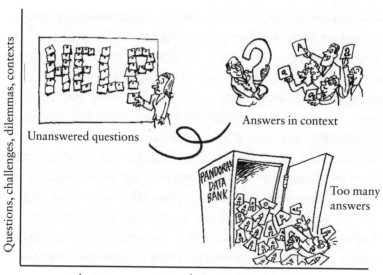

Figure 8.4 Questions versus Answers

At top-left we have employees (vainly) asking for help, with the requisite answers irretrievable from the mass of 'objective' information. Perhaps the answer is somewhere, but where exactly? And does it fulfil our purposes? At bottom-right, we have Pandora's Data Bank, a massive box of answers for which no one has a question and for which the original questions are lost.

Genuine knowledge is portrayed at top-right. It consists of strategic questions answered by employees and customers, or texts within contexts. The whole process of continuing inquiry unwinds in a helical pattern of ever more probing questions answered by the most up-to-date operations of the company, which culminates in vital knowledge about the corporation and its environment.

The process of posing questions and seeking answers is vital to any corporate sense of direction. The world is awash with information, thanks to the Internet, but you tame these floodwaters by having questions that qualify *some* of this information as relevant and the vast bulk of answers are irrelevant to your purposes. You know what you want to know, the fundamentals of your company's success and continued inquiry into this. With a series of clear questions the prospect of a *dialogue among equals* becomes ever more possible. This does not mean that questioners and answerers are of equal status, but rather that leader and subordinates share the truth between them; each is indispensable to a solution. The data must fit the theory; the confirmation or refutation must qualify the hypothesis. Each sees the other as essential to their inquiry.

5 Right-first-time _____ *Error and correction*

In many respects a corporation has a right to expect that things are done properly without errors. A computer that fails to compute is clearly unacceptable. With experience, rules and procedures are laid down and people are expected to follow these. In some cases errors can be life threatening. This habit of getting it right the first time and being ashamed of errors is widespread and understandable.

But corporations who try to innovate almost *never* get it right the first time. A succession of trials and errors is necessary. Famous inventions such as the white profiles on Wedgwood china, Edison's electric bulb and the Dyson vacuum cleaner went through more than a thousand iterations. A wise corporation will arrange for many trials to be simulated cheaply so that the process costs less, but errors there will be and these must be seized upon so that the product or service is quickly corrected over time.

This applies especially to inventive products. After all, these have never been manufactured before, sold before, used before or maintained before. At every stage there will be errors that need to be corrected. Modern manufacturing is such a complex business that improving it never ends. In a process with over three hundred manufacturing steps there is always something that can be done better or several steps that can be eliminated, or worked on in parallel to save time. Some companies, such as HP, aim to be '70% or 80% correct' when they offer a customer a product that has been specified in advance. The reason for this is that making the product 100% right requires input from the customer, who will use it, not just from the supplier. The initial specifications may not have been adequate for complete satisfaction.

The learning system of erring and correcting was originally created by W. Edwards Deming and was taught to Toyota and other Japanese auto companies that are now the most successful in the world. His advice was rejected by Ford, Chrysler and General Motors, with the consequences we now know. Modern factories use the process of continuous improvement widely. It is useful to contrast product innovation with *process* innovation. The latter refers to making near identical products to those already on the market but using less expensive processes and materials in manufacturing to do this. Japan's rise from 1950 to 1992 was largely on the back of process innovation, using new materials and continuously refining these. On a visit to Motorola in Penang, Malaysia, we witnessed pieces of paper entitled 'I Recommend' plastered on all four walls and clear across the ceiling. There were over two thousand recommendations for improvement arising from the workers themselves, not simply the bottom-up participation we commended earlier, but critical insights into how operations might be improved. The papers bore the photograph of the participant.

A prototype is an example of an approximation to the finished product put out specifically to be criticised and improved. Increasingly these take the form of digital films so as to portray the inside and the outside of a product, how it can be used, maintained and repaired and how it might alter the habits of customers and consumers in the market. Customers can change this or that feature and the digital prototype can be used to mobilise enthusiasm among investors, partners, distributors etc. The DVD may cost only a fraction of the finished product, so the price of improvements is kept low.

Teaching by the case method, pioneered at Harvard, is a way of helping learners benefit by mistakes made by those who went before. If we can dramatise in written form, or more recently in filmed drama, some of the more common mistakes made by innovators, those coming after can avoid these. Drama or plays are great teachers. If we err in what we imagine or has been imagined for us, we may avoid making this mistake.

Figure 8.5 shows the dilemma of right-first-time v erring and correcting. The one-eyed giant at top-left symbolises the Dogma of Immaculate Perception, wherein leaders believe they have a perfect theory or strategy that needs only be implemented flawlessly. At bottom-right errors are being repeated and *not* learned from. We call this Muddling Through and it is clearly dysfunctional. The reconciliation essential to an innovative

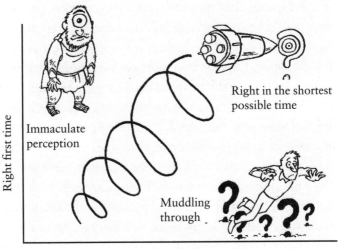

Figure 8.5 'Right the first time' versus 'Errors and corrections'

company is 'Right in the Shortest Possible Time', an aim that reminds us that improvements can be rapid.

In modern Fabs (fabricating plants for microchips) it is customary to measure yields-by-the-day. Yield equals the number of chips that are correctly manufactured. In a matter of weeks the yield rises from around 20% to 99% or higher as thousands of small corrections are made by workers and supervisors.

6 Explicit knowledge _____ Tacit knowledge

One habit of the mature corporation that inhibits innovation, without intending to do so, is identifying the knowledge it has with *explicit and codified* knowledge. Once knowledge is classified and quantified so that you have the totals within each classification, it begins to resist any new knowledge, because new knowledge disrupts existing classifications and codes in which the corporation is now heavily invested. Once you install software that displays the data you have collected it becomes expensive and even confusing to question existing definitions.

Hence hospitals that naturally seek to give new patients early appointments will schedule these in July and August so that the patient on vacation will postpone these 'voluntarily', excusing the hospital from blame for the delay. Explicit measures such as these resist modification, because the insight that the hospital is cheating is initially tacit. What is codified, explicit and measurable tends to dominate over what is tacit, insightful and yet-to-be-measured. Corporations cling to their KPIs (key performance indicators) because everyone's performance is being reported on these indicators and to change these is disruptive and 'unfair'.

Nearly all innovations start with tacit concepts within the mind or shared tacit understandings between persons and team members. Leaders who see only codified knowledge will fail to appreciate the value of ideas yet to be codified. They will say, typically, that the development of this idea is not in the budget and therefore cannot now go forward or is not measured and hence 'does not count'. Explicit knowledge is said to be 'objective', giving it higher status than tacit 'subjective' knowledge. Two Japanese researchers, Ikujiro Nonaka and Hirotaka Takeuchi, have made the distinction between explicit and tacit knowledge crucial to the process of innovation.

Tacit knowledge may be metaphorical, as in the case of an aluminium beer can which gave a team the idea of building a cheap, disposable drum for a home copying machine; or it may be a form of manual dexterity, as when the hands of master bakers twisting dough were filmed and then copied by engineers designing a dough-mixing machine for home baking. The tacit knowledge was in the bakers' hands, which the machine made explicit, just as the analogy was in the empty beer cans, which the disposable drum codified and objectified. This work is important because it reveals that the origins of new knowledge and creativity lie in cultural relationships between people (see Figure 8.6).

'Buried Treasure' lies in the shared meeting of minds at bottom-left. This is codified as the helix spirals to the left, to become 'Intellectual Property' at top-left. Only codes can be legally protected, which is another reason for valuing this more than tacit knowledge. Yet the helix culminates in 'Knowledge Leadership', the Red Sea parting and the 'Land of Milk and Honey' beyond. Leaders need to keep eliciting

Figure 8.6 Explicit knowledge versus tacit knowledge

what is tacit within the corporation, encouraging informal activities and spontaneous activities, but ensuring that these are codified. But they also need to *dissolve existing codes* and ask whether these can be improved upon, whether the letter of the law truly reflects the tacit spirit of the law, its noble intentions. Just because data has been collected does not mean that its classification is unalterable.

Indeed, knowledge often takes the form of stories, like that of Moses crossing the Red Sea. The power of stories is that they elicit many personal and tacit interpretations that inspire followers. You never quite know what the story 'means', because it is there to help you create new meanings. Knowledge leaders embark on journeys of endless discovery, sharing and codifying as they create knowledge. John Sculley of Apple wrote *Odyssey* about his time with the company. His slogan was: 'The journey is the reward'. As with Homer's *Odyssey*, he depicted a wandering adventure without end. Computers were 'the wings of the mind', navigating through turbulent seas of knowledge. You never finally arrive, but you keep inquiring. He called himself the Chief Listener.

7 Authority of leaders _____ *Delegation to creators and teams*

In a very real sense the right to innovate needs to be delegated downwards by leaders and to creative persons and to teams. This is because to innovate *is* to lead. You suggest a new direction and hope the corporation will follow, but this is the responsibility of leaders and attempts to innovate may appear to leaders as attempts to usurp their leadership roles. Every corporation has a responsibility hierarchy. Those at the very top are directly responsible to shareholders and will be removed should they fail. They cannot abdicate this responsibility by saying that employee X had such a wonderful idea that they decided to let him/her lead the organisation instead. A leader may yield to the judgement of an inventive employee only if he or she *delegates* authority to that person. In this case the formal leader is responsible for this delegation and its results, while the inventive employee is responsible to the leader for how that delegation was used.

We begin to see what very real problems are involved in leading an innovative organisation. The creator has the fun, but the formal leader has the responsibility and carries the can if the innovation proves an expensive failure. It is not difficult to understand why a leader might be lukewarm towards innovation. Comprehending and assessing a novel idea is hard work and involves deferring to the creator, a posture the leader may feel weakens his/her authority. Authority is easily lost. It is a necessary quality of successful leadership and in a very real way the leader must be the *servant* of innovative persons in the corporation. Some leaders may feel such humility unbecoming.

The leader of an innovative organisation must be careful not to monopolise innovation. This is what Edwin Land did in the Polaroid Corporation, which promptly collapsed within three years of his retirement. For decades he had been the Sage on the Stage, the one genuinely inventive person in the corporation with everyone else dancing attendance. In Figure 8.7 he wears a magician's hat (see top-left). Magicians, unlike scientists, do not share their secrets with others but flaunt them to impress. At the opposite extreme there is an egalitarian ethos that states that the mentor/leader is a resource person (bottom-right), to be ignored if that is what people want, but that is to trivialise leadership to some kind of hat stand and assumes that employees will never become discordant. The mentor/leader of the innovative learning corporation is the *conductor of talents* (top-right), the person responsible for the symphonic and harmonious function of professional contributors. An orchestra can function briefly without a conductor because the symphony has been internalised, yet the conductor is there to reconcile all instruments on their way to delight the audience and to remind players of the beat and tempo.

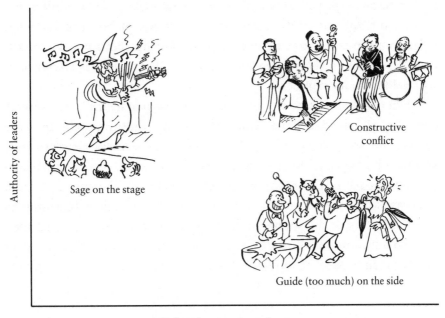

Figure 8.7 Authority of leaders vs Delegation to teams and creators

However, the leader does not deal with creative individuals alone. It will be recalled from Chapter 3 that teams are involved and these constitute a formidable challenge. A team is usually needed to turn an idea into a prototype and then a product and turn it from a mental construct into a fully-fledged innovative venture. Hence the first necessity is for project groups to be *sponsored* by those in authority and given the authority, delegated by the leadership, to give life and shape to an idea. It is necessary that a team includes members with the requisite skills and experience. Some of these members will volunteer but others may need to be appointed. In either event the leader is responsible not simply for authorising the team to go ahead and employ his/her delegated authority, but seeing that the team is properly constituted to undertake the challenge.

It is also the job of the leader to give the team its remit, to describe the challenge, pose the question and to describe what a solution has to accomplish in order to be viable. This is no easy task because the leader does not know what the solution is. The issue is so broad it needs multiple inputs, some of which are beyond the leader's knowledge. One of the characteristics of teams consisting of experts from different functions is that these are expensive. Hence leaders are taking a costly gamble that a particular team will see its venture through to completion and that what it finally proposes is practicable. A team that has been poorly briefed may come up with ventures that will not work for reasons that have been withheld from its members.

Figure 8.8 shows how easily the sponsorship of teams can misfire. A common error is to seed the team with persons whose compliance to the sponsor's wishes can be assured. Such 'yes-persons' are rarely innovative and may be expected to spy on the rest of the team, reporting back to the sponsor secretly. If the sponsor believes s/he has the answer, a team is a waste of time and money, especially one that simply rubber-stamps existing beliefs. If the sponsor admits to not knowing the answer, then only an autonomous team can discover a solution. Either way, keeping the team 'on a leash' at top-left is bound to fail.

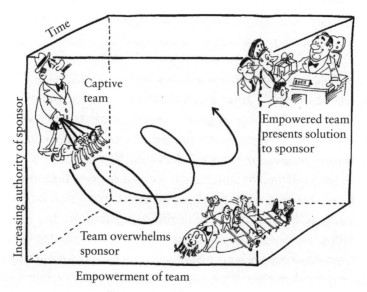

Figure 8.8 Authority of Sponsor versus Empowered Teams

But at bottom-right is what the sponsor dreads, that the team will coerce him/her and s/he will be tied down to a non-viable proposal that brings disgrace to everyone involved. Twelve people committed to a venture are an influential lobby and the sponsor will be roundly condemned if the innovative project the team has worked so hard upon is not appreciated and implemented. In short the 'Team Overwhelms its Sponsor' is a dreaded outcome. The sponsor is unpopular whether the project fails or whether it is abandoned.

The reconciliation is at top-right where an empowered team presents the solution to its sponsor whose authority is enhanced, thereby making both the sponsor and the team feel triumphant. Notice that the helix gets wider as it spirals up and to the right. Teams often check back with their sponsors to make sure they are on the right track, but this must be voluntary and not coerced. Assured that what they are developing is viable, they check back at longer intervals, until the innovation is ready to present.

Perhaps the most famous team sponsor was Jack Welch of General Electric. At the height of team processes at GE, Welch was debriefing four to five teams a week and taking their conclusions on board. He would implement up to 80% of their conclusions unchanged. Sponsorship is no easy task. The sponsor knows the question, the issue or the dilemma but not the answer, and must be prepared to let the team be a source of enlightenment. In such circumstances teams act in the manner of consultants but, unlike consultants, they do not arouse the corporation's 'immune system'. Coming as they do from the corporation itself, the tissue they supply is not rejected by the body of the corporation.

8 Designed strategy and business model _____ Emergent strategy and business model

What helps to mobilise a corporation at the level of people, teams and departments is strategy. The organisation as a whole has a plan that enables it to win, or at least that is its aspiration. But the question then arises as to where the strategy originates. Generally speaking it is thought to originate from the top echelon of the corporation and to cascade top-down upon lower ranks of managers and employees.

When this happens the discouragement of innovation becomes quite severe, unless of course there is a really creative business model in the boardroom, in which case only the ideas of top people get a chance to be implemented. But there are several objections to designing strategy on high, like Alexander the Great, and then issuing the orders of battle. Top management is furthest from the front line and often slow to discover changed circumstances. The time taken to develop strategy and then have the second echelon brief the third and so on down may be as much as six to nine months in which case conditions may have altered radically. Then there is the problem of the corporation's culture, which may enable it to deliver parts of the strategy, but not other parts because its learning is insufficient or its mood is hostile to certain tactics. A corporation needs to respect its limits. But by far the biggest objection is that people throughout the organisation have ideas and initiatives of their own and reducing them to the role of delivery mechanisms for plots hatched on high is to suppress these talents.

On the other hand, those at the apex of the corporation are there for a good reason. They are likely to have excelled in the past and been promoted. Not to let them play an active part in innovative strategising would be perverse. So how should the innovative organisation deploy its strategy in a way that involves all assorted talents, top and bottom, centralised and decentralised? This issue has been powerfully addressed by Henry Mintzberg. He observed that many organisations change almost completely in quite a short time with no orders from the top at all. The Canadian Film Board switched from making films for movie houses to supplying these to TV without any designed strategy. Independent producers noticed where the market was moving and switched over spontaneously.

Honda Motorcycles had intended to launch their heavy machines in the USA but when these leaked oil and needed repair they switched their entire campaign to distributing motor scooters on which they happened to be riding to attend meetings. The switch was initiated by the small US sales team, which, after their meeting was over, found a small crowd of Los Angeles citizens had gathered around their parked scooters.

Mintzberg describes such events as *emergent* strategy. The independent producers and the Honda sales teams took local initiatives that were successful and were then imitated by other business units in their corporations. The advantage of emergent strategy is that it is exceedingly close to the customer and in touch with changing events. It may even consist of co-creation with customers. Moreover, the culture of the corporation has already shown that it can accomplish such feats successfully. You do not have to 'sell' your strategy to lower levels of the company; it is already theirs and you celebrate the spontaneous innovation of your business units to the utmost. Strategy bubbles bottom-up and from the margins to the centre.

But what, then, is the role of top management? It has at least three roles: to search among the most innovative businesses for those setting the best examples; to publicly extol these emerging strategies and ensure that they receive a lot more resources with which to be successful; finally, to take two or three of these emerging strategies and *craft a composite*, which has the advantages of all three but the drawbacks of none. In this way senior managers get to design strategies after all, but out of the clay of the successful industrial experience and out of the corporate strengths already exhibited. Mintzberg calls this *crafted strategy*, using the 'clay' arising from the metaphorical potter's wheel. This makes the most of innovation, wherever it can be found.

In Figure 8.9 we see this dilemma presented, taken to two extremes and reconciled at top-right.

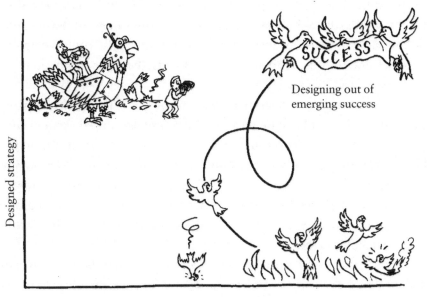

Figure 8.9

At top-left designed strategy is somewhat akin to winding up me-chanical birds. It is curiously artificial and clumsy. At bottom-right we see that not everything that emerges is viable. Several 'birds' have singed tail feathers and rather than rising phoenix-like out of the ashes several are consumed. But some do make it to success and these become exemplars for the kind of strategies that work and the combinations of these can reasonably be thought to work even better. Above all, top managers are scholars of effective innovation and are inspired by palpable successes.

9 Standards/benchmarks of internal order _____ *Chaos of unpredictable customer needs*

Many organisations work hard to maintain a rational internal order. This consists of standards and benchmarks, allegedly common to the industry, which are supposed to tell you what that industry's challenges and best practices are. As can be imagined, such elaborate measures and structures impede innovation, which is of necessity a departure from conventional wisdom. Such benchmarks face backwards. They tell what has been accomplished up to now, against standards established some years earlier. They may or they may not be as relevant as they once were. Ideally standards enable one to exceed what others have established only on the same dimension. Instead of racing with rivals, you race against the clock and the quicker production proceeds, the more competitive you supposedly are.

At least in theory customers want what the benchmarks measure, e.g. high quality and fast delivery, but if no one has asked them in some period of time then the standards the company strives to attain may be but a shrinking part of what customers want. Kaplan and Norton have made internal benchmarks v external customer needs into contrasting ends of their balanced scorecard. They insist that a company gain on both rather than just one and that what customers need should inform what benchmarks measure.

This makes good sense but we reject the idea that these values must 'balance' in the manner of scales or a seesaw. There is no inherent reason why customers should not get more and more of what they need, while internal benchmarks represent this more and more accurately. The two values are synergistic and contribute to each other's development. The problem for the would-be innovative organisation is that while benchmarks and standards are orderly, customers' needs and wants are chaotic, random and 'crazy' in the sense that they follow a logic alien to the supplier who cannot predict what they might want next.

A corporation cannot be innovative *unless it allows this chaos to wash over it*. It needs to let go of its own concepts of internal order in order to engage the unpredictable turbulence of customers' demands. Once you let these engulf you, the chances of finding a new method in this seeming madness are good. We know that 'chaos theory' is not without its own logic, albeit of a very dynamic and cyclical kind.

A company, which supplied earth-moving equipment to those constructing golf courses and other landscapes, asked their customers what their chief pain-points were. They discovered the *real* problem lay in scheduling contractors to arrive and complete on time so the next contractor could begin. Delays were incredibly costly and disruptive, with endless rescheduling. This company still supplies earth-moving equipment, but it also now handles the business of managing subcontractors and has valuable data on the relative reliability of some six hundred contractors across America, together with power to award these contracts or withhold these depending on records of reliability and quality. The margins in this business are five times that of earth-moving equipment. Chaos, pain and frustration among customers can be very profitable for those able to assuage it.

The kind of leader willing to plunge headlong into the turbulence that is nearly drowning the customer is the servant-leader, who thinks first and foremost how s/he can help, rather than what has been traditionally supplied by his company. Figure 8.10 depicts the standardised and benchmarked organisation on the vertical axis and the chaotic, unpredictability of customer needs on the horizontal axis. All the orderly benchmarks in the world are not going to save you if margins are being squeezed and your very traditional enterprise is sinking. Rearranging the deckchairs on the *Titanic* will not save its occupants.

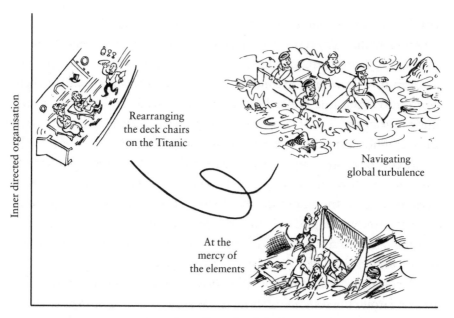

Figure 8.10 Inner directed organisation vs Outer directed organisation

On the other hand, throwing yourself on the mercy of the elements (bottom-right) will not save you either. If your customers cannot solve their own pains, can you? But you will only know this if you share that pain and come to see it from the inside and discover the hidden order within the chaos, a possible clue to innovation itself. We have depicted this at top-right as 'Navigating Global Turbulence'. The senior managers in several Japanese companies call themselves 'white-watermen'. They see themselves as racing the rapids of a wild river, paddling like mad to steer between the rocks. It tells you much about the genuinely innovative corporation.

10 Past financial performance _____ *Future learning goals*

We must not overlook the most common way in which corporations assess how well they are doing. They are legally obliged to produce audited accounts of their financial performance. It is this that gets pored over by financial analysts, who in turn inform shareholders, so that share prices register what a company is supposedly worth.

Financial performance figures are the most detailed and definitive statements of their affairs which companies provide. Many experts think that the bottom line and its effect on share price is the best possible guide to the purpose of business enterprise, which is to enrich its owners. Audited accounts have clarity, specificity, exactitude and meaningful contrast. What else is needed?

Unfortunately financial performance has at least one major drawback. It faces backwards towards a company's past. It is an accumulation of what has happened over the last 25 years. In the case of energy companies and some pharmaceutical companies, investments made more than a decade ago pay off in the current year. The present financial crisis should remind us that banks showing huge profits only a few months ago, figures on which they are now obligated to pay bonuses, can evaporate in a few days to become catastrophic losses. The world's financial industry has backed over a precipice while looking resolutely to the rear instead of forwards, mesmerised by its own historical rise to power.

Here is an industry that has sadly neglected its future learning goals. Indeed, so little has it learned that the larger financial system that has collapsed beneath it is understood by almost no one and those few claiming to understand it cannot agree amongst themselves. There could be no greater demonstration that the precision of financial performance figures come far, far too late to warn us of looming disaster. Credit vanishes long before banks can work out just how grievous are their financial losses. At this time of writing, six months into the crisis originating in September 2008, the full extent of losses has yet to be reported. We still do not know how bad things are. Financial performance is a lagging indicator if ever there was one.

It also has little or nothing to say about innovation or the prospects of new initiatives. Innovation only registers when the venture moves beyond break-even. Those studying performance figures will be the last to know. Only when ideas are turned into products, products into sales, sales into money, will financial experts recognise innovative efforts.

It is once again Kaplan and Norton who argue that unlike financial performance, which looks to the past, learning goals, which the corporation sets for itself, look to the future and the scorecard should balance. Learning has a crucial connection to innovation; because at the leading edge of knowledge many new connections become possible and only those with comprehensive knowledge of key disciplines can see those connections. A corporation that moves to the leading edge of a genuinely scientific discipline, and this may not include economics, is in a powerful position to keep innovating.

In Figure 8.11 we see that when an emphasis on financial performance is pushed too far to the top-left of the grid, the corporation does not only face backwards but suffers paralysis through analysis; the orientation to numbers has the effect of fragmenting the organisation into scores of little pieces. Like Humpty Dumpty, no one is able to reassemble the shattered parts. However, going to the opposite extreme is no help either. If a corporation thinks only of learning and not about the costs of obtaining that knowledge then it risks running subsidised seminars with

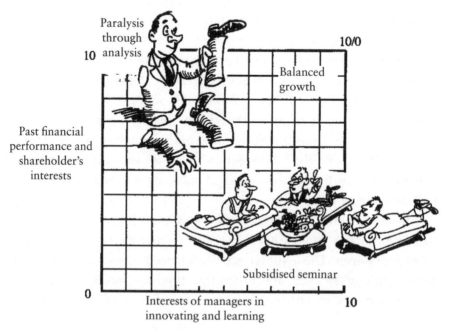

Figure 8.11

no impact on profitability (bottom-right). Learning cannot be an end in itself. What is needed, according to our reinterpretation, is less balanced: *integrated* growth in which better learning informs better earning and higher earnings feed around to stimulate learning in a virtuous cycle.

It is no exaggeration to say that innovative organisations are engaged in a learning race and that keeping up with how customers are changing and how disciplines are expanding is an increasingly strenuous process. The great advantage of innovation is that you do not have to keep up with the pace-setter; you *are* the pace-setter or the race itself.

11 Innovation internal to the corporation _____ *Innovation external to the corporation*

It may not be enough for individuals, teams and the whole organisation to be innovative, if by that is meant generating novelty only from within the company, typically the R&D department. Even while your corporation is innovating, so are scores, perhaps hundreds of others in your field. The notion that only what is invented internally has any merit is one of the great delusions to which corporations are prone.

In the last few years some major companies headed by Proctor & Gamble have appointed twin directors of innovation, a director of internal innovation, responsible for getting new ventures out of the R&D department, and the director of external innovation, responsible for scanning the wider environment and discovering usually small companies with highly valuable innovations. It is often forgotten that Microsoft did not generate Windows but acquired it. The innovative company may either acquire the new development or joint venture with that company. In both cases the innovation comes from the outside.

Of course, the derivation of a new development may be neither exclusively internal nor external but a combination of both. Perhaps the external company has a new material that hugely increases the competitive advantage of some device generated internally. The creative combination may come from the fusion of internal and external elements. External sources may include the network of which the corporation is a member but also stretches beyond the network to any innovation of relevance anywhere in the world. No wonder then that this process is called *open innovation.* Rather than novelty being developed in the sealed confines of the R&D department, which even employees of the rest of the corporation may not enter, the entire process of development from the idea stage onwards is opened up to consultation with the outside. There is a permeable membrane around R&D that admits qualified outsiders and seeks their input.

Figure 8.12 reveals both traps for the unwary and the possibility of reconciling internal with external innovation. At top-left we have the secretive R&D department, with its NIH slogan, 'not invented here', an attitude that rejects and trivialises developments outside 'the holy of holies' which is R&D. Often such departments claim a near exclusive right to innovate. Other members of the corporation are mere followers. Pundits in the early nineties forecast that Germany, France and Sweden would overtake the USA and the UK because of higher spending on R&D. It did not happen. The experts had reckoned without phenomena like Silicon Valley where hundreds of small companies fed into larger ones as innovations were combined.

But external innovation, which is just a shopping trip for the latest gadgets, is not going to work either (see bottom-right). There needs to be a seminal idea to which external developments can be attached. The notion of a portfolio of the kind that business conglomerates used to col-

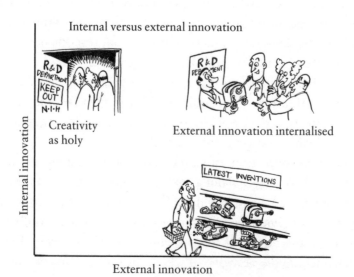

Figure 8.12 Modern corporations increasingly mixing internal with external innovations

lect, a bit like a rare stamp collection, fails entirely to make the necessary connections. What is needed is for external innovation to be internalised and organised within a company (see top-right).

12 Building a profitable company _____ Building an innovative network

Finally we need to ask about the unit that learns, innovates and prospers. Are we speaking of a single corporation, surrounded by rivals, fighting for survival, or are we speaking of entire innovative networks? In short, who is it that prospers and wins, the company or the whole network? Of course, a company cannot neglect its own advantage. It has shareholders who own that company, not the entire network, so earnings accruing to the company itself cannot be ignored. But where the emphasis is on innovations, the number of new combinations possible within a network far exceeds the number of new connections within the confines of a single company.

One important strategy in combining company with network development is to make sure your company becomes the network's hub. In this way, the vast amount of crucial information passes through your company, which essentially centralises the decentralised net (see Figure 8.1). You now know more than other network members know and can learn faster. But you might still be unwise to exploit your position at the expense of your network, because the success of the whole network is what sustains you. An example of sharing information to benefit the entire net is Wal-Mart's statistics on what has been sold through its outlets and where. Within hours of Proctor & Gamble launching a new product Wal-Mart can inform it of how fast that product is moving in every region of America and beyond. Such information is vital to test marketing and can obviate costly failures among new products.

While the American auto industry treats its suppliers in the old-fashioned way, squeezing their margins, forcing concessions and constantly demanding lower-cost bids from rival tenders, the Japanese auto industry nurtures long-term cooperative relationships with its network suppliers and contractors. This is especially important for innovation, since much of the novelty in automobiles comes from electronics and new safety systems. In short, it is the suppliers who innovate most, which they can only do if well treated by the auto manufacturer.

Toyota has gain-sharing and fate-sharing contracts with its suppliers, whereby both companies share the proceeds of innovation. It also guarantees its suppliers a small mark-up, say 5%, and then shares with them gains from joint cost reductions to increase that margin further. This aborts the usual rivalry between the company and its suppliers and subcontractors in which each tries to deceive the other about relative costs. The different fortunes of the Japanese and American auto networks are plain for all to see.

A company that placed itself at the hub of its network and then exploited it ferociously was Enron. It even contrived blackouts for its California customers to keep them paying above the market price for energy. It arranged for generators to go down for 'repairs' and then made money by speculating on the resulting spike in energy prices. But those who exploit their networks can cause these to collapse and this is just what happened to Enron. It was not a Texas 'Lone Ranger' herding mere cattle but rather a net of interdependent units with one common fate.

Summary

An innovative corporation needs to reconcile all or most of these twelve dilemmas. It must better centralise information from ever more decentralised activities. It must link its functions and technical departments with project teams and human processes. Only bottom-up information from participating employees can properly inform top decision-making. No way can the innovator be right first time, but s/he can, via fast corrections, be right in the shortest possible time. This requires that tacit knowledge be codified, made explicit and widely diffused, yet tacit objections to the codes must be carefully considered and re-codified as required.

All innovation is potentially subversive of formal leadership. Leaders must delegate the right to innovate to creators and teams and allow their ideas and strategies to emerge spontaneously from the grass roots of the company and then interface with customers. It is possible to design strategy out of such successes. The company's standards and benchmarks of internal order must yield at times to the clamorous, chaotic needs of customers that wash over these standards, chaotically. Only thus can new order be discovered amid this chaos.

While figures on financial performance may be the most precise and detailed records available, these are historic and face backwards. As such, companies can collapse without warning through reliance on lagging indicators. It must look forward to what needs to be learned apace if the company is to survive. Innovation of itself occurs not simply internal to a company in its R&D department, but externally all around it. Scores of opportunities are lost if internal developments are not combined with external ones in open innovation.

Finally, innovation occurs most readily not just inside one company but also within its surrounding network or ecosystem. It is the entire network that learns, prospers and innovates. Strategy should seek to enhance, not exploit, members of a network, who share their fate in the future.

CULTURE AS THE INTEGRATOR OF INNOVATIVE VALUES

The importance of corporate culture

Thus far we have introduced three levels of innovation: personal creativity and entrepreneurship, innovation in teams, and what the organisation's structure must do to stimulate innovation and achieve renewal. What binds these three levels together and what cuts across their division is culture. Culture pervades the mind, the small group as well as the larger society. It is everywhere in a distributed pattern, so that if you observed a single person, a small group or an entire organisation at work, you could probably tell from what culture your observations derived.

The four cultures we introduce below derive from two dimensions. They are either rather hierarchical or egalitarian on a vertical dimension and either person-centred or task-centred on a lateral dimension. But this does not mean that cultures with an elite hierarchy set no store by equality. There may have been recruitment examinations in which all entrants had an equal chance, but performed differently. Nor are task-oriented cultures completely dismissive of the people who do these tasks. In a very real sense, these four boxes are stereotypes or 'archetypes', to give them a less opprobrious label. Yet we cannot avoid such labels. They are woven into the mythology and symbolism of all cultures and loom large in the minds of members. Cultures, whether corporate or national, stereotype themselves. Big Ben, the Sydney Opera House, the Empire State Building – their images are flashed on to screens to enable audiences to locate the action.

We all form first impressions quickly. We would not be able to function effectively without doing so. It is part of our survival mechanism. Are we being confronted by a friend or an enemy? The point is not to avoid stereotypes; these are everywhere. The point is to go beyond superficial impressions to see what lies deeper and half-submerged and to use our understanding of archetypes as a way to consider the complexities of real world cultures. This is what we will be doing with these four cultural quadrants.

We cannot avoid archetypes because they are in themselves cultural symbols: the Statue of Liberty, standing in lone splendour to welcome those dauntless enough to have crossed an ocean; the Tomb to the Unknown Soldier attempting to compensate for the anonymity of mass slaughter; the Statue of Eros celebrating love. All are static images portraying some heroic postures and so it is with our four cultures (see Figure 9.1).

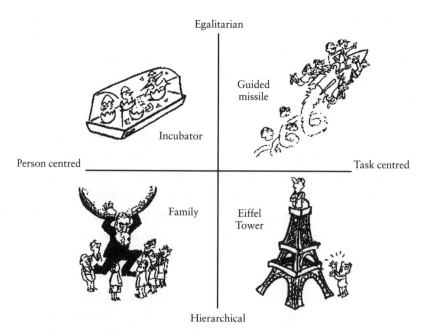

Figure 9.1 Four cultural archetypes

The Incubator

Let's first examine the quadrants, even if only as manifestations. The Incubator, top-left, typical of Silicon Valley, is a culture that is both person-oriented and egalitarian. It is highly creative, 'incubating' new ideas. We're not referring to 'business incubators' *per se*, but using incubation as a metaphor for hatching creative ideas. Such organisations are egalitarian because anyone, at any moment, regardless of their status, may come up with a winning idea. They are person-oriented because the tasks necessary to making and distributing these new products are not yet defined. The Incubator has been given many labels including organic system, loosely coupled system and temporary system, which Mintzberg referred to as an 'adhocracy'. Here people are not controlled but inspired. People are fully committed and love to be challenged. As innovators, the leaders are expected to facilitate change and jump at opportunities. This is management-by-shared-excitement led by the power of ideas, acknowledging the authority less of man than of science and seeking ever-new connections on the leading edges of knowledge. The driving force is a passion for novelty. Customers share this and scramble for early breakthroughs.

Incubator culture revolves around brilliant people and their relationships, all on a first-name basis, but it needs continuing fireworks to maintain itself or its members drift apart and may attempt their own start-ups. When the flame begins to die the company may quickly dissolve unless supported by inputs from the cultures close to it. It is also vulnerable to growing too large. When numbers increase beyond one hundred or so, the intimate, innovative relationships become attenuated. The 'span of control' is not wide enough to value each person's potential and all the ideas.

The Family

Family culture is perhaps the oldest culture, since a large number of companies originate from family lifestyle or livelihood enterprises, even if they eventually go public. On a global scale, there are more family-owned companies than any other. But we are speaking of family *cul-*

tures, not legal ownership. Family culture is hierarchical because the gap between 'parents' (owners) and 'children' (employees) is often wide. The 'old man' may be revered or feared. He – and it is often a 'he' – may regard his employees as members of his family, whose burdens he carries. Mentoring, coaching and developing employees' potentials are borrowed from the family ideal. The family's style is that of mutuality and kinship, the leading personalities have the strongest influence, and the source of cohesion is affinity and trust. Its members are controlled by social pressures. Its guiding star is harmony and its chief currency is persuasion and loyalty. You do what is best for the family.

Family culture is person-oriented, because who you are looms larger than what you do. Family members may not be fully professional. Those most accomplished at tasks may be passed over in favour of closest kin. Insiders have advantages over outsiders. Such cultures are often warm, intimate and friendly, but their internal integration may be achieved at the price of poor external adaptation, and they can 'hug and kiss each other into bankruptcy'. Creative genius rarely passes down a dynasty, so the founder's vision may end up like the Ford Edsel, a car named after Henry's son and equally unimpressive.

Power is exercised *through* people and sometimes *over* them. The danger for family cultures is that their inward orientation may not be matched by enough looking outwards. Cultures with too little differentiation can become 'inbred and incestuous' in their discourse, with too little comprehension of the wider environment. Like the Incubator culture, this is a primary group of people who know each other very well along with each other's personal predispositions. Also like the Incubator culture it has trouble growing larger since only a limited number of persons can constitute a family. In cases where family cultures do grow large there will be an inner circle of people who trust each other and an outer circle of comparative strangers with diminished influence.

The Guided Missile

In contrast, the Guided Missile is an egalitarian, task-oriented culture in which project groups steer towards the accomplishment of team tasks. They are typically multidisciplinary, taking from the various functions of the organisation only those people essential for completing the set task. They are egalitarian because *whose* expertise is relevant to their common problems is an ever-open question. NASA was probably the most famous culture of this kind. It took over 100 disciplines in science and engineering to land on the moon. The relative contributions of each had to be negotiated among equals. The only 'boss' was the task or mission itself. 'Getting the job done' with 'the right person in the right place' were favourite expressions.

Such cultures develop a sense of purpose, sometimes a superordinate goal, like Project Manhattan that built the atom bomb. These cultures are well suited not just to innovation and problem solving but also to customising a complex product or system for a choosy client. As we saw in Chapter 4, teams develop over time and have periods in which they become 'hot', matching their skills against challenges. A team at its best is a microcosm of the problem it is addressing. Its membership can represent all sides in a particular conflict or dispute but bring these persons into sustained and intimate contact long enough to solve the problem.

The chief problem with teams is their high expense. A dozen expert persons meeting for two or more hours is a very costly proposition. Because teams are temporary, lasting only as long as their projects, they lack the deep commitments of the Family or the Incubator, yet they are excellent at combining a diversity of talent with a unity of purpose. They are driven by team goals, generate and discover real knowledge, share a sense of dedication, defer to the authority of a total solution, strive to be broadly effective, are essential to the creation of viable systems and symbolise professionalism and pragmatism.

Increasingly the problems faced by a corporation are complex, multifaceted and interdisciplinary. Teams can provide a valuable opportunity to get functions to help each other and devise new connections. In most bureaucracies the division of labour gets more attention than the integration of labour. Teams are invaluable at these integrative tasks, also at zeroing in on a moving target and achieving a fruitful rendezvous with the customer whose requirements are in flux. But the major value of the Guided Missile team culture is to champion innovative ideas and work these through the various 'gates' described in Chapter 5, taking these ideas from mere mental images to finished products and providing the momentum that carries ventures forward.

The Eiffel Tower

Our final cultural quadrant features the Eiffel Tower. This is what Max Weber described as bureaucracy and what Henry Ford and Frederick Winslow Taylor saw as the most efficient of manufacturing units. This culture is highly structured, detailed, precise and repetitive and emphasises the division of labour. It is by far the cheapest way of producing material goods in great quantities at high speed. Everyone has a pre-defined job description and power derives from one's position in the hierarchy. Common subjection to a boss above you is also its principle of cohesion, while control is exercised through strict rules and practiced procedures. Its watchword is efficiency, machines working in a predictable way and served by people. Its aim is nothing less than to constitute a better system of order.

Yet the downsides of the Eiffel Tower are well established. Work is exhausting, simplified, alienating, automated, machine timed, and even soul-destroying. It is partly responsible for the rise of Communism and for turning the working class against capitalism in many countries. Trade unionism has everything the lonely factory lacks. Indeed, the Eiffel Tower is close to being a highly negative stereotype that has lost business considerable public support.

The need for a new paradigm for corporate culture

While most readers will readily recognise our four archetypal cultures, this recognition comes at the cost of oversimplification. These cultures are close to being caricatures. Any of the four in its purest form would surely be dysfunctional. The Eiffel Tower reminds one of Charlie Chaplin in *Modern Times* or more seriously of Fritz Lang's *Metropolis*. The Family culture corrupted by financial gain is reminiscent of *Bleak House* or *Nicholas Nickleby*. The Incubator culture conjures up mad scientists assisted by sorcerers' apprentices, while Guided Missiles may take on all the mad momentum of an intolerant sectarianism.

We intend to show that each culture in the four quadrants is assisted and maintained by the others to a greater or lesser degree. What we recognise is merely the preponderance of one over the others. In some cases one culture gives birth to another and in other cases a neighbouring culture completes the work begun by another. There are a host of inter-dependencies, many of them quite subtle. Nor should we assume that a corporation has but one culture throughout. The R&D department might be an Incubator. The sales department may deploy teams in the manner of a Guided Missile to sell what the factory has produced in the style of an Eiffel Tower, while the staff in the canteen and kitchen may enjoy a culture akin to the Family.

As might be expected we have found no correlation in our research between the preponderance of one culture and overall performance of the company. This is because cultures must fit the circumstances in which a company finds itself and circumstances differ widely across industrial ecosystems. It is part of the strength of a culture that it can transform it-self from one quadrant to another as circumstances change. When members of a culture are asked in which quadrant they fall, all four quadrants are recognised as being present, although some may be much more salient than others.

Most theorists on corporate culture have fallen into the habit of creating quadrants. For Charles Handy in *The Gods of Management*, it is Dionysus, Athena, Apollo and Zeus, corresponding roughly to Incubator, Guided Missile, Eiffel Tower and Family, a typology much influenced in turn by Roger Harrison. Cameron and Quinn have a similar quadrant, featuring Control–Flexibility, Internal–External. All such schema are readily recognisable, while their essential Western linearity misses what, for us, is the most important difference in the effectiveness and innovative powers of culture.

What ultimately matters most is whether our four quadrants or those of others are *synergistic*, i.e. working with each other in creative combinations, or *schismogenetic*, i.e. split apart, combative and mutu-ally escalating. Synergy, from *syn-ergo* 'to work with', is a concept in-troduced by Ruth Benedict. It means values in a culture are mutually supportive, so that unselfishness by anyone in some cultures is quickly reciprocated and rewarded in a way that fuses the Selfish–Unselfish di-chotomy. Schismogenesis occurs when unselfishness is cruelly exploited with the beneficiary demanding even more sacrifices, so that selfish and unselfish values come apart with the first preying eagerly on the second.

Schismogenesis is a term coined by Gregory Bateson and defined as 'the progressive splitting in the structure of ideas'.

Applying this to our four quadrants we can ask whether these work with each other in mutual support or square off against each other in battle. The conflict between the alienating features of the Eiffel Tower and the Brotherhood of Man, extolled by trade union 'families', occupied much of the twentieth century and brought many businesses and unions to their knees, turning half the world red. In contrast, it is highly desirable, as we shall see, for one corporate culture to help create another and for all four to exist in harmony.

Other creators of quadrants have also noted the danger of splitting; for example, Quinn notes:

> 'When this zealous pursuit of a single set of criteria takes place, a strange inversion can also result. Good things can mysteriously become bad things ... criteria of effectiveness, when pursued blindly, become criteria of ineffectiveness.'

An experienced and innovative leader knows that features of these four cultures must be fused and ways of cleverly combining these are many. Innovation does not simply occur in the Incubator, although new products may originate there; a broader definition of innovation occurs wherever aspects of the four different cultures are combined to form a new business model.

Towards an integral organisation

In this section we argue that a prerequisite for an innovative organisation is the reconciliation of the variety of organisational cultures, in order to face the challenging dynamic world in which it operates. In this way, it can overcome the limitations of the stronger culture into which it will otherwise tend to drift, lurching from crisis to crisis.

Culture consists of more than the four crude extremities detailed earlier, although these make a good starting point. Culture consists in how *contrasting values and conflicts are habitually mediated,* in short, how well our four quadrants can be creatively combined. That these quadrants are highly diverse is important, since innovation creates unity out of diversity, as we have seen. We need Family Missiles, Guided Incubators and Missile-created Towers and so on. Instead of using 'the forced choice' type of questionnaire wherein one quadrant is a negation of the other three, we described each culture in a way that permitted it to be compatible or incompatible with others. Here is an example:

Each person is given a clear definition of their responsibilities in the organisation	Eiffel Tower
Information is shared widely so that everyone can get the information needed when required	Family
We work in flexible networks in which personal development is key	Incubator
There is an orientation to results and achievement to get the job done	Guided Missile

If these four cultures are split, one set of answers will greatly outnumber the others. If they are integrated, all or more of the quadrants will be strongly supported and will be seen as developing together. An overview of the characteristics of the cultures can be seen at http://www.businessacrosscultures.com/corporatecultureoverview.

From intimacy to invention

A very obvious way of integrating the four cultures is to see these as four successive stages of growth and development over time. How does a company begin? The GEM studies conducted jointly by Babson College and the London Business School have discovered two major motives for entrepreneurship in the world: survival and self-expression. Most small companies in the world are started by families and have a Family culture, the purpose of which is to enable entrepreneurs and their families to survive. This helps to explain why so many immigrants, strangers-in-a-strange-land, start up companies. They need to survive and for newcomers this is especially difficult, so they substitute a product for their personalities to give others a good reason for transacting with them. In this case businesses originate from the Family quadrant and the 'family' often includes fellow Arabs, fellow Chinese or fellow Indian immigrants, so that Arabs in America are actually wealthier than the average American, and Chinese immigrants to Great Britain are wealthier than the average Briton.

But businesses can also originate in a powerful need for self-expression. In this case business originates in the Incubator quadrant, often among highly educated electronic engineers, bioengineering experts and similar persons. Silicon Valley, the Cambridge Phenomenon, Shanghai's business incubators and its new eco-city are such examples. To be innovative is intrinsically exciting and adventurous and may be among the best ways to live. Abraham Maslow called it self-actualisation.

There is, of course, no inherent reason why a culture that starts as a Family cannot mutate into an Incubator. Much will depend on how personally creative the founders are. Family cultures with low creativity may remain as Mom and Pop stores but many move on. Anna Lee Saxenian made a survey of Silicon Valley companies in 2000 and found that as many as one-third of these were headed by Indian or Chinese immigrants entering America after 1970. These were worth $58 billion. Indeed, Chinese and Indian immigrants were more numerous at the top of such organisations than at the bottom.

In this case the need for survival has been combined with the need for self-expression and the two cultures have been joined. Many Asians use their high family savings rates to help start new companies, borrowing from relatives. Saxenian's research found many ethnic entrepreneurs were in touch with 'family' in Bangalore, Taipei or Shanghai. Ethnic entrepreneurs need to network with those of similar background. These tend to be 'high-trust' relationships since without these the entrepreneur has no one on whom to rely.

In Figure 9.2 we see how innovation is born out of necessity. Migrant minorities find themselves in a world of strangers. All they have to support them are ethnic family networks which they cannot cheat and avoid sanction. But if ethnicity is *all* they have then they are likely to go no further than Mom and Pop stores in ethnic enclaves. But at least some of them realise that they are perforce different from the rest of society so they might as well *express that difference* voluntarily. They have nothing to lose.

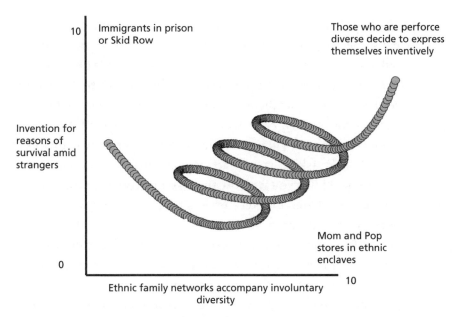

Figure 9.2 Family intimacy v Incubation of innovations

Note that many immigrants finish up at top-left or bottom-right, but some succeed in creating innovative families. Both the Family and the Incubator join to explain the business success of so many migrant, ethnic groups. These are primary groups small enough to know one another well with sufficient intimacy to discover where genius is hiding. For such reasons the Chinese outside China, Indians outside India, Jews throughout the Diaspora and Arabs outside the Middle East, even Koreans in Japan, tend to be more entrepreneurial and fare better than those in their home countries. Should a migrant innovator misbehave it will be all around his/her community by sundown.

From invention to intention

Whether a business starts with a Family, an Incubator or both of these cultures it will face predictable challenges as it grows larger in numbers employed. A culture cannot remain person-centred beyond a certain size because of the impossibility of knowing so many people intimately and because the informal span of control breaks down as numbers increase beyond one hundred.

There are other problems stalking an Incubator culture. When you first invent something much sought after, you have only to 'throw it over your shoulder' metaphorically to have customers scramble to get hold of it. These 'early adopters' will often pay over the odds to try something new. Indeed, the success of Silicon Valley has been attributed to the 'hunger' of hackers for novelty. But this situation is transient. Within a few months your competitors will have similar offerings, prices will drop and customers will start asking you to adapt your product to their special needs. Unless you do this you will lose the revenue from the products you initially introduced. Later adopters are less adaptable. They want you to do the work of customisation.

Such a task requires an intentional Guided Missile culture to carry it through as the novelty wears off. You can only keep your customers by adding features and uses that they particularly want, and this needs a team to respond to new customers' specification and create a solution to whatever problem s/he confronts. For example, two-way radio equipment is no longer a new product, but fitting out a fleet of air ambulances that have to respond to emergency calls needs a team to meet various exigencies on behalf of the customer. It needs to be loud enough to be heard above the noise of rotary blades. It needs text to check that the message was correctly heard. It needs a geographical positioning system to zero in on the site of the accident and accurate estimates of arrival time at the scene, with an automatic relay to the police.

Note that the competitive advantage of a new incubated product has not disappeared but it is beginning to fade. So special designs for special customers are becoming more and more vital to what Clayton Christiansen calls *sustaining innovation*. Creative features are added incrementally to the original product that make this more and more useful to various market segments, so that a mobile phone can listen to broadcasts, send text messages and pick up e-mail. Note that innovation of a kind is the aim of teams in the Guided Missile culture; we have *not* left innovation behind, rather its character has changed to sustaining an existing product line.

In the Guided Missile culture, employees have not just an intention and a mission, but a task. They are there to offer their professional expertise to other professionals and solve the problem at hand. They have been picked because they have the skills to help solve the problem. One of the great powers of a team, as we have seen, is to put its enthusiasm, momentum and critical acumen behind an incubated product and bring it to fruition. The team potentially joins the inventor to the customer and makes sure that the invention has fulfilled its intention of pleasing the customer.

As a product matures the power tends to move from the supplier to the customer who now has more options in choosing a supplier. That customers are helped and supported in their use of the products becomes a major selling point. Feedback from the customers who must use the product becomes crucial and in many cases engineers must confer with engineers over extended periods. There is often an element of co-creation, with customers putting the final touches to the product and ensuring it is 100% right. All this is accomplished in Guided Missile style by teams. Of course, the two cultures may not *always* integrate smoothly. The genius of the original product may be watered down by 'group think' in the team. The customer may be poorly instructed in how the product should be used. The incubated product, although brilliantly inventive scientifically, may be so poorly applied by the team as to be useless to the customer. What seems to matter most is how the two cultures support one another in mutual enhancement. The dilemma is set out below in Figure 9.3.

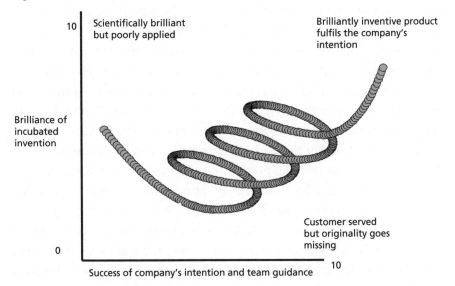

Figure 9.3 The intentional invention

It is clear that at top-left and bottom-right the Incubator and the Guided Missile have split apart, but at top-right they are working together in reconciliation, as outstanding persons fulfil their team tasks in egalitarian fashion. After all, a team is small enough for the creativity of the individual to count. So, far from suppressing the individual creator, a team may celebrate her or him. To be admired by a small group of colleagues is among life's most delightful experiences.

So now we have a really well-working Guided Missile culture that is delighting customers. Surely we do not have to change any further? But we do and must. Remember our once new product is maturing but we do not wish to stop selling it. After all, we invented it and we deserve the income flow. Unfortunately the product is by now so routine that it does not require a team of professionals to guide it towards the customer. A Guided Missile culture is expensive and by now customers are experienced enough so they do not need copious advice from a multi-professional team. Our once ingenious product is on the way to becoming a commodity.

From intention to routine implementation

The time comes when for reasons of economy our product must be handed over to the factory, or processed in some routine way. It needs to be manufactured cheaply and in quantities. The Eiffel Tower, one of the cultures least favoured among those with whom we have consulted, may still be a necessity. Must their lives be governed by machine-timed efficiency? The stereotype of the Eiffel Tower is more feared and avoided than any of our quadrants, so it becomes all the more important to show how it is qualified and humanised by its adjoining quadrants. The 'pure' Eiffel Tower is quite dysfunctional but not with the assistance of other cultures.

Let us suppose that the product *has* become a commodity or near-commodity and must be worked upon at minimal cost in a factory. But factories have changed considerably of late. It is now exceedingly common for workers to meet in teams at the beginning and end of the day to critique the day's operations and seek to improve these under the banner of Quality Circles, Quality of Work Life or Continuous Improvement. In short, workers spend part of their time in Guided Missile teams so that their work on the shop floor will go more smoothly. An American social innovation called the Scanlon Plan, much praised by Douglas McGregor and widely copied in Japan, joins the Incubator culture with the Guided Missile with the Eiffel Tower. Workers are given half an hour a day – and donate another half hour – to brainstorm improvements in their workplace. Where this improves the input–output ratio the workers get half the money and managers, representing shareholders, get the other half. The watchword is 'Every person an entrepreneur'. Innovation is the responsibility of everyone.

Today many factories encourage workers to work in groups rather than strung out in lines. The work process is not simply circular but face to face. This enables everyone to watch out for everyone else and for new workers to be supervised and assisted lest they err. In the famous Hawthorne Experiment six women were taken out of a factory and put in a room face to face where their productivity climbed 38%. That said, their job was the same, assembling telephone relays, but they did it more effectively around one table as a team. At Volvo a team is responsible for assembling a finished automobile and leaves its members' signatures beneath the vehicle.

The Eiffel Tower is also infiltrated on its other side by the Family. German quality manufacturing has been much assisted by the survival of the apprentice system, a 'father–son' relationship in the workplace, often credited with having sparked Britain's Industrial Revolution, propelled by skilled craftsmen. Japanese management celebrates a quality called *amae*. This is not the Latin word for love, but the abiding concern and respect between a superior and a subordinate, an inspiring indulgence. A new employee is often given an 'elder brother' to look after him, known as a *sempai-gohai* relationship, 'elder and younger brother'. These metaphors clearly hark back to the family.

Our consultancy worked for some years for Motorola, which until recently was a family dynasty three generations long. No employee over 60 could be terminated without permission of the CEO. Every employee was encouraged to recruit from among their own families, so that families supported one larger family. One female employee got a prize when the twenty-eighth member of her extended family was offered a job at the company! Motorola gave generously to the Chicago school system and ran children's summer camps for technically oriented youngsters.

When we visited Motorola in Penang, Malaysia, it was the birthday of the female managing director. The bouquets of flowers stretched all the way down the passage to her office – we had to wade through them!

Motorola also binds the Incubator and Guided Missile cultures together. If any section of a team disagrees with the rest of a team, a minority report is written and sent up the hierarchy. This was how mobile phones became a major business. It was a dissenting minority in a team discussion. Yet despite all this, Motorola is a most exacting Eiffel Tower culture, installing Six Sigma quality, a process of such discipline and exactitude that errors on routine operations are reduced to one in a million. This example illustrates that all four cultures can be powerfully intertwined in one corporation to deliver precision where this is needed and flexibility where this is more suitable. The Japanese give the term 'voluntary management' to those cases where blue-collar workers can solve problems on the spot, or meet after the shift to confer on improvements.

Computers now print out what is right or wrong with production processes and workers using algebra make the necessary adjustments. The effectiveness of a modern factory lies in how finely it is coordinated and teams of 'voluntary managers' take responsibility for this. The dilemma below shows how the Guided Missile culture steers and guides the Eiffel Tower culture. We have used the example of the Scanlon Plan.

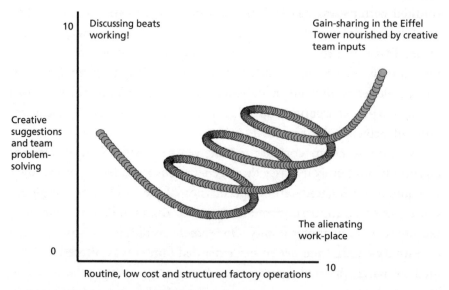

Figure 9.4 The intentional implementation

It is at least probable that the team meetings, occurring at the end of each day in a primary group, take on some of the characteristics of the Family. In the chart above, the creative suggestions and team problem solving on the vertical axis are important, but by themselves not enough. Discussions may beat working (top-left) but the work has to be done. If we have nothing but routine, low-cost operations on the horizontal axis then we are back into the alienating workplace (bottom-right) that the young Karl Marx condemned. What is required is the integration of the Guided Missile and the Eiffel Tower with features of the Incubator and the Family at top-right. Gain-sharing in the Eiffel Tower nourished by creative team inputs is the required recipe.

We consulted at one point with Intel in Malaysia. The CEO was Chinese and very much a servant-leader. He had opened a crèche in the gardens of the factory where infants and toddlers could be cared for and taught English. Their parents could spend the lunch hour with them. He also built an adult activity centre and laid on a free bus service to take workers and their children home from work in the evening and back in the morning. The Works Council discovered what all these amenities cost and met in groups to improve productivity so that the CEO would be repaid for all his trouble. Dynamics of this kind *unite all four quadrants of the culture.* The workers knew that if Intel audited his accounts, these concessions might cease. They were determined to build a business case for their better working conditions and other amenities.

The CEO also started an in-house shop. The shop invested its profits in nearby businesses, mostly lower tech. When a worker was unable to keep up with the algebra needed for the manufacture of Intel chips, he sought a less complicated job in a nearby business and was recommended for the job by a shareholder. In six years no one had ever left the company without another job to go to. Long live the Family!

Leaders who can 'conduct' or 'orchestrate' all four quadrants of the culture, blending each into a symphony, are rare. Among the qualities it requires is the ability to get down into the details and the nitty-gritty of the Eiffel Tower, before returning to a statesman-like view of the big picture and the incubation of an innovative business model.

Jim Morgan, co-founder and former CEO of Applied Materials, created the phrase 'porpoise leadership'. From an Incubator culture he had created, he thought there was a way to get down to details as well. Just as a dolphin leaps and plunges, so must modern leaders move above the fray to see the corporation spread out beneath them, but also dive down deep to make a critical examination of the details. You can't always be at the top of the abstraction ladder at a distance from concrete reality. You need to get your hands on the day-to-day minutiae of organisational life, to walk your talk, and be seen to actually do what you have been articulating.

An overview of leadership dilemmas can be seen at http://www.businessacrosscultures.com/leadershipcrisiscultureoverview.

One powerful influence that comes from the Family is that everyone should cooperate for the common good. A contrasting influence that comes from the other three quadrants is that we are caught in a competitive struggle – we must out-innovate, out-customise and undercut our rivals in costs if we are to survive. Yet only habits of mind and a forty-year Cold War have persuaded us that competing is 'good' and cooperating somehow subversive of our ideals, so that the West persistently accuses the East of 'crony capitalism' and active government assistance to the economy is seen as a fall from grace.

Motorola, during its glory days, instituted a Total Customer Satisfaction Competition in which any team serving customers in any part of the world could enter. At one level this was highly competitive. Heats were held within countries, then the victors went to regional run-offs, and then the fifty best teams in the world came to the Paul Galvin Theatre in Schaumburg, Illinois, for the finals. Countries such as Singapore and Malaysia thought this was such a good idea that they challenged Motorola teams domestically and had them compete against other companies. In such contests we see competition between teams in a Guided Missile form, but also Incubators since many total solutions for customers were highly creative. Employees were encouraged to make pitches from a platform, to show off individually Western-style and be self-assertive as innovators must.

But there was a highly cooperative side to this equation too. Teams shared a common fate that brought them close to each other. They had a shared mission to serve the customers and it was the customers' plaudits and their measurable gains from the solution wrought that helped the teams to win the contest. Indeed, it was a competition *at cooperating*. The components going cheaply into the solution had in all probability been mass-produced in an Eiffel Tower but what won the day was the particular configuration of these components to solve the customers' problems. Every team also embarked on a family adventure that could end up on stage in the USA and find its place in the knowledge generated by Motorola University.

The integration of cooperating and competing is depicted below in Figure 9.5.

Too much competition leads to Tooth and Claw, top-left. Too much cooperation may lead to Cosy Collusion but Motorola's TCS Competition (Total Customer Satisfaction) blends competing with cooperating along with several quadrants of our corporate cultures.

In Chapter 7 on the Singapore Experiment we saw that a classroom of would-be entrepreneurs, all keen to incubate, require a family

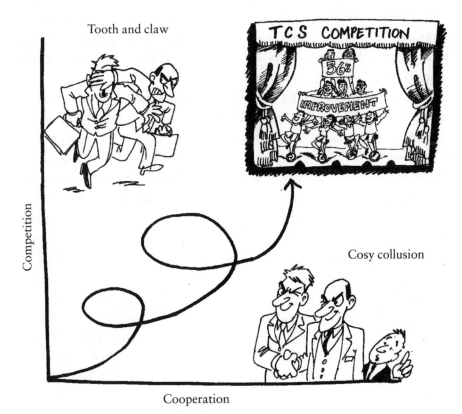

Figure 9.5 The integration of cooperating and competing

atmosphere in the classroom, a cheering section of colleagues to egg them on, but also to criticise constructively, so that the prototypes are improved. The entire class forms teams in a 16-week business simulation, while many products must be designed for low-cost manufacturability in an Eiffel Tower-type factory. Once again all four quadrants are joined. Class members compete but because their visions are so diverse no one's victory detracts from the success of others, so they also help each other.

At Royal Dutch Shell, the Dutch author was able to combine team (or communal) rewards with individual rewards. Half the rewards for good performance were distributed to all team members, while the other half were distributed to individual team members – in accordance with the team members' estimates of their relative contributions. So individuals received half the additional rewards, but only if their co-workers deemed this to be just. Where individuals contribute the winning edge to their teams, their popularity and self-esteem are greatly enhanced by the gratitude of team members. In this way, the social system applauds their individual contributions and does not grudge their subsequent promotion.

The reconciled dilemma is illustrated in Figure 9.6.

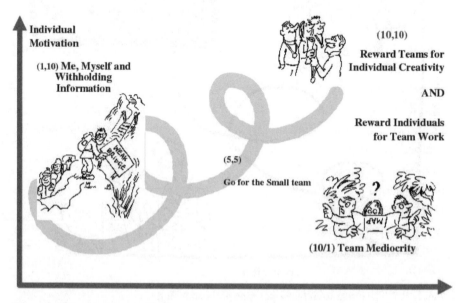

Figure 9.6 Co-opetition at Shell

From implementation to inventing

Now we come to perhaps the most vexed problem. Can a company, having journeyed from Family plus Incubation to an intentional Guided Missile until it was forced to implement this automatically in an Eiffel Tower, now come full circle to be reborn? It is very difficult and quite rare but it has been done.

Corporations have an average life expectancy that is shorter than most human lives, although a few are into their second century. One reason is that an Eiffel Tower, with its highly structured division of labour and its detailed operations, finds it almost impossible to return to a 'childhood state' wherein classifications have not yet been made. We know this in part from the research conducted by Clayton Christiansen at Harvard. He looked at 129 computer companies of which 109 had gone out of business. The main problem they all faced was a constantly shrinking disc drive at one time 18 inches and today around 2.5 inches. The computer is designed around the disc drive so their ever-smaller size renders large computers heavy and obsolete.

At the time the smaller disc drives were introduced they accomplished less than the existing larger ones, so that the companies with larger drives felt justified in sticking with the original size, a decision in which they were joined by customers who did not want to waste their time pioneering an unfamiliar system. Alas, most companies making this decision perished, in many cases dooming their customers also. One reason was that the smaller disc drives, once introduced, improved rapidly, a process called 'sustaining innovation', until they were as good as the larger discs at a lower cost and smaller size. Sustaining innovation is what occurs in Guided Missile teams. Christiansen calls these ever-smaller drives *disruptive innovation*, because a new design with a simpler system incubates and disrupts the Eiffel Tower structure of the current product. Wang, DEC and ICL are among the prominent victims of such disruption.

Christiansen's *The Innovator's Dilemma* has become a best seller and many are the companies that have implored him to find a way out for them. His warning does not simply apply to the computer industry but also to the old-fashioned integrated steel mills, now replaced by mini-mills, to the invasion of the American automobile market by compact, low-cost Japanese autos and the attack on Xerox by Cannon, using a desk duplicator, far more basic than Xerox's finest and quickest machines. What happens to complex technology is that scores of extra features are added by the Guided Missile culture and the Eiffel Tower culture until it *over-serves its customers*. At this point it is vulnerable to disruption by a simpler, relatively 'primitive' technology incubated in a new start-up at a fraction of the cost.

Christiansen's answer to his wide and rather desperate readership is not entirely satisfactory but his may be the only way out of the dilemma. In his most recent work, he advises large companies *to disrupt themselves*.[1] Even while their complex product is expanding and being elaborated by task cultures the company must renew and reinvent itself by asking 'what radically simpler alternative is there to our own current over-elaborated products?' If we were to torpedo ourselves from underneath, how would this be done and should we not do this to ourselves before someone else does? Christiansen has founded a business incubator in Singapore dedicated to disruptive innovation.

The problem of renewal and rebirth by moving once more back to the Incubator quadrant is less serious if that same culture never died and continues to inspire the company. Applied Materials is still run by the original entrepreneurs who founded it and still incubates, develops and manufactures new products. It seems able to come full circle from a mature product in its final years to a reinvented one. Yet this is a rare accomplishment. Hewlett Packard seems to have lost its former innovative flair and has outsourced much of its innovation to Flextronics, which has yet to challenge it, but probably will before long.

A strategy adopted by East Asian companies is to begin as a humble subcontractor and gradually take on more and more complex work until the Eiffel Tower culture has had its invention and intention hollowed out and taken over by the interloper. The Italian silk tie industry succumbed to this invasive strategy by Chinese companies that initially supplied their silk, then cut it, then dyed it, then printed it and then shipped it to where it was sold. When the Chinese had all the requisite knowledge

---

1 Scott D Anthony and Erik A. Roth, *Seeing What's Next*, Boston: Harvard Business School Publishing, 2004.

they entered the market and easily wrested it away. So, although moving from the Eiffel Tower back to the Incubator or the Family is very difficult indeed, it may be possible to be disrupted by a subcontractor or preferably to disrupt oneself and grow a new business model to replace the older one.

Summary

Figure 9.7 summarises the argument of this chapter. Company cultures move from Family to Incubator, although high-tech companies may start with the Incubator and not all Families make the transition. They next move in turn from Incubator to Guided Missile to Eiffel Tower as the products they supply turn into commodities. Finally, they have an outside chance of renewing themselves, disrupting their own technologies and incubating a new conception.

Even so, they are rarely in one place at one time. The Family may be nurturing its more creative members to invent something. The Incubator almost certainly has the intention of serving some customer out there in the environment. The Guided Missile remains faithful to its incubated products even as it prepares itself for the coming of the Eiffel Tower. Finally, the Eiffel Tower confronting an elephant's death may be capable of renewing itself and incubating once more. In the meantime, the Family culture has pervaded the three other cultures with its ethic of trust, goodwill and effective ties.

The cultures may not, of course, be fused and integrated and may not carry with them the legacy of the phases through which they have moved. The Family may, on occasion, shut out all other influences and suckle its own mediocrities. The Incubator may enjoy the process of creation more than any result or benefit to others. If so it will bloom briefly and die. The team process may be so intoxicating that members cannot let go. They will price themselves out of the market. Finally, the Eiffel

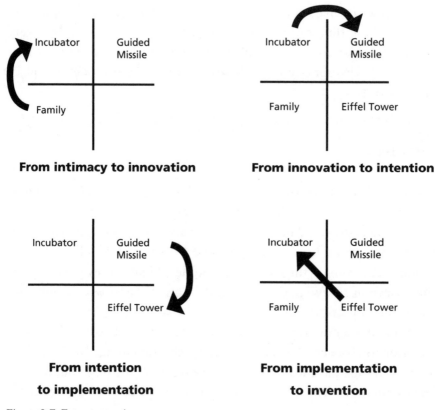

Figure 9.7 Four successive stages

Tower may become a Kafkaesque nightmare of those inhabiting cages of their own design.

What ultimately works, although you need social innovation to bring it about, is the orchestration of all four cultures, excited by the Incubator, committed to Guiding the Missile, structured by the Eiffel Tower and healed by the bonds of the Family. We have described the leader who can do all these things as the servant-leader, looking always towards what the culture needs. S/he manages the culture and the culture manages the people. Whatever may appear on the surface of a corporate culture, the truth is that all other cultures are working 'behind the scenes' to sustain it or inflame it and that the culture carries the legacy of the phases through which it has passed and the future to which it aspires.

WHAT SHOULD A LEADER DO NOW?

If you have read this far you will know there is no magic formula, no action, or even series of actions that can be counted on to be right in all circumstances. There are *no* ready-made techniques that can be pulled out of the toolbox. The best we can do is help you to diagnose the state of your organisation so as to repair serious imbalances. In tragic drama the protagonists often limp as a sign of their imperfection. It is in repairing this uneven gait, in balancing values so that they are equal, that a novel integrity can then be wrought. The best help we can give is to pose key *questions* which leaders can pose to their organisations and to themselves and so spot what is weak or lacking.

1 When you compare the creative potentials of your people with the opportunities given them to create, which of these two is lagging? Possibly as a result of the present recession, do your people seek occupational and financial security above all things? Or is the business environment insufficiently stimulating so that they are not drawn out?

   In our view, creative ability is widely, not narrowly, distributed and most employees are seriously underestimated. However, threat and insecurity are great dampeners. The instruments outlined in Chapters 1–3 should be of assistance in measuring, recruiting and assessing creative potential. If such persons are present but not performing, you need to look at the stimuli in the environment. Are you challenging them sufficiently?

2 Are your employees sufficiently *aware* that you wish them to be creative? Are they free to experiment, take risks, improvise and err? What happens to them when they do this?

It is all too easy to talk up innovation and extol it, but too often this is just rhetoric. It is very easy to praise innovation but much harder to do it. Many ways of punishing innovation are inadvertent. Blaming people rather than the learning process for any mistakes may harm creativity. Pay for performance rewards only what is recognised and innovation may not be seen as valuable. Deadlines, pressures, crises, cost cutting and redundancies may drive your best and brightest to leave, as they have better options. Big bonuses fail to work when you do not know what you want. They rather drive conformity to present goals.

3 Have you acted to take the danger and high cost out of experimental behaviour? Are there tools for modelling, simulation, prototyping that permit learning by mistakes to be inexpensive as opposed to dangerous and costly?

No company can afford expensive, dangerous or reckless mistakes. That is the reason for counting 'insufficient separation' between planes and counting 'unsafe acts'. But if you want to learn without endangering people, you need to simulate and render 'mistakes' harmless. A company either provides these opportunities to learn or it does not. It either allows people to 'play' with prototypes or not.

4 Assuming some 'play' is permitted, does your company err on the side of preferring 'toys' to real life or on the side of preferring the serious business of launching products to first playing with them? Does it get the transition from play to seriousness right? Do your people have a sense of humour or is it deficient? Do they have the capacity to laugh at themselves and does the laughing stop in the face of challenge?

The balance of 'playful seriousness' is vital. Those without a sense of humour are invariably sterile. So much repetition may be required that unless you are enjoying yourself and having fun you will fail to persevere.

5 Is the bottleneck in your organisation that slows down innovation the shortage of people willing to hazard themselves or show off, or

the shortage of people willing to listen long and patiently to others? Are they able to criticise the *project* without discouraging the *person*?

There is often a chronic shortage of mentors who are willing to nurture the innovation in others. Some successful courses on innovation have twice as many mentors as potential entrepreneurs. Many managers believe that listening is low status as opposed to articulating. Also they do not know how to sustain the innovator while improving the project s/he is working on.

6 Does your company have a regularised process for creating project-based teams that join various functions and help these contribute? Do teams in part self-organise around projects they have created and push this from idea to reality in a stage-gate process? Does the team accept responsibility for the ultimate profitability of the project?

The individual creator is too weak without a team to champion her idea and see it though to launch and payback. Teams rarely spring up unbidden and even where they are spontaneous they need to be legitimised, resourced, briefed, presented with their challenge and given the time, space, resources and autonomy to act. Their solutions need to be evaluated and implemented where possible.

7 Are there senior managers able and willing to sponsor teams and take the responsibility for their success, giving them sufficient delegated powers to achieve solutions? What is the ratio of implemented solutions versus those that fall by the wayside? Do you trust teams too little or too much?

Teams are expert-intensive and quite expensive to mobilise. Shelved recommendations are unaffordable in any numbers. It is part of a senior manager's competence to brief a team on the challenge facing it and what any solution must accomplish *without* infringing its autonomy of thought.

8 Are team members carefully selected so that their capacities match the profile of the problem? Are their abilities sufficient for the challenge of the problem they confront?

'Hot' teams and exciting innovation emerge from teams whose skills are stretched but not overstretched by the challenges. Problem solving is inherently thrilling and monitoring the morale of teams and their *esprit de corps* is instructive.

9   Is learning elevated to the status of a super-ordinate goal in your organisation so that generating knowledge is part of this? Are routine operations treated as questions deserving new and significant answers?

Leaders must see themselves and be seen as leading a process of inquiry, posing questions to which employees and customers can find the answers. You are in a 'learning race' with your competitors to master learning goals before they can. You respect those persons with whom you are in dialogue.

10 Does your organisation value knowledge regardless of its origins in other cultures and companies? Do those at the borders of the system receive the attention of those at its centre regardless of how decentralised their activities are? Would sudden success in any part of the system inform the whole?

Good decisions can only flow down and out if good information flows up and in. There should be decentralised centres of excellence in those cultures that excel at these kinds of task.

11 Are you sufficiently open to tacit, intuitive, informal, un-codified forms of knowledge or do you only pay attention to what can be counted and can measure performance?

Novel concepts start their life in un-codified forms and a company full of performance indicators can easily overlook these. It is typically informal groups and unusual relationships that create new insights. You ignore these at your peril.

12 Do you have leaders that are willing to delegate resources and power to creative persons and teams and accept responsibility for doing this, despite the danger of undermining their own authority and nurturing rival forms of 'leadership'?

All innovation is an attempt to lead and may arouse the hostility, not the support, of those in positions of power. Historically the 'creative minority' have had a hard time.

13 Do you look for innovation both inside *and* outside you own company and try to put these new developments together? Do you seek to make syntheses across disciplines, across nations and with venture partners? Are your innovative processes open, or secret and confined within your company?

The process of creating new combinations never stops and unless you look outside your own R&D you will not spot these.

14 Is your main concern to enrich your own company, if necessary at the expense of companies in your network, or is your main concern to benefit and build up your entire network and develop this as an innovative ecosystem?

Those who pursue the latter aim are able to form new, co-creative partnerships with suppliers, contractors and other companies in the network. The willingness to treat these as equals opens up a larger array of possibilities.

15 Has your company the ability to resemble a family, an incubator, a guided missile and an Eiffel tower all at the same time, keeping touch with the history through which it has passed and the future to which it aspires? Can you 'change cultures' to take on the form required by new challenges and environments? Are you, at heart, all these metaphors and more?

We have to get beyond stereotypes to bring the family and the missile team into the factory, the process of incubation into the project teams, and order and discipline into innovation. Realty is cyclical and the circle never ends. It is our very business model and our vision of the culture that needs to be creative and to discover a myriad of new connections.

INDEX

INDEX OF DILEMMAS AND RECONCILIATIONS

A guide to the language of innovation

Unless the key value distinctions which we make can be reconciled they may constitute lasting dilemmas and confront us with conflict, impasse, contradiction and mounting anxiety.

Below are some of the polarities used in this book and beneath each is a brief summary of how it might be reconciled. There are five principles used in reconciliation. The first is to convert nouns into present participles ending in '-ing'. Instead of Abstraction, say abstracting. Instead of Concrete say concretising. The second is to place one polarity in the context of the second, so that concrete detailing is subsumed by abstracting principles, the former being examples of the latter. The third principle is to sequence the values, first to examine concrete details then to consider what abstraction would make better sense of these, or to think deductively from abstract propositions to concrete pieces of evidence that would verify these. The fourth step is to make a virtuous circle out of these, concretising the data so as better to create abstract generalisations. Finally, the polarities must be synergistic, from syn-ergo to work together. Better concretising makes possible better abstracting and theory building.